Democracy

MW01284609

The School for Advanced Research gratefully acknowledges the support
of the Wenner-Gren Foundation for Anthropological Research
for the seminar from which this book sprang.

Publication of the advanced seminar series is made possible
by generous support from The Brown Foundation, Inc., of Houston, Texas.

**School for Advanced Research
Advanced Seminar Series**

James F. Brooks
General Editor

Democracy

Contributors

Mukulika Banerjee
Department of Anthropology, University College London

Kimberley Coles
Department of Sociology and Anthropology, University of Redlands

Carol J. Greenhouse
Department of Anthropology, Princeton University

Akhil Gupta
Department of Anthropology, University of California, Los Angeles

David Nugent
Department of Anthropology, Emory University

Julia Paley
Department of Anthropology, University of Michigan

Jennifer Schirmer
Centre for Development and the Environment, University of Oslo

Harry G. West
Department of Anthropology, SOAS, University of London

Democracy

Anthropological Approaches

Edited by Julia Paley

School for Advanced Research Press

Santa Fe

School for Advanced Research Press
Post Office Box 2188
Santa Fe, New Mexico 87504-2188
www.sarpress.sarweb.org

Co-director and Executive Editor: Catherine Cocks
Manuscript Editor: Kate Whelan
Designer and Production Manager: Cynthia Dyer
Proofreader: Sarah Soliz
Indexer: Catherine Fox
Printer: Thomson Shore, Inc.

Library of Congress Cataloging-in-Publication Data:

Democracy : anthropological approaches / edited by Julia Paley. – 1st ed.
        p. cm. – (School for Advanced Research advanced seminar series)
    Includes bibliographical references and index.
    ISBN 978-1-934691-07-6 (pa : alk. paper)
    1. Democracy—Cross-cultural studies. 2. Political anthropology. I. Paley, Julia, 1964–
JC423 .D439842
    321.8—dc22

                                        2008024800

♻ This book was printed on 30% PCR paper.

Cover illustration: Untitled, 2007–2008, 18" x 40", oilstick and colored pencil on board
© Patrick Dodd, www.artistpatrickdodd.com.

Contents

Acknowledgments

This book is the product of an advanced seminar at the School of American Research, now named the School for Advanced Research (SAR), in Santa Fe. The Wenner-Gren Foundation generously contributed additional funds. In Santa Fe, Mukulika Banerjee, Carol Greenhouse, David Nugent, Jennifer Schirmer, Kay Warren, Harry West, and I engaged in a lively exchange of ideas. We were pleased to include discussion of Akhil Gupta and Kimberley Coles's work. We thank SAR's James F. Brooks, Catherine Cocks, Richard Levanthal, Nancy Owen Lewis, and Leslie Shipman for their support, as well as Lynn Baca and Kate Whelan at the press. Two anonymous reviewers provided valuable comments. I extend my thanks to the student research assistants at the University of Michigan who helped in the preparation of the edited volume—Sheena Ardeshna, Ellen Block, Michelle Hunscher, Nidhi Mahajan, Viviana Quintero, and Katherine Sheets—and gratefully acknowledge the office assistance of Kim Cramer, Renee Heath, and Roxanne Loy. Deep appreciation goes to the anthropology writers group at the University of Michigan, Rebecca Hardin, Eduardo Kohn, Nadine Naber, Damani Partridge, Elizabeth Roberts, Gayle Rubin, and Miriam Ticktin, as well as to Keith Brown, Ayako Kano, Christi Merrill, and Gordon Whitman, for their thoughtful input.

Democracy

1

Introduction

Julia Paley

On the front page of newspapers daily, at the heart of foreign policy agendas, at the center of debates, democracy is a central theme of our times. And in its international salience, in the confidence with which it is parlayed across the globe, it is often taken as a truth held to be self-evident, easily defined by its most prominent features: free and fair elections, a multi-party system, and freedoms of expression and the press.

Yet as recent events have highlighted and as long-standing debates have underscored, democracy is not nearly so clear-cut. Indeed, its complexity requires new forms of understanding. With that in mind, I invited a set of prominent political anthropologists to participate in an advanced seminar on democracy at the School for Advanced Research in Santa Fe in 2005, and that seminar became the basis for this book.[1] Like the article "Toward an Anthropology of Democracy" published in the *Annual Review of Anthropology* (Paley 2002), the seminar aimed to explore how anthropological perspectives might take understandings of democracy in new and unanticipated directions. While the article offered lenses for viewing the array of anthropological interventions on democracy available at the time,[2] the SAR advanced seminar provided a forum for interactive conversation about democracy, with particular attention to theoretical directions, methodological approaches, and reinterpretations of political events. It invited anthropologists to share their work investigating local understandings, official discourses, transnational processes, and transformative possibilities in relation to democracy. Collectively, we had a sense that we were working "toward" something—that is, contributing to a still emerging field.

From the start, the intellectual approach at the seminar involved relinquishing preconceived notions of what democracy is or should be. Throughout the week, we moved further and further away from seeking a core definition of democracy and closer, instead, to an awareness of democracy's open-ended construction. Through a heightened alertness to what we saw emerging in our ethnographic work, we engaged in a constant process of opening up new questions. It became evident that our dialogues with people in our field sites, beyond illuminating different understandings of democracy (which they did as well), continually generated new ways of framing our inquiries. This analytic openness is what we see as the contribution of anthropological approaches to democracy.

As input into this ongoing exploration and as a way of offering pathways into the chapters of the book, this introduction brings together ideas circulating within the collective discussion and interactive dialogue during that week in Santa Fe. In the introduction, my own synthesis and analysis interweaves with a set of thoughts that emerged, inextricably, through engaged conversation and animated debate. To give a window into these interactions, at moments I quote not only from the volume's chapters but also from the participants' verbal comments at the seminar and their earlier written texts. The introduction, moreover, is arranged in thematic sections that connect chapters by various authors to one another: multiplicities; political language; institutions and practices; the people's will; conversation and discourse; mediation and textualization; markets and commodification; transnationalism; methods, ethics, and transformations.

MULTIPLICITIES

Foreign policy makers and those engaged in promoting democracy internationally identify characteristics needed for a political system to be labeled a democracy and apply those criteria to countries worldwide. They maintain that programs and political systems can be replicated in vastly varying circumstances, for example, by implementing democracy promotion projects in one region and then using the knowledge gained to expand them to others. In activities such as these, a common vocabulary becomes available to everyone from policy makers, to researchers, to nongovernmental actors, to media. Explicit in setting forth criteria, it gains effectiveness by exerting a commonsensical grip on the social and political imagination.

An anthropological approach is not about developing a somehow more precise set of mechanisms for determining whether a country is or is not a democracy. That would cordon off definitions of democracy precisely at the moment we seek to open them up. Instead of developing new criteria, in this volume the authors are interested in two main things: first, detecting the many variations associated with the term *democracy* in a broad array of contexts and, second, understanding the way democracy has been conceptualized in public discourse and practice—both the *logic* underlying the idea that democracy is definable by discrete features and infinitely replicable and the *process* through which this notion of democracy has been generated and has come to predominate.

Notions of democracy prevailing at present are but one manifestation of a broader phenomenon that David Nugent (chapter 2) has called "normative democracy," a term he uses to describe the dominant status bestowed upon a particular form of liberal democracy. Nugent urges us to take note of the particularities of Western liberal democracy by understanding it to be one project among many, its distinguished status residing primarily in its having been generalized as a norm.

What becomes crucial for analysis is not just the observation that one form of democracy is normative, but also that any dominant form emanates from and is reconfigured in particular places and times and through particular nexuses of institutions and power relations. Instead of a single trans-historical norm, there are ongoing processes of making or maintaining assertions of normativity amid a field of contestants. Moreover, even those forms with dominant status experience a range of variations and disputes internally. The studies in this volume are attuned, therefore, to the temporality, agency, and processual nature of normativity; rather than take it as a given, they trace its historical emergence and its trajectory in specific situations.

This processual approach applies as well to what Nugent calls "alternative" democracies. He draws an example from Peru a century ago, when leaders of the Alianza Popular Revolucionaria Americana (Popular American Revolutionary Alliance, known as APRA) redefined democracy to entail equality and unity and maintained that economic decisions should be made by organized communities.

In these instances, alternative democracies should not be viewed as an array of bounded systems mapped onto places or groups, each distinguished by its own unique configuration and placed in a relativistic frame. Such a construct would logically lead to categorization and the creation of typologies, a project in which we do not seek to be engaged. The emphasis on discrete, contrasting systems would also tend toward positing alternative democracies as both atemporal (or unchanging in time) and mutually isolated. Moreover, it would risk reducing complex phenomena to "distinctive features"—decontextualized elements that stand for and highlight difference. Instead, the point of analysis should be to trace the history through which alternative democratic forms came to be, as well as the directions in which they are headed.

Because distinct democratic forms continually contest one another for dominance, a valuable analytic approach is to situate powerful and non-powerful actors within the same frame, by examining how they selectively choose and resignify elements of a globally circulating discourse. APRA's leaders chose to call their project "functional democracy," despite the fact that they could have called it (and also did call it) something else, "Latin American socialism." Their selecting the term *democracy* indicates that they considered using a globally circulating discourse and reworking it with another set of meanings to have strategic benefit at their time.

The potential effectiveness of that kind of politics varies with circumstances. In contrast to the case of APRA, grassroots shantytown health promoters in my study of Chile (Paley 2004) found the term *democracy* to be so captured by a post-dictatorship politics of neoliberal accommodation in the 1990s, that the term emerged in health promoters' discourse mainly as critique ("This is not democracy!"). Instead, the language of human rights, equally a globally circulating discourse and one that had also predominated during the period of military dictatorship, became more useful for their purposes at a time of formal political democracy. Here, we are analyzing the ebb and flow of a discourse—fluctuations in moments, places, and historical circumstances when the term *democracy* seems either particularly apt or not useful at all. In so doing, we are analyzing the outer edges of discourse, the shifting borderline between the instances in which democracy discourse is picked up and used and those in which it is cast aside in favor of other possibilities.[3]

Anthropologists gain analytic leverage in this project from ethnography enriched through historical inquiry. The unique conceptions of democracy emerging among subaltern peoples enable a contrast with prevailing norms that allows us to think outside of dominant assumptions. That analytic perspective, in turn, permits a denaturalization of actions of major international powers themselves—the internationals doing election monitoring in Bosnia-Herzegovina in Kimberley Coles's chapter 5, the Bush administration's discourse on the Iraq war in Carol Greenhouse's chapter 8, or the Colombian military officers in Jennifer Schirmer's chapter 9. Such anthropological projects take with utmost seriousness the injunction to "study up" (Nader 1972; also, Gusterson 1997) among powerful groups, while studying "down" and "across" as well. In fact, the juxtaposition—at times a face-to-face encounter, at times an evasion—of Ford Foundation staff with Mozambiquan Muedans in Harry West's chapter 4 or ex-guerrillas and military personnel in Jennifer Schirmer's chapter 9 shows the interface in these various conceptions of democracy. Moreover, the contemporary world reveals examples of thoroughgoing, mutual imbrication in which subaltern and dominant groups construct forms of democracy in conjunction with each other—evidenced, for example, in the interwoven strategies of the World Bank and the Ecuadorian Indigenous Movement in the development projects explored in my own research (chapter 6).

POLITICAL LANGUAGE

Because groups siphon vocabulary from internationally circulating discourses and enact distinctive meanings and practices, one goal is to understand the resulting variations. A key entry point for this inquiry is linguistic: an analysis of the vocabulary people use to describe political processes in which they are engaged. Mukulika Banerjee (chapter 3), calling her broader project "popular perceptions of democracy," recommends taking common political terms such as *state, power, administration,* and *bureaucracy* and examining how people interpret and use them. Conversely, one might listen for the colloquial terms people use to describe the state, bureaucracy, political parties, and other political institutions, to see where the overlap occurs.

One way to grasp internal diversity and transformation is to follow situations in which people are frustrated by the categories available to them. We might pay attention to moments when someone is actively trying to articulate a political distinction but finds herself without the vocabulary to do so, or occasions in which an opposition party makes headway in a political campaign by drawing on otherwise unheard-of vocabulary. We should be sensitive, too, to the mechanisms through which people change their political language. These issues resonate with phenomena in post-socialist Eastern Europe, where continuities in meanings seem to predominate because vocabulary remains the same, even though words are used to describe very different phenomena (Burawoy and Verdery 1999), or the reverse, as when the adoption of a new glossary obscures entrenched continuities in meaning systems.

Whereas some groups bestow unique meanings upon internationally circulating political vocabulary, others express themselves in a language all their own. Harry West (chapter 4) finds value in Cameroonian intellectual

Achille Mbembe's notion of "languages of power," by which he means forms of political expression that "emerge from the daily life of the people" (Geschiere 1997:7). This concept, instead of identifying an enduring mode of expression, highlights the openness and transformative nature of political thought, in that a language of power is "constantly sought and never arrived at," in Harry West's words during the seminar. The talk that captures people's attention in this part of Mozambique is not of elections, but rather of lions, and experiences of sorcery infuse Muedans' subjectivity. Ironically, this was a form of engagement with international politics, for it "afforded [Muedans] profound insights and allowed them to formulate a nuanced critique of democracy as they experienced it" and, moreover, to articulate "their own vision of, and for, the working of power in the world they inhabit."

The notion "languages of power" and the multiplicity that West perceives can be applied not just to subaltern groups but also to the democracy promoters themselves—the Ford Foundation, USAID, and other agencies operating in Mozambique. The overt language and logic the practitioners use may or may not intersect with their own experiences. As Greenhouse's chapter 8 suggests, discourses may be shifting and tactically oriented toward any number of audiences, some of them internal to the organizations themselves. Coles's chapter 5, too, portrays internationals working in Bosnia-Herzegovina as enacting one official set of activities but having a significance and self-understanding that transcend or circumvent those explicit tasks. As ethnographers of democracy who are placing many disparate and intersecting actors into the same analytical frame, we might productively ask, How do we describe the cosmology or cultural idioms of people who are doing international democracy promotion work? What assumptions about democracy—such as the idea that it can be transplanted from one locale to another—are embedded in particular formulations?

STUDYING POLITICS: INSTITUTIONS AND PRACTICES

Although meaning-centered analysis is crucial, it does not suffice for the study of democracy. Instead, drawing on a history of practice theory in anthropology (Ortner 1984), an analysis of democracy benefits from attention to the intersection of meaning and practice—what is *done* with meaning, how politics operate. Therefore, it is essential to examine the day-to-day activities people engage in and the consequences, both intended and unintended, of their actions with regard to such topics as election monitoring, governmental offices, and democracy promotion programs.

Mukulika Banerjee's work (chapter 3) forwards a hybrid methodology that takes up where survey research leaves off, forging an anthropological intervention in the most large-scale and central of questions about democracy. Banerjee starts with a puzzle that she derives directly from questions at the heart of the electoral scenario: why are illiterate rural villagers among the most avid voters in India? Her ethnography of West Bengal brings us immediately to the electoral scene—the polling machines, the lines of voters waiting in the sun, the publicity promoting candidacies. In the best anthropological fashion, Banerjee reveals to us the meaning systems for these villagers. Yet as Banerjee inhabits the village in many different seasons, she finds that talk of politics recedes outside the electoral moment and that its silent operation infuses daily interpersonal encounters that cannot audibly be commented upon. She is thereby led to explore how politics is constituted in these non-electoral scenarios—something that would be invisible to a researcher appearing only at the time of the vote or asking questions only about institutional politics.

Banerjee's chapter 3 complements Kimberley Coles's chapter 5 on Bosnia-Herzegovina, where it is not silence but presence that provides the analytic subject with regard to recent elections. For Coles, just as for Banerjee, passive presence has ramifications far beyond explicit activity: silence speaks louder than a proliferation of words. In Bosnia, election monitors officially have jobs to do, and Coles shows them implementing a dizzying array of procedures. But it is the internationals' non-activity that may be their most significant work. Coles explores what might be termed the "agency of passivity"—the experienced utility and strategic intent of "just being there." She holds that "being there" operates in three registers: sheer (vast in numbers), mere (pure existence), and peer (or pedagogical, that is, teaching democratic values and behavior by example). These assessments are shared. They are explicit intentions of the countries and agencies providing the monitors, as well as the experiences of Bosnian recipients of assistance.

Together, Banerjee and Coles's entry point for studying democracy is elections, yet each reveals that politics occurs in the most imperceptible of ways—unspoken in one case, unacted in the other. Because of their anthropological approach and their ethnographic method, they identify phenomena that standard studies of politics would be unlikely to discern. Because of their closeness to the scene, they ask questions that would otherwise not be asked. But equally important is that neither author shirks from studying politics in its most widely recognizable forms, using commonly accepted vocabulary, cooperating with colleagues in political science, and asking questions that derive from the most pressing public questions of our time.

My own chapter (6) reveals that, in contemporary Ecuador, the impact of electoral politics on the strength of the indigenous movement is the subject of continual internal debate. Through an electoral strategy beginning in 1996, the national indigenous confederation and its allies have placed in office numerous congressional representatives, governors, mayors, and council people. At face value, this is a victory for the movement and enables a greater influence of indigenous peoples over public policy. But questions linger for indigenous organizations, in both the national and the local arenas. Has landing officials in elected office fortified the movement and advanced broader goals? Does gaining elected office result in the absorption of the indigenous organizations' major leaders into established structures that undercut their commitment to and connection with the "communities" that constitute the movement's base? Although elections have classically been seen as a defining element of democracy, questions remain for social movements about whether an electoral strategy may actually weaken democratic representation.

POPULAR SOVEREIGNTY AND THE PEOPLE'S WILL

In democracy, the government's authority (in theory) derives from the people's will. The famous statement that democracy is "of the people, by the people, and for the people" explicitly postulates the existence of a *people*. But so does APRA (Nugent, chapter 2), which perceives its program as a counterweight to liberal democracy. By the same token, socialist systems (for example, those present historically in Mozambique) also claim to be speaking on the people's behalf (West, chapter 4). Such invocations take strategy and effort on the part of political leaders, but the idea of "the people" may, in other circumstances, be taken for granted.

Invocations of "the people" and its will do not refer to a people that actually preexists; rather, the act of constituting a people happens within political action and public rhetoric on an ongoing basis. This leads to ethnographic inquiry about how "a people" comes into being in particular situations labeled democracy. We might ask, what are the range of conditions in which this occurs, the situations in which it does not, and the complex and often contested processes through which it happens? A number of chapters in this volume investigate the complex processes involved in asserting the representation of the people's will.

In Ecuador and Peru, constructions of identity work explicitly through ethnic categories, precisely because stigma and exclusion have been embedded in racial constructs. Commonly, democracies put forth universalist claims about peoplehood, despite the fact that they are situated in systems that denigrate subordinated groups. Because racial hierarchies are at the foundation of many political democracies, the explicit invocation of ethnicity is often used on the part of social movements to redress general power imbalances. Social movements' discourses may also be framed in terms of inter-ethnic relations and cross-cultural dialogue or may find ways of articulating commonalities that otherwise would not occur. Centrally, social movements have used these mechanisms to shape a different form of peoplehood and democracy.

At times, social movements create identities and demands; in other instances, there is neither clear articulation of a platform nor organizational membership. The degree to which peoplehood and its expressed interests solidify and cohere varies widely. Mukulika Banerjee, in reflecting on her field site in West Bengal (chapter 3) during the seminar, noted that an articulation of the "people's will" is relatively straightforward and consistent. The catch is, what people are communicating is "so simple that it's not worth the politicians' while." Harry West (chapter 4) highlighted, instead, an abiding fluctuation: a "will" that is hard to pin down precisely because of people's own mixed feelings, morphing desires, and multiple responses to systems and events.

Not only might the people's will be ambivalent, but it might also be unarticulated. Drawing on Veena Das's observation, West said, "People often don't express suffering in the kinds of confessional modes that truth and reconciliation commissions call for." West postulates that a people's will might not be expressed in clearly spoken or plainly written forms (of the kinds social movements often produce), but instead in subtle, unvocalized practices.

CONVERSATION AND DISCOURSE

US politicians frequently make assertions about what "the American People" want. In claiming to know the people's will, officials marshal opinion polls, conversations with constituents, or common sense. The degree to which such claims convince listeners varies, but convincing might not be the primary goal.

In chapter 8, on the Bush administration's arguments in favor of military intervention in Iraq, articulated prior to the war, Carol Greenhouse cautions against reading politicians' speeches and government documents as if they reflect anyone's actual views, as if state discourse could somehow express the will of the people in a way similar to ordinary conversation. In the seminar, she commented, "Such taken for granted ideas about the embeddedness of official texts in culture, legal consciousness, and everyday storytelling...encourage the tendency to assume a collective subject, as if such texts were extracts of normal conversation." The problem here is not just the construction of a singular collective subject that may or may not exist, but also the notion that state discourse follows normal conversational patterns. Conversation, an interactive and dialogic process in which people exchange views, is "constrained by the conventions of grammar, syntax, narrative, and logic" that make it resonate and cohere. Embedded in interaction, it involves moral and ethical dimensions.

Greenhouse proposes that, although officials may echo key terms and logics from everyday speech in their public pronouncements, high political discourse operates through a different mode of power in some circumstances. It may, at times, succeed precisely because of its malleability or lack of coherence. Not bound by the rules of conversation, it sometimes functions by way of "discursive fracture," a negative form of intertextuality that functions by controlling the oppositional force of competing framings. Discourse becomes fractured as politicians make different arguments to different audiences such that no single argument can effectively counter the politicians' position. This creates the appearance that agreement exists within the public, thereby giving the impression that the absence of opposition equals the presence of consensus.

Greenhouse argues that under some circumstances, high public officials maintain an institutional control (for example, through protocol) that enables them to limit their accountability, if only temporarily. She commented at the seminar that in such cases, "discourse is so outside the political order that there is not immediately obvious within the political order a place to answer back and say, 'No, not that.'" It is important to note that discursive fracture is not limited to the realm of government; nor does Greenhouse claim it as a defining feature of government. Still, the notion that high officials in democratic states can in some circumstances block dissent by selectively reconfiguring the oppositional force of their constituents' language signals an aspect of power and representation not classically associated with democracy. The further notion that the people do not speak through the state means that high official discourse in some circumstances replaces or even precludes the very articulation of will that liberal theory imagines it to internalize and convey.

MEDIATION AND TEXTUALIZATION

The discussion of discourse in Greenhouse's chapter 8 invites us into a broader consideration of political language, in its spoken and written forms. What kinds of de facto rules guide communication, and how are they interdigitated with relations of power? How might the "will of the people"—and the actions of the state—be mediated and textualized?

Whereas, in Greenhouse's chapter 8, high-level officials evade accountability to constituents by way of discursive maneuver, in Akhil Gupta's chapter 7, on literacy, low-level bureaucrats prevent rural residents from registering complaints and voicing demands—and thus making their will known—by insisting that all claims be made in writing. In a context in which a majority is unable to write, this calls into question the idea of a state representing a people. In fact, not unlike Greenhouse, Gupta shows how officials manipulate the form language must take in order to produce evasion and inaccessibility.

In Gupta's chapter 7, rural villagers and bureaucrats talk past each other. The villagers' oral complaints fall on deaf ears when they remain uninscribed in official registries, and the villagers' presumptive representatives meet surreptitiously, at times and places unknown to constituents. Gupta contends that the supposed binary between oral and written—present among his informants and in the literature—misses the degree to which these intermingle. More common historically have been conditions of "restricted literacy," in which people have *some* experience with the written word (ways of dealing with documents, encounters with texts). Instead of reflecting an essential distinction between written and oral, the bureaucrats' insistence on writing is an exercise in power—one complicated by strategies available to subaltern actors, including mimicry, forgery, and counterfeiting. In all cases, textualization is a mediating mechanism through which state power is brought into relation with citizens.

MARKETS AND COMMODIFICATION

Democracy is now so deeply embedded in a prolonged moment of economic and philosophical liberalism that democracy (as ideology, as experience, as expectation, as policy) is co-produced with market economics, a phenomenon neatly captured by the phrase "free market democracies." Parallel to expectations about the former Soviet Union, where socialism was to be replaced by the twin "freedoms" of market opportunity and political voice, elsewhere this entanglement has been an explicit effort of international agencies' democracy promotion programs, in which electoral politics are paired with a contraction of public services and an export-oriented economic model. Ironically, the undoing of the welfare state drives the stakes for democracy higher: where the population's necessities are intensified and unmet, the need for political representation to resolve their problems is all the more acute. The process of marketization, however, has undermined safeguards of political expression.

Because free market reforms intensify inequality, they must be justified publicly in some cases. Here, democracy can become a legitimating mechanism to facilitate structural adjustment. In some cases, nondemocratic political systems have been breeding grounds in which market reforms are implemented, then continued by subsequent elected governments or exported to long-standing political democracies. In others, economic success stories are used to legitimate the authoritarian systems that spawned them.

This overpowering sense of the present moment creates a need to historicize—to trace how these conditions came to be and where they might be headed. We are especially alert to the ways that neoliberalism itself has specific histories in each of these locales. We note that neoliberalism is not a single, universalized project but rather a set of processes that have arisen in very particular contexts and therefore have taken on different configurations in the settings in which we work. Similarly, acts of racialization construct distinct categories of people and possibilities for identity, as is evident in my own work on Ecuador (chapter 6). Situated in regional particularities, these histories are not bound by national borders.

Notably, market-inflected democracies are often experienced in relation to what came before them, be it socialism, communism, or right-wing authoritarianism. To take just one example, the Mozambiquan state has virtually exited from the countryside: schools are now without books, medical clinics without supplies. In the Mozambiquan context, democracy is associated with the end of socialism and the retraction of state services, as noted in Harry West's chapter 4. In this case, as in others, democracy is defined locally in relation to what preceded it and what accompanies its arrival.

At the center of debates about economic restructuring is the question of whether "the state" is *withdrawing* from interference in the economy or is *maintaining and reasserting* its strength but in other forms. In places such as Mozambique, where public services have simply disappeared, the state can be characterized as withdrawing. In other places, state functions are not absent, but rather transformed; the state ventures into areas of persuasion, selective subsidization, or cooptation that reinforce export economics. In Ecuador, the country's participation in the international economy hinges on exporting oil. To further this project, the government co-opts indigenous groups resisting oil extraction, by offering them places within government. There, they bring into cooperation a whole set of social organizations whose resistance to oil extraction thereby diminishes. In this instance, activity by the state facilitates the country's insertion into the international economy.

What we also see is a reconfiguration of the mix of provision of services, with nongovernmental organizations, bilateral donors and multilateral lenders, and volunteers stepping in where government-provided public services once stood. Carol Greenhouse's chapter 8, in particular, reveals the commingling of public entities and private interests, what she calls "the hybrid zone," in which "the government operates through the private sector." That these mixes of public and private occur has huge ramifications for democracy, for it means, in Greenhouse's spoken words, that "there are...anti-democratic currents even at the core of broadly democratic institutions" and that "there is a way in which state government now is thoroughly imbricated with the private sector," which "has its own modes of governance that are *not* democratic." This has important ramifications for democratic theory. It reminds us that democracy is not a single whole, but an array of institutions and power relations, not all of which are controlled by the public.

TRANSNATIONALISM

If conditions in our field sites hold in common an economic backdrop, they are also interwoven, highlighting the transnationality of political processes. Although elections remain largely national affairs, the processes orchestrating them, as well as the ramifications of these processes, far transcend countries' limits, as do aid agencies' democracy promotion programs, world courts, international conventions, indigenous movements' coordinating bodies, and more. In Bosnia-Herzegovina, Colombia, Ecuador, India, and Mozambique, and amid the texts produced in Washington DC, we catch sight of connected forces: election monitoring, the Ford Foundation, the World Bank. Manifestations of these institutions and discourses vary across our studies, depending on the geographic site of our research and on the training of our lens, yet they are interconnected.

The extranational nature of democracy promotion becomes evident in chapter 5, by Kimberley Coles. Her essay opens by introducing "Charles," a man who comes to Bosnia-Herzgovina to engage in election monitoring. Coursing through his story are innumerable transnational dynamics, from the diverse set of places to which he has traveled to the organizations that have employed him and the work he is engaged in. The very term used to describe his position—an "international"—highlights the arrival of individuals from a range of countries, sponsored by not only national governments but also supranational institutions and both non- and intergovernmental organizations. And the phrase "international aid circuit" underscores the rhythm of maneuvers, patterns of travel, and creation of opportunities for people from a wide variety of professional backgrounds to move across locales, staying any one place for only a relatively short period of time. Coles emphasizes that the significance of the "presence" of these internationals goes beyond the aims of the sponsoring organizations to take on unanticipated meanings for both Bosnians and the "internationals" themselves.

Jennifer Schirmer's chapter (9) explores cross-national activities by describing a project designed to draw Colombian armed actors into peace processes. The project, called "Skilling the Armed Actors for Peace in Colombia," operates through confidence-building dialogues, or *Conversatorios*, in which officers, ex-guerrillas, and others, such as politicians, human rights lawyers, business people, and representatives of international organizations, gather to talk. Funding comes from the foreign ministry of Norway, a country that has engaged in conflict resolution efforts in many regions of the world. The approach is noteworthy for engaging armed actors at an early stage in peace-building on the premise that transforming conflict into politics requires including those who have the most capacity to wage war. The aim is to create a neutral space in which dialogues between armed actors and civil society can be sustained even if formal peace processes take longer than expected. In this context, Norway's presence in Colombia is not so much direct and proactive as indirect and low profile.

My own essay on indigenous movement strategy in Ecuador (chapter 6) takes up the question of why social movement organizations remain important after local governments have established participatory democracies. I argue that the organizations are, among other things, crucial for creating ties with groups distant from the locale, such that the broader networks and organizations might have the agility to confront supralocal issues raised by the global circulation of capital and the operation of international financial institutions. Because indigenous movements and development agencies each transcend nation-state boundaries and constitute transnational entities, my broader project is thoroughly multisited. Traveling between Quito and Cotacachi in Ecuador, Washington, DC, and beyond, I seek to follow discourses, logics, and pressures from different interest groups between locales of policy construction, places of policy implementation, and spaces of publicity where organizations seek to reap symbolic and monetary rewards for work done. Such work requires placing seemingly disparate events and entities into the same analytic frame.

As these capsule descriptions suggest, processes generating democracy exceed the limits of any country; therefore, studying democracy ethnographically calls for fieldwork that can trace people and events beyond pre-set borders. The projects require not only linking agendas and institutions across regions but also taking as objects of study transnational agencies and networks themselves. Studying democracy may therefore involve engaging with an eclectic array of situations, including international regulatory systems, virtual communities, coalition politics, and international finance, among others. To that end, the studies need to transcend the divide commonly established between the categories "domestic" and "international" to set phenomena of different orders and scales into relation with each other and make evident their connections.

METHODS, ETHICS, TRANSFORMATIONS

In anthropology, democracy is not a unique site for these reflections, but because of its encounters with dispersion, dialogue, violence, and social mobilization, it is an excellent location from which to explore the potentials of ethnographic inquiry and expression that could have wider implications for the field. The transnational dynamics researched in these chapters produce intriguing challenges: how to untangle the web of complicities in state department pronouncements and relate foreign policy justifications to events in the Middle East (Greenhouse, chapter 8), how to relate the "presence" of internationals in Bosnia to the other locations of their work and lives (Coles, chapter 5), what to make of the cynical advice that the best place to find an Ecuadorian indigenous leader is in the airport (Paley, chapter 6).

And then there is the issue of temporalities: how to capture situations of rapid change in which government regulations undergo revisions repeatedly, electronic messages make but a momentary appearance before being erased forever, and conversations, scraps of paper, and logics are fleeting, changing as they are at a quickened pace. And how to reconcile the incongruous "time frames" of the different actors involved: the short-, medium-, and long-term strategies of an international coalition pressing for change and coordinating across time zones with the "time-space" of a national bureaucracy implementing regulations.

In this array of circumstances, our information is often mediated. Researching in these transnational arenas, we cannot always be participant-observers (although many of the authors in this volume are). Instead, we at times deal with "brokered data" acquired from third parties such as nongovernmental organizations or from governmental archives. For Jennifer Schirmer (chapter 9), the issue is "brokered working conditions" in which nongovernmental organizations are the access points to relationships.

Dealing with NGOs means working at first through their modus operandi—"learning how to use different strategies at certain moments and not pushing the limits too much at certain points." For Carol Greenhouse (chapter 8), the tension is around using composite documents that are highly negotiated and highly pre-tested, as opposed to conversational speech.

What do these new conditions of research mean for writing? The possibilities for generating written forms that embody the content of analysis are intriguing. Given that there are moments in research, as in life, when it is appropriate to talk politics and moments when it most definitely is not, how can our genres similarly create and defer to these pressures, generating variegated texts that tread deftly through protocol in one moment, try out oblique references to politics in another, and speak truth to power in a third? Writing about Mozambique might involve generating a stylistic surrealism to convey the experience of sorcery or a nondeclarative writing style to communicate the ambivalence in Muedans' political desire. Prose about Bosnia-Herzegovina might include textualized "presences," a literary manifestation of *just being there*. In all cases, the authors struggle to find forms to convey the intangible: the ironies, the co-presence of seemingly contradictory emotions, fluctuation and instability, incongruous temporalities—phenomena that escape, unruly and unkempt, from standardized argument.

Considering these possibilities entails grappling with the elasticity of ethnography as a genre. There is no immediate resolution to the quandaries presented here, but there is the ability to shine a spotlight on the dilemmas themselves—methodological, ethical, interpersonal—in the text. Because the theme of democracy has such acute political salience, ethnographies of democracy often exceed the boundaries of writing. Here, methods and ethics are tightly wed. Engaged anthropologists set up arenas, ranging from the very public to the more discreet, in which to be in conversation with the subjects and interlocutors of our studies. At times, it is possible to contribute ethically by transferring crucial information from one place and one set of people to another. In these instances, the ethnographer herself becomes part of the multi-sitedness.

Jennifer Schirmer (chapter 9) takes on the ethical challenges by engaging in potentially transformative work in Colombia. There, she has created a program of Conversatorios between otherwise antagonistic parties in the armed conflict. In contrast to the bureaucrats in Gupta's chapter 7, who evade dialogue by refusing to receive villagers' oral complaints, in Schirmer's program military officers and ex-guerrillas sit in the same room to listen to each other's experiences. Taking in a new direction anthropology's classic mission to grasp the "native's point of view," the Conversatorios ask each party to "respect and listen to one another's opinions." Schirmer notes in chapter 9, "Conversatorios work anthropologically by framing the dialogue in terms of the multiple mindsets present in the room." That is, each participant tries to grasp the others' mental frameworks—their experiences, their histories, their logics and ideas. In doing this, Schirmer aims for what she called, in our discussion, "the original idea of democratic pluralism, of opening yourself up to listening and to dialoguing." The goal is consciously to generate new political possibilities by cultivating an awareness that making purposeful choices about society is possible.

CONCLUSION

For many interlocutors—academic, policy oriented, in the media, or in the broader public—a starting point for discussions of democracy is one of definitions: how is democracy defined? In this volume, we take a different approach, one that engages in a continuing process of exploring a wide variety of lived meanings and practices. The precise phenomenon we are studying is not predetermined but rather emerges within the various field sites in which we do our research. Our process of inquiry allows the very questions we are investigating to develop through a dialogic engagement with people in the places we study. Such an analytic openness is at the very heart of anthropological approaches to democracy.

Notes

1. At the time, SAR was known as the School of American Research. Mukulika Banerjee, Carol Greenhouse, David Nugent, Julia Paley, Jennifer Schirmer, Kay Warren, and Harry West were present at the seminar. We discussed Akhil Gupta's paper in his absence; Kimberley Coles's paper was later added to the collection. At the seminar, we read and commented on an early rendition of Kay Warren's paper, but her work was at too early a stage to become part of the book.

2. For a recent compendium of essays on "cultures of democracy," see *Public Culture* 19(1), winter 2007.

3. This approach provides challenges for the analyst of democracy because it demands vigilance: our vocabulary and categories often operate within existing naturalized conceptions, and much writing on democracy functions within frameworks deriving from Western liberal thought. Adoption of such language is, at times, due to

moral commitments to social change and the impulse to cooperate with agencies promoting the establishment and strengthening of political democracies. Alternatively, it may be a result of political institutions and processes' appropriation of widely circulating discourses for their own ends, such that words are imbued with meanings from contradictory political stands. When the vocabulary available to us has already been claimed, we struggle to find words and conceptual frameworks that are not overdetermined by prevailing understandings and pragmatic uses.

2

Democracy Otherwise

Struggles over Popular Rule in the Northern Peruvian Andes

David Nugent

In the middle decades of the twentieth century, the Chachapoyas region of northern Peru saw the emergence of a transnational movement of participatory democracy based on a unique vision of continent-wide citizenship and on a public sphere made up of cooperative organizations in which the mass of the population would be actively involved in determining the conditions of their everyday lives. Although this movement drew on discourses of the European Enlightenment and the rights talk of the "bourgeois" revolutions, it was not a democratic revolution of the liberal European kind. In this chapter, I discuss the social and political forces that gave rise to this "alternative" democracy, in particular, the fragmented and incomplete nature of Peruvian state formation, the state's consistent disregard for the principles of popular sovereignty, and the efforts of subaltern groups to forge a political community that would make a reality of their understanding of those principles. I contrast these developments in northern Peru with processes of democratization and state formation in Western Europe in the centuries leading up to the Industrial Revolution. This was the historical context that produced the forms of democracy, rights, citizenship, and public sphere that much of the contemporary world has come to regard as normative—forms of liberal democratic life that have virtually nothing in common with their northern Peruvian counterparts.[1] In juxtaposing distinctive historical trajectories of politics and culture that have produced radically different forms of democracy and citizenship, I question the normative status of the European form by drawing attention to its highly idiosyncratic nature. I also draw attention to a problem that has received relatively little anthropological attention: the existence of a broad range of democracies and the social conditions out of which distinct democracies have emerged.

Although democracy is the focus of this chapter, I also consider the broader political structure in which movements of democratization are embedded, a political structure that is "state-like." Democracies vary widely in form and content, but a major preoccupation of virtually all is to establish the parameters for inclusion in and exclusion from a state-like polity. That is, democracies are generally based on the assertion of political rights and obligations (often glossed as "citizenship") that establish the terms of participation in a political community that exercises the powers we associate with states. Without a consideration of the power structure in which negotiations over inclusion/exclusion and participation take place, it is difficult to understand what democracy is in any given context.

When discussing alternative democracies, a consideration of state activities is important for another reason. Most scholarship concerning what democracy is, where it emerged, and why it came into being comes from a particular historical context, that is, Western Europe in the centuries leading up to the Industrial Revolution.[2] In other words, our normative or modal conception of democracy derives from a quite singular set of historical and political developments—the efforts of particular social groups to claim particular rights for themselves in relationship to state polities of a very specific kind. The significance of this fact is highly underappreciated. Because this historical sequence has come to define the normative version of democracy, it is important to understand who the groups were that asserted the rights we have come to view as democratic and in the context of what kind of state polity they asserted these rights. Only then will we be in a position to identify and understand alternative historical sequences of state formation and democratization.

Before going into the details of my argument, I would like to offer some general thoughts about democratization itself. I find it useful to approach democratization as a particular example of a more general political and cultural process in which self-identified (and at times spatially localized) groups seize upon discourses circulating in the global arena and generate "vernacularized" versions of global discourse to suit particular circumstances. In the case of democratization, the discourses circulating globally emerged initially out of the European colonial encounter with the non-European world, out of the Enlightenment, out of the French, Haitian, and US revolutions, later out of the Russian and Mexican revolutions, and still later out of anti-colonial movements. As shown later in the chapter, stories about the Inca Empire played a key role in the construction of democracy in Andean Peru. These discourses have provided a rich, complex, and also contradictory set of concepts and terms that invoke some form of popular sovereignty and have been seized upon by a variety of groups around the world in mounting their struggles. The particular rights seized upon in any given context, as well as the interpretation given to these rights, have depended on the nature of local political struggles and on the set of power relations in which local groups are embedded.

That these groups will find *any* aspect of liberal democracy to their liking is not a foregone conclusion. As Harry West reminds us (chapter 4), the very notion of popular sovereignty implies its own political and moral referents, which may be viewed with great hostility and suspicion. Indeed, the myriad responses around the world to liberal democratic practice—from rejection (West, chapter 4), to reconstitution (this chapter), to acceptance (Banerjee, chapter 3)—reveal just how much this political form is contested terrain. So, too, do ongoing attempts to reconfigure the moral fault lines of actually existing democracy. The efforts of multiple groups to reject or reconfigure liberal democracy, in the past and in the present, reveal that a moral geography of democracy has been continually evolving on a global scale.

In making these points, I would like to emphasize that no "pure" principles of the Enlightenment, the French Revolution, and the like, were originally centered in Western Europe and subsequently "altered" in a spatial plane removed from "the West." That is, it is important to disrupt the assumption of core and periphery that is implicit in much writing about alternative modernities and democracies. Instead of a core and a periphery, multiple and contradictory versions of democracy, modernity, rights, and freedoms have emerged from within, as well as beyond, Western Europe. Of these, some have achieved normative status; others have been vernacularized. As Kimberley Coles (chapter 5) and Julia Paley (chapter 6) show in their contributions to the present volume, whether any given version of democracy and citizenship has become normative or vernacular has been the result of *political* processes within "the West," as well as beyond it.

As I use the term, *democratization* refers to the assertion of rights and obligations that are based loosely on the principles of popular sovereignty but that vary widely in scope and content. Furthermore, as the chapters in this volume show, these principles can be advanced by a variety of social groups in different times and places. They are generally asserted in order to establish the nature of people's relationship to a state-like polity, real or imagined (this is an important distinction for the case I will discuss).

With this in mind, I will now contrast the process by which nation-states and democracies have formed in two contexts. One of these is Western Europe, the contemporary birthplace of liberal democracy. The other is northern Peru in the post-colonial period (after 1824), where I examine the emergence of an alternative democracy. The point is to understand the nature of the power structure that groups were forced to confront in asserting political rights and in defining the nature of their membership in the political community. This will make it possible to understand which groups actually claimed "democratic" rights in the two contexts, as well as the nature of the rights they claimed.

THE FORMATION OF NATION-STATES AND THE EMERGENCE OF DEMOCRACY IN WESTERN EUROPE

The period since the early 1970s is now widely recognized as one of major reorganization (if not crisis) in the powers and prerogatives of nation-states (Brenner 1997; Sassen 1996). During this same period, there has been a veritable explosion of academic interest in "the state." Much of this work has focused on the genealogy of European nation-states. Based on the influential scholarship of Michael Mann (1986, 1988, 1993) and also of Charles Tilly (1975a, 1975b) and his associates, who draw on the work of Weber (1950) and Hintze (1975), many scholars view state making as being analogous to a "protection racket" (Tilly 1985). In this view, state control has much in common with the Mafia's infamous "offer that cannot be refused." State makers—specialists in wielding violence—insist on providing "protection" to all who come within their purview. Although it is not at all clear that this protection is either needed or desired, state makers demand a "rent" in return for services rendered. The essence of state control is thus seen as being the threat of violence (Centeno 2001; Lutz 2004).

Modern state structures began to emerge in Europe with the "military revolution" of the sixteenth and seventeenth centuries (Parker 1976; Roberts 1967),[3] a revolution in the organization of violence that helped initiate what is referred to as the "extraction-coercion cycle" (Finer 1975). This cycle was crucial to the growth of states because it enabled those who wielded violence to extract resources more effectively from the societies of which they were a part and to convert these resources into enhanced war-making capacity. This, in turn, made it possible to eliminate violence-wielding competitors and to extract resources from ever-larger territorial domains.

The extraction-coercion cycle did more than concentrate the means of violence and expropriation in the hands of a select group of power holders. The cycle was also directly associated with the growth of fiscal institutions that could manage this process (Ardant 1975; Tilly 1990:131). These institutions were responsible for overseeing taxation and for channeling the resources thus obtained into increased war-making capacity. They acted as the core of complex absolutist states capable of the extraction of resources, the conscription of human beings, and the regulation of increasingly broad areas of social life.[4]

The development of the agrarian bureaucracies associated with these royal absolutist states transformed the organization of political space, replacing the partial and overlapping jurisdictional sovereignties of the feudal era with territorially based sovereignty (P. Anderson 1974; Mattingly 1988[1955]; Ruggie 1998). As a result of this process, states came to oversee mutually exclusive, geographically continuous domains with clear "insides" and "outsides" and unambiguous, linear boundaries (Biolsi 2005). Within these domains, states claimed a monopoly over physical and symbolic violence (Weber 1950) and used this control to organize multiple spheres of life—economic, political, and cultural—on a national/territorial basis (Bourdieu 1999).[5]

The "governmentalization" of the state during the nineteenth century (Foucault 1991; Rose and Miller 1992) built upon these earlier processes of state formation. This period saw the emergence of a veritable army of experts and an even larger number of specially trained government functionaries (Osborne 1994), who were collectively responsible for knowing and maintaining the wealth, health, and happiness of their respective national populations. Drawing on carefully constructed rationalities of rule, they monitored the well-being of schools, homes, factories, prisons, and psyches. They also codified their knowledge in the form of the positive sciences of economics, statistics, sociology, medicine, biology, psychiatry, and psychology (Rose 1996). The knowledge they produced and the surveillance they provided played a crucial role in translating knowledge into power—by means of technologies, apparatuses, and procedures that concretized the ways in which the exercise of power was conceptualized.

Against a background of this centuries-long process of state formation, the rights and protections that we now view as "democratic" emerged in some countries of Europe but not in others. To oversimplify a series of complex arguments, most scholars make a distinction between two national contexts in Europe. On the one hand, coercive state power was used to bolster the position of aristocratic, labor-repressive, agrarian elites, who controlled large numbers of dependent rural laborers, and systematically to exclude subaltern groups from the political community (Moore 1966; Tilly 2004). In these contexts (Brandenburg-Prussia), what emerged was not democracy but, ultimately, fascism.

On the other hand, in national contexts where an urban-based bourgeoisie helped lead a commercial revolution, the pact between centralizing states and powerful agrarian elites was broken. Here, the commercial classes were able to open a new political space by consolidating a group of entitlements (which we call "individual rights and protections"), a set of social institutions (civil society; see Keane 1998), and also a public sphere (see Habermas 1989) that was autonomous of, and set real limits to, state power. These entitlements, institutions, and social spheres formed the core of modern democratic citizenship, helped establish the institutions of political democracy, and remain central to what democracy means to most people today. These liberal entitlements included, for example, the "freedoms of" (speech, religion, and movement [of people, commodities, ideas, messages]). They included, as well, the "freedoms from" (arbitrary search and seizure, for example) and protections of person and property. They also established the autonomous (male!) *individual* as the sovereign holder of jural rights. Overall, these entitlements set legal and practical limits on the ability of government officials to interfere with everyday social life.[6]

Part of the origin myth of European democracy is that it is the most recent manifestation of a millennia-long democratic tradition originating with the Greeks in ancient Athens. It is interesting to compare democracy in these two settings; such a comparison brings out just how distinctive European democracy is. Actually, the liberal rights that make up European democracy have little, if anything, to do with popular understandings of Athenian democracy. What we are taught about democracy in ancient Athens is that it was based on *citizen control*, on ensuring that the citizenry exercised a direct and powerful voice in all community affairs.[7] That is, Athenian democracy guaranteed extensive "input from below," from the mass of the population, who were to determine the conditions of their own existence. Liberal rights, however, address a quite different problem. They are focused on the state rather than the citizenry and limit "input from above." In other words, liberal rights map out a terrain where state power may *not* be exercised. They are intended as, and developed historically as, brakes on the unrestrained use of state power (Wood 1994). As Carol Greenhouse (chapter 8) and Jennifer Schirmer (chapter 9) show in the present volume, this is one reason they remain salient today, in the context of highly repressive state structures and institutions of global governance.

It is important to recognize that this is a very specific definition of democracy, one that has to be understood in context.

THE "COMPROMISED" NATION-STATE AND DYSFUNCTIONAL DEMOCRACY

It is hard to imagine a social context that differs more from Western Europe in the centuries bracketing the Industrial Revolution than Peru during the post-colonial period (after 1824). The nineteenth century in Peru was characterized not by the consolidation but by the disintegration of absolutist state power, not by the concentration but by the diffusion of the means of violence into multiple and antagonistic hands.[8] This century was characterized not by the unification but by the parcelization of sovereignty, not by broad agreement over the principles and procedures of government—or even agreement about what would be the focus of disagreement (see Roseberry 1994)—but by fundamental dispute over the nature of legitimate rule. It is as if the historical trajectories of these two parts of the world were moving in opposite, if interdependent, directions.

These conditions extended into the twentieth century in many parts of Peru, resulting in conditions of "relative statelessness." Symptomatic of this state of affairs was the following: the quarter-century immediately before and after 1900 was characterized by frequent coup attempts, the repeated threat of civil war and movements of secession (which threatened the unity and integrity of the polity), and the widespread use of private violence to achieve private ends. The following further reflect the degree to which Peru differed from European states: Those in the national capital could not effectively tax the general population, so there could be no extraction-coercion cycle. Nor were they effective at conscription. They exercised little control over the national territory, had only a small standing army, and were ineffectual at defending the boundaries of the nation against foreign aggression.

Nor did Peru have an army of experts and an extensive cohort of specially trained government functionaries who were collectively responsible for monitoring and maintaining the health and well-being of the national population.[9] To the contrary, expertise was highly underdeveloped, and government functionaries were few in number. The Peruvian state bureaucracy was quite "thin," and many posts that existed on paper were left vacant. At times, vacancies occurred because no one was willing to fill the posts in question (Lima lawyers were unwilling to take up judgeships in remote Andean provinces). At other times, the positions remained unoccupied because higher state authorities found it to their advantage to leave lower posts vacant, to claim that these were filled, and to pocket the salaries of the imaginary public employees.[10] Needless to say, such practices further thinned a complement of state functionaries that was already quite emaciated, left major "holes" in public administration, and contributed to the state's general inability to monopolize physical or symbolic violence.

Beyond the fact that state employees were few in number and could be more virtual than real, those who were real flesh and blood had little or no training relevant to the positions they occupied, and the majority received no salary for the work they performed.[11] Rarely was there any pretense that state offices were there to serve "the public good" or that these offices operated according to impartial rules that applied equally to all. Instead, positions in the state bureaucracy were commonly used for the personal aggrandizement and profit of those who occupied them, as well as those who controlled appointments to these posts. Actually, the ability to name people to positions in the state bureaucracy could be quite lucrative. In Chachapoyas, those who exercised this power often charged a fee to those who were thus appointed, who were, in turn, left to recoup their investment (and more) in their day-to-day interactions with the populace under their jurisdiction.[12]

Nor did the Peruvian state exercise even a relative monopoly on the exercise of symbolic violence, which would have enabled the state to engage in what Corrigan and Sayer refer to as moral regulation:

> Out of the vast range of human social capacities—possible ways in which social life could be lived—state activities more or less forcibly "encourage" some while suppressing, marginalizing, eroding, undermining others....We call this moral regulation: a project of normalizing, rendering natural, taken for granted, in a word "obvious", what are in fact ontological and epistemological premises of a particular...form of social order. [Corrigan and Sayer 1985:4]

The central government's inability to regulate the moral domain was partly a function of its underdeveloped bureaucracy and the limited range of social activities it could effectively monitor. In addition, peculiarities of Peru's post-colonial history contributed to the state's difficulties in attempting to develop a truly national citizenry or culture.[13] Particularly important in this regard was the relationship between the actual practice of class-based and racially based domination in the many regional domains that dotted the Peruvian landscape and the egalitarian discourse of the still largely imaginary Peruvian nation-state.

Although Peru had been founded as an independent republic in the 1820s on liberal principles of democracy, citizenship, private property, and individual rights and protections, the central government was not remotely able to make good on these arrangements even one hundred years later. Such principles were uniformly invoked in all political ritual and dis-course—there was a language of the nation-state—but everyday life in much of the country was organized according to principles that were directly opposed to these precepts of popular sovereignty.

Chachapoyas, in the northern sierra, was one such region.[14] Dominat-ing the social and political landscape of this region was a group of white, aristocratic families of putatively Spanish descent who saw it as their birthright to rule over the region's large mestizo (in local slang, *cholo*) and Indian peasant populations. These elite families rejected any and all asser-tions of equality between themselves and the subaltern groups over which they ruled. In fact, the elite regarded themselves as a separate aristocratic caste—the *casta española*—that was naturally entitled to power and privilege because of its racial purity and cultural superiority. Even social interaction with cholos and *Indios* was kept to a minimum and was structured in such a way as to require public deference and subservience from these "lesser" peoples.

The practical problems of governing forced the central regime in Lima to ally with the aristocratic families to maintain even a semblance of con-trol in the outlying sections of its territory. The weakness of central state authority, the diffusion of the means of violence into multiple and antago-nistic hands, and widespread disagreement over the nature of legitimate rule rendered the central government unable to control the national terri-tory directly during this period. Those who controlled the central state apparatus were compelled to seek out clients among rural aristocratic fam-ilies who would rule in the name of the central regime.

In other words, although the independent republic of Peru had been born of armed struggle against absolutist Spain and although the central government embraced precepts that had emerged out of the Enlighten-ment, the actual operation of the state apparatus depended crucially on maintaining social structures of the ancien régime. At any one point in time, select elements of the landed class in Chachapoyas enjoyed the back-ing of the central government, but this class was far from unified. Rather, all members of the elite saw themselves as having the inherited right to rule, which no one, neither the central government nor other members of the elite, could legitimately deny them. Furthermore, in order to exercise these rights, the elite did not hesitate to use violence. Those who interfered with elite privilege did so at their own peril, as is attested to by elite families down to the present:

> In 1913 the president [of Peru]...was [Coronel Oscar] Benavides, an old friend of my great uncle Pablo M. Pizarro, who was senator of Amazonas. The two had gone to military school together.... Benavides appointed a new prefect for Amazonas, who traveled from Lima to Chachapoyas, where he expected to begin his duties. My great uncle [who, as senator, was living in Lima], however, was opposed to the appointment...and when the new prefect attempted to take up his post, he was informed that Senator Pizarro would not allow it. He [the new prefect] was denied entrance to the prefecture. After waiting for several weeks at El Molino [a hacienda of an opposing family, located just outside Chachapoyas], he returned to Lima. Shortly thereafter, the president called my great uncle into his office for an explanation. Challengingly, he asked my great uncle, "Who rules in Amazonas, you or me?" My uncle replied, "It looks like I do, doesn't it!" [Mariano Rubio Pizarro, June 27, 1991]

As this suggests, elite men regarded themselves as having no true peers, and certainly no masters. Rather, each believed that he had the right to use power in defense of prerogatives that were legitimately his because of the elite station in life he enjoyed by right of birth.

As a result, in the opening decades of the century, the operation of the state apparatus and the imagined community of the nation were "compromised" in two senses. First, the region's landed elite (people like Senator Pizarro) took conscious and systematic steps to contradict publicly what the "state stated" (Corrigan and Sayer 1985). The elite used state powers and public institutions to subvert the very forms of egalitarian personhood and homogenous public imagined in national discourse. The elite were compelled to do so for two reasons. On the one hand, national discourse emphasized equality before the law, citizenship, and constitutional rights as the only legitimate basis for national life. These principles blatantly contradicted the racial hierarchy and inherited privilege of the elite and the violent struggles for power that occurred as different factions of the elite— each with its own extensive clientele of cholos and Indios—battled for regional control. On the other hand, state institutions were designed from the center to support the public sphere imagined in national discourse, one consisting of a mass of formally identical (albeit male) citizens, each jurally indistinguishable from the next, all of whom were united behind the national cause of promoting "progress." This public sphere, as well as the institutions meant to support it, also offered an explicit critique of a social order in which local aristocratic elites and their clients used unlicensed violence on an endemic scale to defend their privileges.

To address the threat posed by the institutional and discursive presence of the nation-state, the ruling faction of the elite (referred to as the ruling *casta*) repeatedly and publicly demonstrated its ability to *ridicule* national injunctions about proper behavior. The ruling elite faction took great care to violate the constitutional protections of those belonging to the opposing, elite-led faction (the opposing casta) and to do great harm to their person and property. As important as the actual violation of these rights, however, was the ability of the ruling faction to show that it could do so with impunity. In other words, the ruling faction went to great lengths to compromise state institutions and national discourse, using both to further the aims of social groupings (their own faction), statuses (superordinate racial categories), and forms of interaction (violence and domination) that were unthinkable (or deemed "archaic") within the discourse of the nation-state.

The nation-state was further compromised by the dysfunctional nature of the "democracy" that emerged out of these conditions. To protect itself from the ruling casta, the opposing casta organized itself into a set of positions that replicated the state apparatus—a shadow state (see Nugent 1999b). This alternative structure of governance included individuals whose positions mirrored those of the departmental prefect, provincial subprefects, and district governors, thus replicating the posts of the executive branch of government. It included, as well, individuals and corporate bodies (mayors and municipal councils) that replicated the structure of municipal government, complete with councilors for each of the areas distinguished therein. It even included senators and congressional deputies; the manner in which they were chosen indicates just how dysfunctional this democracy was.

Elections for senator and congressional deputy (other than the presidency, the only posts for which elections were held) were violent affairs, the first stage in their outcome being decided only when one casta managed to defeat the other in an armed battle for control of the voting booths on election day (Basadre 1980; Nugent 1997; Taylor 1986). Despite this initial setback, the losing casta was rarely willing to concede defeat and went on to organize new elections for the same posts. In this new electoral contest, only its own clients could vote.

The losing casta justified its actions by making the quite accurate claim that the electoral victory of the winning faction had been based on violence and intimidation. It therefore violated democratic procedure and should be considered null and void. Oddly enough, in this second expression of the people's will, the candidates of the losing casta were uniformly victorious. As a result, the elected representatives of both castas attempted to take up their posts in Congress in the national capital, all claiming to be the democratically elected senators or deputies. It was then up to Congress as a whole to decide who had actually won the election (see Basadre 1980). The process by which Congress did so was anything but rapid or straightforward, because of which it often remained unclear for months at a time who was in the shadows and who was not. Even when Congress did reach a decision, the casta whose representatives had been disqualified was unlikely to concede defeat.

As a result, at any given point in time, both the ruling and the opposing factions sought to occupy the same political space, and both claimed to be "the legally constituted authority." Neither of these factions could hold on to the state apparatus for more than five to ten years before being deposed by the other. Furthermore, in that the rise of one faction inevitably meant persecution, decline, and even demise for the other, each faction fought viciously to protect its own interests.

In these conditions, the populace could not possibly view elected representatives as having been chosen according to neutral and impartial procedures. Nor could the population view the outcome of elections as an expression of the collective will of the people. That contending elite factions used the state apparatus to advance their own interests in the most blatant of manners also made it very difficult for people to regard the state as a discrete entity that stood above and beyond society or to view the nation as an entity with a general will or interest. Not only did intercasta struggles to control the apparatus of state compromise the integrity of normative democratic procedures, but these same struggles also ridiculed and undermined the very precepts of state and nationhood.

Involved in violent encounters with members of opposing factions on an ongoing basis, the ruling faction was nonetheless the official representative of the independent republic of Peru within the department of Amazonas—a republic founded on liberal, Enlightenment principles of individual rights and protections, the sanctity of person and property, and equality under the law. As a result, the ruling faction, while committed to making constant attacks upon the life and property of the opposition, was equally compelled to present itself in all political ritual and in all political discourse as the sole and true defender of state-endorsed principles of popular sovereignty.[15] In these rhetorical and ritual spaces, the ruling elite faction elaborated a mythical social order that was the antithesis of factional politics and aristocratic hierarchy. In place of violence, insecurity, and privilege, everyday life was depicted as consensual and orderly, and individuals were portrayed as universally enjoying the protections of life, liberty, and property granted them by the Constitution. In ritual and discourse, unity and harmony prevailed, and distinctions of race, gender, and class—upon which the entire aristocratic order was based—ceased to exist. In their stead, the ruling faction asserted the existence of a mass of identical (male) "citizens," all of whom were united behind the cause of promoting "progress."

The particular elite faction that controlled the apparatus of state was forced to offer public accounts of its deeds by invoking notions of equality, individual rights, and the "common good" that directly contradicted its own actions. Aristocratic "sovereignty," which was being played out on the ground, could not be celebrated or even acknowledged in formal political spheres. There was no space for it within the language of the nation-state. Popular sovereignty had to be celebrated, despite the fact that it had virtually no relation to any existing social reality.

In other words, the attempts of warring, elite-led factions to legitimate aristocratic sovereignty, when popular sovereignty represented the sole terms in which political life could be represented, compromised the nation-state and made it very difficult for the state to "forcibly 'encourage' the forms of social life imagined in national discourse" (Corrigan and Sayer 1985:4). The state could not become the very organ of social thought and moral discipline (see Durkheim 1904) because those responsible for "translating" state discourse into actual practice were determined to contradict what the state stated.

Elite efforts to compromise the nation-state were internally contradictory. The more elites "misused" state institutions to undermine the egalitarian forms of personhood and public imagined in national discourse, the more powerfully they generated the image of a state form that was an inversion of their own compromised creation. The very fact that the elite devoted such unceasing attention to compromising the nation-state suggests the existence of something of which the elite were deathly afraid, something so powerful and so dangerous to elite power that it had to be compromised and negated at every opportunity. The "thing" in question was a nation-state liberated from the abuses of the local elite, one that truly did represent justice, equality, and the common good.

There were important spatial and temporal dimensions to this process. The public demonstrations in which the elite showed their ability to hold the liberated nation-state at bay—that is, the success of the elite in compromising the state apparatus regionally—created the illusion (and illusion it was) that a liberated nation-state existed in a different spatial domain, lying beyond the reach of regional power holders. And because the liberated nation-state had been distanced from local affairs, it was possible for the popular classes to conceive of the liberated nation-state not only as a "thing" that could arrive from afar but also as a thing whose arrival was being thwarted by the elite. And because the liberated nation-state was associated with democracy, modernity, and the future and because the elite self-consciously harkened back to tradition and the past, the spatial plane became a temporal one as well. Not only were the elite holding the liberated nation-state at bay geographically, but also backwardness and tradition were thwarting the advance of democracy, modernity, and progress.

In sum, elite efforts to compromise the nation-state helped produce a distinctive version of the "state effect" (Abrams 1988). Unlike the situation in the highly bureaucratized and governmentalized polities of Western Europe, in the Chachapoyas region, it was the absence instead of the presence of state institutions and government experts that created the illusion that the state was a real thing. Furthermore, because the elite placed themselves in opposition to the principles of popular sovereignty, poor and marginalized groups could seize upon the image of an absent nation-state as a moral alternative to aristocratic and authoritarian rule.

APRA'S FUNCTIONAL DEMOCRACY

> If everyone is equal, when someone says, "Let's get together, a group of us, to build this irrigation canal. Let's do it, all of us, united," then people work together. This is democracy. People [are willing to] do this because they know that when everyone is equal, working together helps everyone. But the anti-democratic system is that the governor [the local state functionary] appears and says, "Listen, you shitty cholos, damn it, if you haven't finished this canal by Monday morning at 8:00 a.m., you're all going to spend twenty-four hours in jail." [Silvestre Rodriguez Goivín, May 11, 1983]

In the 1930s the aristocratic order of Chachapoyas came undone in the face of pressure exerted by APRA,[16] a proscribed political party that organized extensively among subaltern groups and succeeded in establishing underground party cells throughout the region.[17] In bringing its message to the regional population, APRA seized upon the very ideals that the elite had been at such pains to ridicule—and that had therefore been so notable through *absence*—and tried to make these present. The party generated new, vernacularized meanings for these terms that had great appeal to subaltern groups. In so doing, APRA gave expression to an alternative form of democracy that implied sweeping change in relations of race, gender, property, and politics. Despite the very real dangers involved in party membership (imprisonment, blacklisting, even torture and execution), APRA succeeded in attracting much of the regional population to its cause. As a result, the party was able to survive long periods of political repression and eventually became a permanent part of the Peruvian political scene.[18]

APRA generated a scathing critique of the aristocratic order and its injustices, a critique sufficiently grounded in truth to make it compelling. Drawing on these injustices, the party framed its alternative vision of democracy. According to APRA, casta leaders were brutal and rapacious individuals, wholly lacking in culture or humanity, who had used claims of racial superiority and noble lineage to visit upon society at large the most outrageous forms of abuse. With support from collaborators amongst the common people, casta leaders had employed indiscriminate violence to terrorize the general populace, placing people in a constant state of insecurity and fear. A population so intimidated and internally divided, APRA argued, was easy prey for the casta families, who used their positions to deprive even the most humble people of their wealth, labor, and dignity. The aristocratic families treated the region's Indios and cholos like beasts of burden whose sole purpose in life was to do the bidding of the elite.

As a result, the party asserted, a region rich in resources, with abundant fertile land and an industrious, hardworking population, had been reduced to the sorriest of states. The central government had long recognized the region's potential and had provided funds to build highways, airports, and hydroelectric plants. It had given money to construct hospitals and schools, to increase agricultural production, and to expand industry. These efforts, however, had come to naught. The monies sent for projects of improvement always seemed to disappear into the pockets of the aristocratic families. Although these families represented themselves as the sole and true defenders of the public good, their only concern was to maintain their own lavish lifestyles. They had never hesitated to steal public funds, subvert the intentions of government officials, or betray the public trust.

In the meantime, APRA argued, subordinate groups were unable to provide their families with even the basic necessities of life—nutritious food, clean water, adequate housing, medical attention. They were unable to educate their children or defend their rights. In the grips of such an oppressive power structure, with no one to take up their cause, the masses had been unable to change their life circumstances. Generation after generation, they lived in extreme ignorance and abject poverty.

The plight of brutish Indios and cholos was of no concern to the aristocratic families, despite public claims to the contrary. The elite believed themselves to be separated from these uncouth creatures by an enormous gulf of history, civilization, race, refinement, and culture. It was this attitude of extreme noblesse oblige, APRA claimed, that had inflicted such enormous damage on the region and its people. It was not just the poverty of the majority that could be laid at the feet of the elite, the party asserted, or even the highly factionalized and violent condition of regional society. In addition, the extreme state of abandonment and decay that characterized Chachapoyas could be directly attributed to the baleful influence of the aristocratic families.

APRA represented Chachapoyas as a region with enormous potential for prosperity, whose poverty, dysfunction, and backwardness had been forced upon it by an aristocratic elite (mis)representing itself as "the people," as patriotic citizens who were united behind the cause of advancing the common good. According to APRA, "the people" did *not* refer to the privileged minority of literate, property-owning white males who had long dominated political life. Instead of *being* the people, the elite had *betrayed* the people, had betrayed the masses of illiterate and semiliterate peasants, artisans, and workers who performed the labor upon which social life depended.[19]

> When speaking to the country folk, we had to be very careful not to use abstract terms that they would not understand, that would make it appear that we thought we were superior to them. We had to speak in simple, direct terms....We would say [to the peasants], "*Society* means 'the people.' Instead of treating us like we are ignorant, like Indios, none of this! *We* are society! *We* are the people! Or did you think that 'the people' referred only to princes or kings, who have money, or to the merchants, who also have money? No! 'The people' are the humble, uneducated folk who want to live better lives, who want to help their neighbors so that they can help themselves." [Nicolas Tuesta Valenzuela, August 17, 1985]

These people, the despised Indios and cholos, the party argued, were responsible for whatever progress the region had made. As descendents of the great Inca Empire, the laboring masses had always recognized the importance of the common good, had always understood the necessity of individual sacrifice to achieve collectively agreed-upon goals. They were only waiting for the opportunity to be free of the elite yoke so that they could develop their potential to the fullest.

APRA's belief in the need for progress and the importance of sacrifice framed the party's ideas about "participation," ideas that were directly at odds with those of the old elite. According to the casta families, their right-ful positions of leadership at the head of regional society entitled them, and them alone, to exercise the right to vote—the sine qua non of democ-ratic participation. Only individuals whose race, class, and gender qualified them as fully rational, responsible, and adult could be entrusted with such an important task.

APRA insisted that participation in a real democracy had little to do with the right to vote—or with any of the rights of liberal democracy per se. These rights pertained only to the political realm. Limiting participation to the exercise of these rights, APRA argued, denied the majority the ability to control the most important aspects of their everyday lives, especially their conditions of work. It also reproduced the fissures of race, gender, and class that so deeply divided regional society, and it left elite control over politics uncontested. The dysfunctional democracy of the casta fami-lies, the party asserted, was little more than a contest among bullies to decide who would be given the opportunity to mistreat the masses.

According to APRA, *participation* was a far broader, far more inclusive term than the aristocratic families allowed. Contrary to the claims of the elite, it did not refer to a narrow political right (the vote) that conferred upon a fortunate few the unilateral power to determine the fate of all oth-ers. Rather, *participation* referred to a broad set of complex *duties* that ensured that everyone would be actively involved in making decisions about, and in sharing responsibility for, the well-being of everyone else. In its broadest sense, *participation* referred to the obligation of all citizens to come together collectively to determine the conditions of their own exis-tence. It implied, as well, the duty to work steadfastly toward the realization of these collectively established goals.

The collective duties implied by the term *participation* took on special meaning with respect to the rural populace, most of whom belonged to indigenous peasant communities that exercised collective tenure over large areas of land (or so APRA believed). In carrying the party's message about participation to these communities, APRA emphasized to people the cooperative nature of work under their ancestors, the Inca, and the importance of strengthening the "primitive communism" the Incas had practiced.[20]

> We stressed to people the *communal* nature of the Inca, that they had practiced a form of communism. We explained that we wanted to strengthen the [Inca] system of cooperativism in the communities to help people overcome their problems—economic, social, and political. This was the only way they could achieve prosperity. [Máximo Rodriguez Culqui, September 3, 1985]
>
> We would say to them, "The *cacique* [the local notable responsible for carrying out state decrees] was a true democrat....He gathered the groups together and built roads, bringing progress to his community. What is a community? What is the meaning of community? Why do they exist? They exist to work the land cooperatively so that we can harvest our fields, so that we can help one another." This democracy [of the Inca] was a democracy in *practice*. [Mario Reina Fernandez, July 8, 2001]

Along with industrial, mining, and agricultural collectives (the latter being former plantations), APRA intended to make cooperative indigenous communities one of the pillars of a peculiarly Latin American form of socialism. Indeed, according to the party, the presence of large numbers of indigenous communities distinguished Latin America from Europe. Communism as envisioned by Karl Marx was therefore inappropriate to the New World, which required a distinctive type of socialism based on the specificities of the region's history and land tenure.[21]

> The party wanted to preserve cooperativism as a way of uniting the people so that they could improve their lives. Party members spoke to peasants often about these plans. When the community had turned out to work together to put the roof on a house [for example], with the men working and women preparing the food, at night, after the work was done, there would be a *fiesta*. The Apristas would work with the community during the day, and at night we would speak. We would say, "Only united as we were today and only with this joy in working for the common good can we ensure the happiness and prosperity of our peo-

ple." This is what APRA wanted to do, and in all the Spanish-speaking countries of America. [Nicolas Tuesta Valenzuela, July 23, 1985]

APRA worked out quite detailed plans concerning how to strengthen the cooperative structures of the indigenous communities—plans that shed much light on what the party meant by participation.[22]

> In the communities, APRA wanted to preserve the existing communal system, but to strengthen it and modernize it. We wanted to make modern farming machinery available to people so that they could produce more food. We wanted to help them build schools and clinics and improve roads. Our goal was to increase output without changing the internal organization of production. [Victor Santillan Gutierrez, January 22, 2001]

APRA intended to strengthen and expand existing deliberative processes in the communities. The purpose was to involve the entire population, women and men alike, in the decision-making process:

> Cooperatives were to function according to laws that *all* the *comuneros* would debate and establish, even the women....We believed that by involving *everyone* in making decisions, people would learn to trust one another, to work together toward common goals....People outside the community would not be able to interfere in its internal affairs. [Victor Santillan Gutierrez, January 22, 2001]

The party also sought to ensure that power would not become concentrated in the hands of a small political elite:[23]

> There would be a managing council for the community that would be responsible for implementing the decisions made collectively by the members. Membership on the council would rotate, and the council would sit for only two years before being changed. Because the community would always develop new problems, there would be the need for new leaders to address them. [Victor Santillan Gutierrez, January 22, 2001]

APRA believed that involving the entire community in collective decision making would strengthen cooperative relations among people and create in each person a sense of duty and commitment to the well-being of the community as a whole, what the party referred to as "civic morality."

The party sought to give communities the autonomy they would need to develop civic morality, by breaking their dependence on the privileged classes that exploited them, especially merchants and hacendados.[24]

> We used to tell the peasants, "Cooperativism means to cooperate, to unite, to join together in order to liberate ourselves from those who exploit us. The goal of the merchant is profit. When he sells you something, he charges you double what it cost him to buy it. Or when he lends you money, he makes you pay back twice as much as he lent you. *Business* is the word the merchants use to describe this. *Business* means only one thing—to rob people scandalously." But the cooperatives we formed were institutions that benefited the *group*. If one talks about business, one does so in order to exploit people, and never did we talk about business in cooperativism. We placed ourselves in opposition to business, in opposition to this way of robbing the people. [Victor Santillan Gutierrez, February 20, 2001]

Independence from their exploiters, however, would not be sufficient to establish true unity among the people. APRA believed that it was imperative for all community members to become actively involved in making collective decisions about their own economic affairs. In particular, party organizers stressed the importance of what would now be referred to as "participatory budgeting." Only by engaging in this practice could the community overcome the divisive effects of individual economic strategizing.

> Each community was to establish its own savings cooperative, which was to operate like a bank for members of the community...but with one important difference [compared with normal banks]. The goal of the savings cooperative was not to make a profit, but to help community members....We believed that increased [agricultural] output in the communities [from the use of modern production techniques] would...mean more money in the savings cooperative, which could be used for whatever purpose the people chose...to build schools, clinics, potable water systems, better roads. In democracy, it is the people's will that matters. The *people* choose, and that is the end of the matter. [Victor Santillan Gutierrez, January 22, 2001]

APRA also developed ideas about how the reinforced cooperative structures could be used to promote the collective use of productive resources, which, in turn, would strengthen interdependence among community members.

> Each community was to have its own truck or other means of transport and also its own farm machinery. The machinery could be rented to any community member, and whatever the person paid would go into the savings cooperative. Or families would work together to farm each family's plot [using manual labor]. This would help preserve the communal structure....
>
> The community would work some land in common, sell the crops from their land, and use the profits to purchase tools for the common use of the community. When a community member wanted to host a *faena* [a community-wide cooperative work party], he could save money by renting the tools from the communal storehouse. Or the community as a whole could borrow the money from its own savings cooperative to purchase barbed wire to fence off pasture—to ensure proper pasture rotation— and could later repay the loan. A single community member could also borrow money, at low interest rates. Whatever community members spent when they rented tools or paid interest would benefit the *community* instead of going to outsiders. Just imagine! The community could also purchase barbed wire in quantity and could sell it at a reduced rate to community members. This would eliminate the middlemen, the town merchants, who overcharged peasants so scandalously. [Victor Santillan Gutierrez, January 22, 2001]

APRA believed that establishing cooperative structures of this kind would help unify people and, in the process, help them overcome the most serious problems they confronted in their everyday lives. The goal was "progress," but not strictly in material terms. "We told people, 'We should not try to live like the rich. No! We should live in moderation so that we have clean water, so that we do not suffer from disease, so that our houses are made of adobe instead of wood, so that our homes have roofs of tile instead of straw. We can do it, but only if everyone is *united*'" (Mario Reina Fernandez, July 14, 2001).

In other words, APRA believed that the challenges people faced were as much political and cultural as they were material. Only "education" could bring about true progress.

Education is the basis of everything, but a transformed education, an education that stresses practical skills and the principles behind the practices people already know. Only education that allows people to recognize their basic equality can bring about progress. Education of this kind helps establish a way of life that is cultured, in which people are brought together rather than divided. True progress helps [people] develop [a sense of] civic morality and mutual responsibility for one another....In cooperatives, civic morality can be learned simply and directly, as a result of people's experience. They [are able to] learn about their obligations to the land and to their community. [Carlosmagno Guevarra Santillan, September 4, 1986]

APRA referred to this form of pedagogy as "really useful education." In later years, when party members discovered the writings of Brazilian philosopher Paulo Freire, they believed that they had found a kindred spirit. When speaking among themselves, Apristas were fond of quoting Freire:[25] "Every community is a production unit, a place where people cooperate to produce what they all need to survive. But it should be far more than that. It should also be a *pedagogical* unit, a place where people learn what is most important for them to know, what is most important for them to value" (Nicolas Muñoz Valenzuela, August 1, 1985).

As the foregoing suggests, an "ethics of participation" permeated virtually every aspect of APRA's vision of popular rule. Indeed, those who were unwilling to work toward collectively established goals were, in the party's view, guilty of the worst kind of crime. During the reign of the Inca, they had been summarily executed, and in the most brutal of ways.

The Inca Empire was based on *equality*. A single call from a cacique [a local elite] would bring out all the people to work together to build terraces, redirect rivers, harvest the fields. This was the period of savage democracy [*democracia salvaje*]....We were united at this time, and we were equal, so we were democratic, but we relied on systems of violence. Brutal punishments were used then, especially for the lazy person, the one who thought he was better than others, who refused to work like the rest. The caciques would grab people like this and march them to the top of a fortress, lie them down on the wall of the fortress, and—PA!—smash their heads in with a large rock. This was how they carried out justice. This was how they protected their democracy. [Nicolas Muñoz Valenzuela, August 19, 1985]

Because APRA's democracy was not so primitive—the party advocated due process of law—Apristas did not argue that such people should be summarily executed. Nevertheless, the party regarded them much as did the Inca. At times, they were likened to poisonous snakes, as in *Race of Vipers*, a book written about the casta families. At other times, they were described as parasites, as creatures that lived off the energy and vitality of other beings. They might even be pitied, despite their wealth and the negative influence they exercised on their fellows, because they condemned themselves to lives of isolation. This isolation, born of their attachment to *things*, made them fearful of their neighbors and unable to know the kind of freedom that can only come from the security of strong, community-based ties. APRA told people that

> the man who doesn't work and who lives off the sweat of others doesn't understand freedom or democracy. He doesn't understand freedom because he lives in fear, that others will take back from him what he has taken from them. He doesn't understand democracy because he is afraid to cooperate with his neighbors. He cannot really participate in the social world that surrounds him. Imagine the spiritual poverty of such a person! Despite his riches, he lacks culture. He must live cut off from his community. [Victor Castilla Pizarro, August 3, 1990]

The alternative form of democratic practice that APRA sought to bring into being was based on a distinctive notion of participation, conceived of as a duty instead of a right. The participatory structures the party worked to establish as the basis of this democracy were intended to promote unity and cooperation that was at once moral, ethical, political, cultural, and material. Only such structures, APRA believed, could act as the basis of real progress.

The party also developed concrete plans concerning how to establish its alternative democracy at the national level. The party envisioned a structure of political and economic life in which productive resources (especially land, mines, and industry) would be expropriated and converted into collective property.[26] The rural and urban laboring classes as a whole would be grouped into cooperatives, at the enterprise level, in each major branch of the economy (production, distribution, consumption). Egalitarian political structures would be established within these cooperatives, which would enjoy autonomous decision-making powers.[27]

The cooperatives were to do more than manage their own economic affairs. Cooperative representatives were to assemble on a regular basis in local, departmental, regional, and national congresses (referred to collectively as the National Economic Congress, NEC) to decide national priorities and policies (Nugent 1999a). The NEC was to replace Peru's existing legislative bodies (the Senate and the Chamber of Deputies), which were seen as organizations that allowed the elite to reproduce their own narrow, class interests. Only an entirely new governing body such as the NEC, APRA argued, could involve the population as a whole in deciding how the wealth of the nation would be used. This would bring to an end the irrational use of the nation's resources and the perpetuation of poverty for the majority.

APRA thus sought to collapse the boundary between domains whose separation and autonomy were built into the very evolution of liberal democracy in Western Europe, the political and the economic (Nugent 1999a). The party wanted to institutionalize a form of democratic practice in which economic processes would be subordinated to and embedded in community-based social and political structures (see Polanyi 1944, 1957). APRA referred to this organization as "functional democracy" and argued that it was an important alternative to the liberal democracy of the United States and Europe. The party claimed that liberal democracy had proven itself a failure in Peru (Nugent 1999a).

APRA'S PRIESTS OF DEMOCRACY

> We Apristas wanted to establish equality in *all* things so that the poor man, who is made to grovel in shame before the wealthy man, realizes that he is not an insignificant worm who is condemned to drag himself along the ground, but is a being fully equal to the rich man, who treads on fancy carpets and dines off of fine china in the grandest of homes. [Mario Reina Fernandez, July 8, 2001]
>
> We did not tell people, "Compañeros, if you join us, when we come to power, we will give *your* son a job in the prefect's office and *yours* a position in the courts." We didn't try to appeal to people's greed or take advantage of their poverty. That was what the castas did....We didn't tell people, "APRA will set you free" or "APRA will put food on your table." Instead, APRA had a different message....We told people, "We ourselves will gain our own freedom. We will enjoy the fruit of our own labor. We will work as

we always have and as we should, but without *hu-mi-li-a-tion*...without having to answer to those with money...[but] first, we have to become *united*. We have to begin by learning to work together. We have to begin [for example] by building our own *horno* [kiln] here in the community so that we can make our own roof tiles, so that we can help one another bring the clay and make the fire, together. We have to become strong. Only in this way, by beginning with one another in our own communities, can we become united. Only in this way will we be ready when our time comes to take power." [Victor Santillan Gutierrez, February 13, 2001]

APRA fervently believed that real democracy could be achieved only if all the people came together collectively to determine the conditions of their own lives in a unified and equal manner. In bringing the party's message about democracy to subordinate groups, APRA stressed the need for unity and equality above all other themes. Party organizers never tired of expounding on these topics and were gratified to find what was generally a receptive audience. At the same time, the Apristas discovered that they had to repeat their message again and again. APRA believed that both the appeal of its discourse on unity and equality and the need for its endless repetition were symptomatic of broader social problems—problems that presented the party with enormous challenges in its efforts to bring about social transformation. Most of these problems revolved around the lingering influence of the divisive, hierarchical, cultural logic of aristocratic rule.

In the party's assessment, among the most damaging legacies of the casta order was that the population had been deeply scarred by a cultural politics of *difference*. This did more than simply force people to accept lives of humiliation and abuse, tragic and intolerable as that was. So terrorized had the populace been by the violence of casta rule and so long had they labored under its yoke that the invidious distinctions of the aristocratic order had lodged themselves deep in people's emotions and psyches, distorting their entire system of values and their life aspirations. Indios and cholos had come to believe in their own inferiority. They strove to be like the rich—pampered, indulgent, and abusive. Although the nationalization of land and industry and the formation of cooperatives were essential to bring about democratic transformation, APRA believed, structural reform would be insufficient unless the people were first led through a series of profound personal and cultural transformations. In other words, only the most sweeping and systematic of assaults on the entire notion of difference could lay the groundwork necessary for democratic transformation.[28]

APRA saw it as the party's special task to seek out and destroy any and all manifestations of difference, material or cultural, associated with the reproduction of the old, aristocratic order. Apristas were particularly concerned with practices that allowed one person or group to assert superiority over another. The party approached the elimination of these practices with nothing short of missionary zeal, treating virtually any expression of distinction as a form of depravity or moral outrage that simply had to be effaced from the earth.[29] To take but one example:

> A person should always behave in a respectful, polite manner with respect to others and not spit in a scandalous manner. If you want to spit, you first excuse yourself, and go outside and spit. Can I be called a *caballero* if I spit right in front of you, at your very feet? I would not be a caballero. Rather, you are the real caballero, and I am a mere cholo. Why? Because I spit at your feet. This is the democracy of individual behavior. [Máximo Rodriguez Culqui, September 5, 1985]

It is not difficult to understand why the party took such an extreme position with respect to assertions of difference. APRA believed itself to be locked in a battle of world historical proportions with the most repressive and backward of social elements imaginable—Peru's aristocratic elites and the deeply stratified social order from which they had long benefited. Nothing less than justice and democracy for the masses hung in the balance. Material and cultural difference alike threatened to undermine the unity upon which the success of APRA's war with the old order depended. It therefore could not be tolerated in any form.

Considering what was at stake, APRA believed that its assault on difference could not be undertaken by just anyone. Rather, it could be entrusted only to the most worthy of individuals. Only people who had shown that they fully understood the gravity of the situation could even be considered for such a task. Only those who had been specially trained could be allowed to "wage war for democracy" (a favorite expression of party leaders). Only individuals who had demonstrated beyond any doubt that they were prepared to make the enormous sacrifices required of them could be trusted to lead APRA's assault on difference.

To prove themselves worthy of being included in this noble effort, in the early 1930s a vanguard of young Apristas subjected themselves to several years of secret training at the hands of more experienced party organizers (see Nugent 2008).[30] During their training, these "novices" learned essential new disciplines of the mind and body that were intended to free them of the cultural weight of casta rule so that they no longer feared the elite, no longer felt awe of aristocratic pretensions, and no longer coveted the wealth or power of the casta families. Indeed, one of the central goals of APRA's indoctrination process was to produce highly disciplined subjects who would be wholly committed to the principles of democracy, equality, and freedom for which the party stood (Nugent 2006).

The training of this elite vanguard of Apristas was broad and rigorous. To learn new disciplines of the mind, the novices read, discussed, and critiqued major works of political and economic theory that had bearing on the problems of Latin America. Party organizers were careful to place special emphasis on the ability to explain the strengths and weaknesses of different doctrines to simple, untutored folk and constantly tested and assessed the novices' abilities to do so. To assist the novices in developing new disciplines of the body, organizers taught that the excesses considered typical of youth—sex and alcohol, in particular—should be avoided. They encouraged good hygiene, regular sleeping habits, and moderation in alcohol consumption. They taught the young Apristas to do calisthenics daily upon waking, helped them organize soccer and volleyball teams, and insisted that they practice and compete on a regular basis. Party organizers also carefully monitored the conduct of their charges in these areas and had them monitor one another's conduct as well (Nugent 2008).[31]

APRA organizers sought to make their novices as "cultured" as possible. There were two dimensions to this process. On the one hand, aspiring party leaders had to acquire the knowledge and master the skills needed to defend their rights. For example, they had to master self-defense techniques, become proficient in the use of firearms and explosives, and learn how to evade the police. They also had to have a thorough grasp of the works of Marx, Proudhon, Gonzalez Prada, and Gandhi and be able to explain these succinctly and spontaneously to a variety of audiences.[32]

On the other hand, the future APRA leaders had to develop the courage and integrity necessary to face the dangers involved in challenging injustice. Party organizers involved their apprentices in "missions" to perform important tasks for the party, from delivering secret messages to Apristas in other towns, to spreading party propaganda in the dead of night, to gathering intelligence from the police and other government functionaries, to organizing new party cells. The missions were graded by level of difficulty, and organizers were careful to expose their fledgling party leaders to progressively more risk. In this way, they were able to gauge the degree to which the novices developed the courage necessary to assume positions of party leadership (Nugent 2008).

As the training continued, APRA organizers carefully evaluated their novices' progress, paying special attention to each person's strengths and weaknesses. They did so with an eye to who would be best suited to fill each of the fifteen secretariats of which the party was composed (see below). After training these apprentices for half a decade and observing their behavior in increasingly trying circumstances, party leaders decided that they had matured to the point that they could assume direct control over the party apparatus. At this point, when their education was complete, these individuals began to refer to themselves as "priests of democracy" (*sacerdotes de la democracia*), a term of deep respect that only the most committed Apristas used with one another.[33] The "priests" were entrusted with the difficult task of preparing the masses for democratic transformation.

APRA'S LIBERATED NATION-STATE

The way the party was organized greatly assisted APRA's priests of democracy in their efforts to wage war on difference and prepare the masses for democracy. APRA was subject to intense persecution by government authorities, and its strategy for survival was based on the elaboration of a complex, subterranean party structure. APRA organized itself explicitly as an underground state apparatus, one that reproduced the national territorial grid. In principle, there were APRA cells or committees for each district, province, and department in Peru and a national committee (located in Lima) for the country as a whole.[34] The subterranean party-state was made up of the secretariats of the interior, organization, propaganda, discipline, culture, popular education, higher education, economy, social welfare, unions, labor, cooperatives, municipal government, indigenous and peasant affairs, and youth, responsible for attending to the affairs of particular categories of the population. Furthermore, the prerogatives and responsibilities of each secretariat were carefully spelled out.

Even though APRA was forced to operate in secret, beyond the gaze of the legally constituted authorities, its subterranean party-state succeeded in involving itself directly and extensively in the everyday lives of the population. APRA's ability to do so stemmed, in part, from the way the party organized its cells and the activities of cell members. These were made up of secretaries, each of which represented one of the fifteen secretariats composing the APRA party-state. The party attempted to have secretaries for as many of its secretariats as possible in every cell or committee, whether it was in a remote rural district or a large urban center.

It was this organizational structure that party priests drew upon in launching their assault on difference and in preparing the masses for democracy. There were several elements to this strategy. First, Apristas tried to provide the humblest of their members with a concrete sense of the more exalted position they would enjoy in the party's alternative democracy. Party priests did so by giving people glimpses of what APRA meant by the term *citizenship*—by providing them with at least some of the freedoms that the party regarded as the foundation of a true democracy. The Aprista vanguard argued that among the most important of these was the freedom from *fear*, especially the fear of coercion. The rural populace was subject to many kinds of fear, but the party leadership believed that people lived in constant dread that the family members would be forced to abandon their homes for extended periods of time on a moment's notice to serve as military conscripts in the armed forces or as labor conscripts for the government's endless public works projects.[35]

To provide humble party members with glimpses of the freedom from fear, the priests of democracy disrupted government efforts to extort peasant labor. They did so by drawing on the party's disciplined membership and its widely dispersed party apparatus to subject the formal apparatus of state to a kind of countersurveillance. This surveillance was intended to enable party priests to generate detailed knowledge about government plans and to translate that knowledge into methods of control. In the process, the Apristas worked to subvert the normal operation of the state.

The party focused much of its countersurveillance activities on the public employees who formulated state plans to conscript labor for military and civilian purposes alike. APRA assigned a select group of party priests the task of becoming the close confidants of these government planners, to such an extent that the Apristas were compelled to socialize, drink, and gamble with them on a regular basis.[36] APRA focused its remaining countersurveillance energies on the Guardia Civil (National Police). These government functionaries were responsible for traveling to the rural districts to apprehend conscripts (who often attempted to flee and had to be brought in at the point of a bayonet). Initially, party priests developed friendships only with members of the Guardia Civil. They were so successful, however, that they ended up establishing a secret party cell among members of the National Police.[37] One party organizer explained:

> I have real admiration for the Guardias [who were Apristas] ...who helped the party during the [years when APRA was subject to] persecution [by the government]. They risked a great deal for us....They were like a CIA Aprista [an APRA Central Intelligence Agency]. Whenever they could, they would ignore us when they saw us carrying out our [nighttime] missions. They

would also report to [APRA's] Departmental Command about their [upcoming] assignments to the countryside [to conscript labor]. Every time they [did so], they put their careers at risk. They showed great courage, and they provided us with information that was crucial to our cause. We owe them much. [Nicolas Muñoz Valenzuela, August 18, 1985]

By carefully cultivating these contacts, the party was often able to learn where and when the government planned to extort labor. An important part of APRA's day-to-day activities consisted of collecting and processing this "secret intelligence" and, when necessary, sending party messengers on emergency missions to the rural districts to warn the Apristas under threat. They were then able to go into hiding, thus avoiding forced labor and military conscription without provoking a confrontation with government officials.[38]

The priests of democracy advanced their assault on difference by offering people glimpses of a different kind of freedom—freedom from hopelessness. Much of the population occupied the bottom rung of a hierarchical social structure that denied them access to the basic necessities of life—medical care, legal protections, material assistance during times of hardship or crisis (the sickness or death of family members, for example). The Aprista leadership believed that these people were so isolated, so poor, and faced such systematic discrimination that they had been made to feel utterly powerless. This distorted people's psyches, condemning them to profound feelings of despair.

The party vanguard worked to lift the veil of hopelessness from people's lives by providing them with much needed services that would make people realize that they could control their own destiny. The party was fortunate to count among its members a considerable number of professionals—doctors, nurses, lawyers, notary publics, court scribes, even judges—who were more than willing to make their talents available to their less fortunate fellow travelers. It was a relatively simple matter for party priests to make the services of these professionals available to party faithful, because of APRA's internally differentiated, widely dispersed party structure. If a peasant party member in one of the rural districts needed a doctor, for example, she could inform the district-level secretary of social welfare. He would send a secret message to the secretary of social welfare for the entire province, and this secretary was usually able to find a party doctor who would treat the peasant, either for free or at a greatly reduced cost.[39]

The party did more than simply provide people with services. A key dimension to APRA's assault on difference consisted of its efforts to establish *organizations* that would help people do the same. Party priests invested much energy in forming new social institutions based on egalitarian involvement, democratic decision making, and generalized participation. A great many people joined these organizations, which varied widely in form and function. They included sports clubs (soccer and volleyball), neighborhood associations, social clubs, reading groups, discussion circles, and debating societies—organizations with a predominantly social or cultural orientation. They also included cooperatives, labor unions, and mutual aid societies—organizations that were more economic and political in nature. As noted above, the party put major emphasis on strengthening the institutions in peasant communities that involved cooperative exchanges of labor and the communal ownership of land.

Party priests played an important supervisory role in virtually all of these organizations. This gave them the opportunity to speak at length to people about the importance of other freedoms that the party regarded as integral to real democracy—freedom from poverty, ignorance, dependency, servitude, and humiliation. Underlying the party's entire discourse on these freedoms was its assertion that every human being is the equal of every other:

> APRA believed that democracy is based on the mutual recognition of all people that all other people are autonomous and equal beings, that each is an individual like oneself. We told this to the peasants, that all people are brothers, that what unites us is that we all suffer, that we all have needs, and that we should help one another overcome our suffering. [Máximo Rodriguez Culqui, September 5, 1985]

This fundamental equality of all people, the party asserted, made it impossible to justify privileges, exclusions, and distinctions of any kind. In the context of the new institutions they formed, party priests continually raised these points with their followers. They explained what APRA meant by freedom from servitude:

> We Apristas would tell the peasants, "All of us are equal, with the only difference that the poor are unable to dress like the rich, that the poor have to sweat in the fields in order to eat while the rich have all of the advantages because of their haciendas. Why should you have to work for the hacendados? Why should you have to leave your own fields just at harvest time or at planting time so that they can plant more land or have a bigger harvest?

> Why should you not be free to work your own land, to help your
> neighbors, to work together with your community? What do you
> think would happen if the hacendados had to harvest their own
> crops? What if they had to work and sweat like you do? Where do
> you think they would be then?" [Victor Castilla Pizarro, August
> 3, 1990]

To convey what the party meant by freedom from denigration, APRA likewise drew upon concrete experiences from the everyday lives of the rank and file:

> We used to ask people, "Why should I not be able to go to a [reli-
> gious] service just because I have no shoes, as long as my feet are
> clean and presentable? Why must I be afraid of entering the
> cathedral when those with shoes can do so freely without being
> afraid? No, Señor! All may enter. I may not have shoes, but I have
> the same spirit as the man with shoes. As a poor person, I am
> closer to God than he, the rich man, who helps no one!" [Mario
> Reina Fernandez, July 14, 2001]

Freedom from humiliation was a right whose importance party priests returned to time and again: "We told people never to show subservience. When a peasant arrived in the city, he could always be identified by his dress. He had to give up the sidewalk and bow his head in respect, as a ritual, as an obligation, to the wealthy. We told people, 'A greeting is fine. It is democratic. But without humiliating oneself, without lowering one's head'" (Nicolas Tuesta Valenzuela, August 17, 1985).

Within the new institutions they formed, APRA organizers went to great lengths to heal the wounds inflicted upon people by the divisive cultural politics of casta rule. Above all else, party priests encouraged even the humblest of folk to recognize that they were the equal of anyone else. The Apristas also encouraged their followers to be prepared to assert that equality in public:

> We told people not to fear the *blancos*, or those who are well
> dressed. We told them to greet people directly, without humilia-
> tion. "Speak as you are. Speak with a little force so that your per-
> sonality asserts itself, so that when you say 'Buenos días,' it is well
> spoken. You should assert your presence by speaking firmly, but
> not too much. And *never* say 'Buenos días' in a subservient or
> meek way. To do so means that you have humiliated yourself.

What does humiliation mean? It means to feel that you are less than someone else. He has a tongue like you. He has teeth. He eats just like you do. He has no other way of eating, or of shitting, because even though he pretends to be better than you are, from his buttocks comes that thing that smells. Or perhaps you think that, when he is shitting, what comes out of him smells like perfume!" [Victor Santillan Gutierrez, February 16, 2001]

Underlying all of APRA's efforts was a single purpose: to familiarize people with forms of interaction and ways of reaching decisions that were based on group cooperation and equality of participation. The party also generalized its new organizations as much as possible so that an egalitarian, cooperative ethos replaced the hierarchical public culture of the elite. In the long run (that is, after the party came to power), APRA planned to make a number of these institutions part of the state structure itself (these were to become part of the National Economic Congress). That is, the party planned to include these institutions within a nested hierarchy of decentralized decision-making bodies that would collectively make up the state. Within these institutions, a mobilized and politicized populace not only would debate questions of the public good but also would establish public policy to advance the public good.[40]

In other words, APRA drew on its internally differentiated, widely dispersed underground party apparatus to form new kinds of subaltern political subjects. It did so, in part, by instilling in its followers new standards of individual behavior, personal affect, and group interaction. Toward this end, APRA authored a code of ethical behavior, to which it expected all members to adhere. The code regulated a very wide range of everyday social behaviors. To help make a reality of these novel forms and standards of behavior, party cadres inculcated in the rank and file new forms of discipline—mental, emotional, and physical—the aim of which was to produce "cultured" individuals. Party priests passed on to their followers the same lessons that they themselves had learned during their own apprenticeships.

APRA's regulation of social life did not end here. Monitoring people's progress toward becoming "cultured" required an ongoing assessment of their everyday behavior, in all walks of life. Party priests developed a comprehensive security apparatus that employed extensive means of surveillance—over the masses and over one another. APRA innovated its own court system to bring the force of the party down upon those who strayed from prescribed forms of behavior. APRA's court generated extensive records of its activities, as did all party offices. Court officers and party sec-retaries were scrupulous about maintaining and safeguarding the "archives" of APRA's activities. These archives provided a permanent record of APRA's successes and failures in meeting its long-term goal, the wholesale transformation of Peru and of Peruvians.[41]

APRA was thus able to link its subterranean state-in-the-making with select elements of Peru's state-already-made so as to effect a shift in how state power was articulated among (some) poor and marginalized groups. Individuals and groups who would otherwise have had few protections found themselves with new options (and also proscriptions). By offering an alternative to local state institutions at their ongoing point of contact with the populace, by using the party apparatus in the defense of principles that were blatantly disregarded by the state, and by adopting procedures that seemed neutral and impartial, APRA helped generate a novel version of the "state effect." That is, the party provided people with a very different view of what an alternative democracy could look like, of what a truly democratic polity could do on their behalf, and of what their relationship to such a polity might be. Although this alternative democracy was more absent than present, APRA's ability to subvert the normal operation of the state, and to do so in ways that produced tangible results for marginalized groups, provided glimpses of the democratic APRA state-to-be. Brief though these flashes were, they left a powerful impression on the imaginations of many people, of all social classes, who felt drawn to the alternative moral and political universe the party appeared to represent.

The sense that APRA represented a moral alternative to the existing state of affairs was reinforced by the "disinterested" nature of its activities. The party was always very careful not to charge for the services it made available to the general populace, and Apristas who tried to use their positions to enrich themselves were summarily expelled from the party (after a trial by their peers).[42] And finally, even if the momentary flashes of the future alternative democracy were more virtual than real—even if the party's humbler members did not always succeed in avoiding corvée labor, for example—people were left with the impression that there was something "out there" struggling to defend their rights, a structure of governance that made present the just social order that was absent.

APRA's goal in creating these new forms of social interaction was *not* to establish a boundary between state and civil society that would set limits on the exercise of state power (as occurred in Europe). Nor were the party's efforts focused on creating a public sphere beyond the gaze of the state, where rational debate about public policy could take place (as in Europe).

To the contrary, APRA clearly involved people in egalitarian forms of association but did so in an effort to *eliminate* the boundary between state and civil society. Put differently, APRA envisioned a form of state and democracy in which a distinctive set of freedoms and a novel group of sociopolitical institutions would allow a mobilized and politicized population to engage in rational debate about the public good. This debate would take place *within* rather than beyond the state apparatus—a state apparatus that would incorporate the participatory social institutions the party forged. The boundary between state and civil society so central to the liberal democracy of Europe was the target of APRA's efforts. The independence of what might be called "elite civil society" and the inability of the state to curb elite excesses were seen as being responsible for the plight of the majority. An uncompromised state and a functional democracy were what APRA sought to create.

CONCLUSION

The alternative democracy that emerged in Chachapoyas in the 1930s represents a specific example of a more general political and cultural process, in which spatially localized groups seize upon discourses of popular sovereignty that circulate throughout the global arena, generate vernacularized versions of these global discourses, and use them to mount local political struggles. The particular rights seized upon in any given context and the interpretation given to these rights depend on the nature of local political struggles and the relations of power and culture in which local groups are embedded. This is as true of European democracy as it is of so-called alternative democracies.

By comparing two historical trajectories of politics and culture that have produced radically different forms of democracy and citizenship, I have tried to draw attention to the highly idiosyncratic nature of the European case and, in this way, to undermine its normative status. In closing, I would like to suggest two other significant points raised by this comparison. The first concerns the importance of "provincializing Europe," to quote the Indian scholar Dipesh Chakrabarty (2000), of viewing Europe as just one more province in a world of provinces. The second point concerns the importance of "deconstructing Europe," of ceasing to view Europe, Western or otherwise, as an internally homogenous unit of analysis. This, in turn, suggests the importance of paying greater attention to the multiple forms of citizenship, public sphere, and democracy that have emerged within the European arena, as well as to the political processes that have resulted in some forms of European democracy and citizenship achieving normative status and others being relegated to a debased, vernacularized form. Taking this approach would allow anthropologists to recognize and analyze a problem that has received little attention: the existence of a broad range of *democracies* and the social conditions out of which they have emerged.

Acknowledgments

I would like to thank Julia Paley, the seminar organizer, for inviting me to participate in the advanced seminar at the School of American Research in March 2005. I would also like to thank the seminar participants—Mukulika Banerjee, Carol Greenhouse, Akhil Gupta, Julia Paley, Jennifer Schirmer, Kay Warren, and Harry West—for their invaluable feedback on the paper and for an exceptionally stimulating and rewarding week of discussions. Conversations with and written commentary from Peggy Barlett, Tom Biolsi, Ben Fallaw, Carla Freeman, Bruce Knauft, Chris Krupa, Joseph Roisman, Brad Shore, Gavin Smith, and Joan Vincent were also invaluable in improving the chapter. The research and writing upon which this chapter is based was generously funded by the National Endowment for the Humanities Summer Stipend Program, the National Endowment for the Humanities Research Fellowship Program, the School of American Research, and the Colby College Social Science Grants Committee. I gratefully acknowledge the support of these programs.

Notes

1. The form of democracy that has become normative in much of the contemporary world is generally referred to as liberal representative democracy (LRD). Briefly, LRD has the following three components. The *liberal* component refers to the rights and protections enshrined in the constitutions of many countries of the North Atlantic—the "freedoms of" (speech) and the "freedoms from" (arbitrary search and seizure). These freedoms seek to establish a state-free topography by limiting the exercise of government power. They are not concerned, however, with the ability of the citizenry to exercise a voice in political affairs; therefore, these freedoms have little to do with the original meaning of democracy (rule by the people). The *representative* component refers to individuals ceding direct decision-making power to others, who make all decisions in the political arena. As has been widely noted, representation disempowers those who relinquish their voice and was designed with this purpose in mind. The *delineation of spheres* component refers to a formal realm of politics that is open to some popular decision making while other realms are not. Particularly important in

this regard is the structure of class, property, and exchange, which many argue would be quickly transformed if these could be changed by popular will (see Nugent 1999a).

2. There is an enormous literature on the diffusion of "Western democracy" outward from the countries of the North Atlantic (see Nugent 2002 for a discussion of this literature).

3. Fernando Lopez-Alves (2000) and Miguel Angel Centeno (1997, 2001) have written very persuasively about the distinctiveness of state formation in nineteenth-century Latin America (from quite different points of view). Lopez-Alves, who focuses on Uruguay, Colombia, and Argentina (with Paraguay and Venezuela as "controls"), uses a modified version of Tilly's "war made states and states made wars" model (Tilly 1975b, 1985, 1990, 1993). Centeno, whose perspective is more continent-wide, finds that Tilly's model has limited application to Latin America. He argues that "the consolidation of central authority and the creation of a modicum of bureaucracy appear to have preceded the state-making stage of war," even in Western Europe (Centeno 1997:1570). "Wars make states" only when "adequate administrative mechanisms [are] in place to manage...revenues and expenditures" stemming from war (Centeno 1997:1569). Such mechanisms, he shows, have generally been lacking in Latin America.

4. Tilly (1990, 1993) and Mann (1986) identify a continuum in the relation between coercion and capital in early modern European state formation (a conceptualization that has much in common with Barrington Moore's pathbreaking work [1966]). At one end of the continuum is the "coercion-intensive" route to state formation. In this route (exemplified by Brandenburg-Prussia), the requirements of war drive state makers to increase revenues and enlarge their bureaucracies by forcing taxation on rural populations. At the other end of the continuum is the "capital-intensive" mode (exemplified by the Dutch Republic), in which state makers and capitalists strike a bargain: capitalists exchange resources with state makers and, in return, receive protection. Also on the continuum is an intermediate position, the "capitalized-coercion" path (exemplified by England and France).

5. This form of territorial sovereignty was institutionalized in the Treaty of Westphalia in 1648 (Ruggie 1998).

6. Rose (1996:46) views liberal governmentality as consisting of acts of rule that intervene in realms considered beyond the purview of the state.

7. See Wood 1988 for a perceptive discussion of the relative status of peasant-citizen and slave in the constitution of Athenian democracy.

8. Until 1824, when Peru won independence, it was a colony of absolutist Spain.

9. See Gupta 1995 and Herzfeld 1993 for insightful critiques of the Weberian model of disinterested, rational bureaucracy.

10. This was an especially common practice with the *gendarmes*, who were responsible for maintaining public order. High-ranking political appointees would often maintain a small force of gendarmes even though the central government had provided funds for a considerably larger number. In this way, the appointees were able to enrich themselves far beyond what would have been possible from their salaries alone.

11. Peru was divided into a nested hierarchy of territorial-administrative units. From smallest to largest, these were districts, provinces, and departments (the latter akin to states in the United States). The district-level government functionaries were responsible for day-to-day public administration and represented the key point of contact between the general population and the government (Nugent 2006). These very functionaries were the ones who received no salary.

12. This was a practice well known from the colonial period, when the Spanish Crown auctioned off the post of *corregidor* (governor) to the highest bidder and then turned these individuals loose on the indigenous population (Larson 1988; Spalding 1984).

13. The inability of the state to engage the general population in a project of national moral regulation—to produce a national discursive field—is shown with exceptional insight and skill by Mallon (1983, 1995), Stern (1998), and Thorner (1997). See also Nugent 1997.

14. Peru is divided into a nested hierarchy of administrative units, from district, to province, to department, to nation. Chachapoyas is the capital of the department of Amazonas.

15. Why castas felt compelled to employ the language of popular sovereignty and liberal rights in political ritual and discourse is an important question for future research.

16. The account of APRA in the remainder of this chapter describes party activities in the Chachapoyas region during the 1930s and 1940s. The account is based on the following sources: interviews (many with Apristas) carried out over a twenty-five-year period during annual visits to Chachapoyas, Peru, beginning in 1983; newspapers, leaflets, and pamphlets printed by Chachapoyas Apristas and circulated throughout the region in the 1930s and 1940s (some of which I encountered in the Archivo Prefectural de Amazonas and some of which were shown to me during the course of my fieldwork by elderly Apristas who had been carefully guarding the documents for decades); and works published by prominent Apristas or by the party during the 1920s, 1930s, and 1940s. Although there were some struggles over regional leadership positions during this period, there was broad agreement among party leaders about ideological and organizational matters. The same could not be said of APRA at the national level. The party's national leadership became less and less radical through

time, leading to generational and ideological splits. These became severe by the early 1950s, when elements of the national leadership still committed to APRA's original radical vision splintered off to engage in more "revolutionary" political activity (see Cárdenas et al. 1952). A discussion of the differences between the regional and national variants of APRA is beyond the scope of this chapter.

17. *APRA (Alianza Popular Revolucionaria Americana)* translates as the "Popular American Revolutionary Alliance." The party was founded in Mexico City in 1924 by Víctor Raúl Haya de la Torre, a Peruvian forced into exile by Peru's dictator, Augusto Leguía. Haya de la Torre's original vision was that all the republics of Latin America would aggregate into a single, continent-wide "superstate"—a United States of Latin America. Only such a polity, he believed, would be capable of maintaining sovereign control over its resources, populations, and productive potential in the face of pressure exerted by the United States of North America. For reasons that are beyond the scope of this chapter, APRA took on an increasingly national focus through time. Haya de la Torre's native land, Peru, became the center of APRA's activities.

18. It is important to emphasize that, in the course of becoming a permanent part of the Peruvian political scene, APRA transformed in fundamental ways. At this writing (2008), an Aprista (Alan García) is the president of Peru, but the APRA of today has virtually nothing in common with the APRA of the 1930s and 1940s.

19. APRA sought to forge alliances between what it referred to as manual and intellectual workers.

20. The indigenous population of the Chachapoyas region was not, in fact, descended from the Inca. See Nugent 1997.

21. APRA was highly critical of, and had no relationship with, the official communist parties associated with the Soviet Union.

22. Victor Santillan Gutierrez was APRA's subsecretary for cooperatives in the early 1930s and was specially trained in this area. I have relied heavily on his testimony in the following sections of the chapter.

23. Inequalities among community members, APRA recognized, threatened the democratic functioning of the cooperative.

24. Despite APRA's rhetoric of empowerment and inclusion regarding the Indian population, indigenous cultivators exercised positions of leadership only in the context of their own communities. Positions of power and authority in the party beyond the community were filled predominantly by mestizo (and, occasionally, white) youth.

25. Party organizers attribute the quote in the text to Freire. Although the perspective reflected in the quote is reminiscent of Freire, I have been unable to determine whether it is a specific quotation or a paraphrase.

26. APRA's early, radical vision emphasized the nationalization of land, mining,

and industry (Haya de la Torre 1927). As time passed, the party became less and less radical.

27. Party documents were always vague as to the precise powers these cooperatives would enjoy. What matters for the purposes of this chapter is the *vision* of autonomy and self-determination APRA offered to marginalized groups.

28. The Apristas of Chachapoyas read and discussed a wide range of political writings, which had to be smuggled into the region to avoid detection by the authorities. The authors whose work they consulted included Marx and Engels, Proudhon, Gandhi, and Freud, in addition to Peruvian writers (especially anarchist Manuel Gonzalez Prada).

29. The only exceptions concerned indigenous language and elements of culture that the party did not regard as obstacles to progress (see Nugent 2008). Apristas were very concerned about preserving indigenous patterns of communal ownership of land and cooperative labor exchanges—practices that the party used as sources of inspiration for its own plans for social transformation. At the same time, Apristas were determined to eliminate what they regarded as the abuse (as distinguished from the use) of coca, which they believed could become a vice if consumed in large quantities.

30. Many of the young people who subjected themselves to this training and went on to assume positions of leadership in the party came from lower-class urban backgrounds. Some were born of illegitimate unions between elite men and humble women. Others were the children of upwardly mobile merchant families whose efforts to rise in the regional social structure had been frustrated by powerful casta families. Still others belonged to landed families that had been denied positions of influence within the casta structure. What they all shared was the experience of being on the fringes of the casta order—of having its benefits within their sights but beyond their grasp.

31. Party practices also had a dark side. At all times, in all aspects of their lives, Apristas were expected to exemplify the principles for which the party stood and to "assist" one another in this regard. That is, they were told to monitor the other members' behavior on an ongoing basis and to report any failings to party superiors. Repeated failings could result in a trial before an APRA court and, depending on the number and gravity of the offenses, suspension and even expulsion from the party (see Nugent 2008; Vega-Centeno 1991).

32. Manuel Gonzalez Prada was an influential Peruvian anarchist who wrote during the opening decades of the twentieth century.

33. "Priests of democracy" is what the Apristas of the Chachapoyas region of northern Peru called one another. The activities of APRA in Chachapoyas are discussed below.

34. *District, province,* and *department* refer to the nested hierarchy of the territorial-administrative units, from smallest to largest, into which Peru is divided. In addition to having cells for each of these units, APRA had regional commands intermediate between individual departments and the nation as a whole. In this regard, APRA appears to have mimicked the Peruvian military, which also had regional commands.

35. The labor demands of the Peruvian military were enormous (see Nugent 2004, 2008). The exactions of civilian planners were comparable. From 1930 onward, the central government sought to "modernize" the Chachapoyas region with public works projects, all of which relied on coerced labor from the rural population. These military and civilian labor exactions threatened to undermine the ability of rural society to reproduce itself (see Nugent 2004).

36. Close parallels exist between these activities of APRA and those of the Sicilian Mafia, which "conditioned" politicians in a quite similar manner (although with very different goals; see Schneider and Schneider 2003).

37. APRA had considerable success in infiltrating the National Police and the armed forces throughout Peru during this period (see Gerlach 1973; Masterson 1976; Villanueva 1973).

38. Needless to say, APRA was not always successful in helping people avoid corvée labor and military conscription. Indeed, it is difficult to ascertain to what degree the party was successful. Clearly, however, government authorities believed that the party's success knew no bounds, that it was thwarting their efforts to carry out even the most basic of governing activities (see Nugent 2007).

39. Party organizers were also able to provide the rank and file with the assistance of lawyers, dentists, court scribes, and other interlocutors who mediated between the rural, agrarian world and that of urban powerbrokers. In the same vein, the House of the People (La Casa del Pueblo), the party headquarters in Lima, provided the party faithful with medical and dental services, legal advice, and subsidized food.

40. APRA never had the opportunity to implement these plans because party members and APRA leader Haya de la Torre were (with few exceptions) not allowed to run for political office. Despite the party's popularity, not until 1985 did an Aprista assume the presidency. By that time, APRA had transformed in fundamental ways and had little connection with its early, radical roots.

41. Party priests were obsessed with the security of their "archive" and went to elaborate lengths to keep it out of the clutches of the authorities, who were equally obsessed with seizing it. To safeguard the documentary record of their progress toward remaking Peru, the Apristas would bury their documents in locales where they believed the authorities would never look (cemeteries were an especially favored location). Subsequently, they would dig up their archive and hide it in the rafters of the

home of someone they thought the police would consider beyond suspicion (especially elderly widows). See Gupta (chapter 7) for a fascinating analysis of written documents, official seals, diplomas, and the like, as fetishes, as well as the role these played in the construction of "the people."

42. There were some exceptions to this rule. For example, when the secretary of welfare interceded with a doctor in order to make medical care available to someone who would not otherwise have access to it, the doctor was not expected to subsidize the cost of medicine (although he usually provided his services without charge).

3

Democracy, Sacred and Everyday

An Ethnographic Case from India

Mukulika Banerjee

In this chapter, I examine aspects of democracy in its various settings of everyday politics and at the extraordinary time of elections. The state of West Bengal, where this study is set, consistently produces some of the highest voter turnouts in India, despite high levels of illiteracy and poverty. The average turnout is 80 percent, compared with the national average of just 60 percent, and West Bengal also has the highest per capita attendance at political rallies in India (Lokniti 1999). Democracy here is a well-grounded phenomenon in which political participation and engagement are widespread. Further, the government in this eastern state is led by the Left Front (LF), a coalition of communist and socialist parties that has governed since 1977. This is a unique case of electoral success in the sixty-one-year history of Indian democracy (or, in fact, in any other). No other elected government or political party has remained continuously in power for so long in a free and fair electoral setting.

The overwhelming enthusiasm for participation in the democratic process among the most socially disadvantaged groups, on the one hand, and the LF's unprecedented scale of electoral success in a country where anti-incumbency is widespread, on the other, have proved something of a conundrum for political analysts. When we examine the nature of democracy in this setting, two major questions confront us: *why* do people vote? and why do people *repeatedly* vote for the Left Front? In this chapter, I show

how an ethnographic study of democracy can provide worthwhile answers to these questions.

Two important features of an ethnographic approach to democracy should be kept in mind. One, popular perceptions of democracy are expressed in both discursive and nondiscursive ways. With great fluency, the villagers among whom this study was carried out presented their views about politics generally and about democracy more specifically, but only in and around election times was a specialized language of "duty," "rights," and "citizenship" articulated. Being in the village during several elections, as well as just before and after, I was able to tap into this discourse. I present these findings in the first section of the chapter, titled "Why Do People Vote?" In the months and years between elections, however, people were more likely to reply to any direct questions about politics with nervousness and hushed whispers and warnings that it is not safe to talk about these things. Instead, they tried to deflect my interest by discussing the intricacies of rituals or rice farming, or anything else that normally would not be considered "political." The silence was not due to a fear of voicing a view contrary to that of the local Communist Party cadre, but of voicing a view about politics without the excuse of an election campaign. To air spontaneous opinion was to risk charges of presumptuousness and getting above one's self and could draw the wrath of the cadres or the envy and disapproval of neighbors.

Therefore, the task of the anthropologist working on popular perceptions of democracy was to be as aware of the muted, nondiscursive arenas as of the more loquacious statements made during elections. When people were unwilling to "talk" about politics, the way to ascertain their ideas and opinions was to watch them "do" politics. Recognizing these actions required a close observation of and participation in the everyday life of events (outside of formal electoral politics) relating to kinship, marriage, and religion, for instance, which anthropologists call ethnography. Through the periodic, voting-inspired reviews of morality and their lingering impact, the realm of the political infused the arenas of social, economic, and familial life, where it was continuously contested and expressed. In discussions about these seemingly apolitical events, informants elaborated on their motivations, strategies, and outcomes more freely than they would have if I had asked for their opinions about the functioning of local politicians, for instance. Doing fieldwork that involved constant engagement in mundane quotidian life for eight years (1998–2006), as opposed to restricting oneself to interviewing people for their opinions, became the only way to generate any insightful data. Only by closely observing these ordinary and everyday contexts alongside elections could I could hope to depict power and its disguises, along with democracy and its sensibilities.

The second feature of an ethnographic study of democracy is to recognize the utility of other kinds of data and methodologies that study the same phenomenon. I propose that an effective way to provide answers to our conundrum is to combine the methods of survey research with those of ethnographic analysis. Well-designed surveys give us useful figures and overall trends; ethnographic research helps us explain them.[1] The surveys used for this research show that what is most striking about the Indian elections is the pattern of political participation that defies commonsensical expectations and academic theories alike in at least three respects.

First, turnout in the Indian elections contradicts the general trend, especially in older democracies, of decline over time. In the past five decades, the overall pattern is that of stable and even increasing turnout for elections. Second, the turnout tends to go up as one goes down the tiers of democracy; the turnout in the local and state elections tends to be substantially higher than that in the national elections. Third, and finally, the turnout is not lower among citizens at the lower end of the social and economic hierarchy; if anything, the reverse is true. A poor, low-caste person is more likely to vote here than is an upper-caste, upper-class person. Also, the rural electorate votes more than its urban counterpart; voting in the tribal areas has caught up with the rest of the country; and the gap between the turnout of men and women has reduced substantially in recent years (Yadav 1999).

Much of this goes against the standard image of "political man" presented by political science research (Lipset 1981). It is important to note that we are not dealing merely with a curious turnout pattern. This pattern, which reflects a robust level of belief in the efficacy of one's vote and a strong support for democracy, is supported by available data on wider political attitudes. In this respect, the underprivileged groups have become stronger supporters of the democratic system than ever before (Linz, Stepan, and Yadav 2007).

By providing a useful snapshot of the political culture of India, the findings of these surveys serve as the ideal starting point for an investigation into popular perceptions of democracy in India. But surveys, although they reveal correlations and assessments of the general trends in a society, rarely explain the reasons behind observed trends. For instance, we now know that a poor, illiterate, village-dwelling voter in India is more likely to turn up at the polling booth at an election, but we have no idea of exactly why. For this, we need a study that is more qualitative and participatory. To ascertain the location of such a study, the random survey sample can determine a wide variety of potential field sites with different social and political profiles. For each of these sites, long-term data on changing economic and social criteria are available (through the sample panel), and these add historical depth to any investigation. Most important, the surveys produce a set of questions that are immediately identifiable as significant topics to pursue during ethnographic research.

With this intention, I chose to locate my ethnographic study on popular perceptions of democracy in two villages that displayed the national trend in its high voter-turnout rates despite high levels of adult illiteracy. My initial question to all informants was one that no survey could ask, namely, "*Why* do you vote?" My intention was to understand why people whose lives improve very little from election to election nonetheless continue to think of elections as important events that *demand* their participation. Why does their faith in their votes persist despite the continued subjection of the vast rural poor's interests to those of the minority urbanites? Why do the disadvantaged and socially exploited turn out to be the staunchest and most vociferous supporters of elections? Put bluntly, *why* on earth do India's "poor of the earth" bother to vote at all?

WHY DO PEOPLE VOTE?

Usually, two sorts of explanations are offered for why people anywhere vote. First, the one derived from rational choice theory is that the vote is a rational and instrumental tool to maximize self-interest and that the voters use it to improve the material condition of their lives. A good example is Kanchan Chandra's discussion (2004) of what she calls "patronage democracy." For instance, she argues, voters in the Indian state of Uttar Pradesh routinely assess the chances of "their" party, defined by caste and ethnicity, in deciding whether to vote for a particular party or alliance. Here, democracy is all about "patronage," the government in power delivering even the most basic of entitlements as handouts to its clients. In this assessment, voting strategically and often therefore increases one's chances of accruing these benefits. According to this instrumentalist view, elections are arenas for transactional behavior, and the skillful deployment of one's vote as an instrument can lead to tangible rewards.

A second kind of explanation is the symbolic view of elections. From this perspective, democracy is really an untrue but vitally important myth in support of social cohesion, with elections being the central and regular ritual enactment that helps maintain and restore equilibrium. The ability to vote is seen as a necessary safety valve that allows for the airing of popular disaffection and opinion but ultimately restores the status quo. In such a reading, elections require the complicity of all participants in a deliberate *mis*recognition of the emptiness of these procedures, the lack of any significant changes that this ritual brings about, and the necessity of this charade to mollify a restless electorate.

Let us now turn to the ethnographic data, to what an election day is like in a village in contemporary India, before we judge the utility of the preceding explanations. Local politics in the two villages of Madanpur and Chishti were dominated by one man, the local Communist Party representative, who was universally known as "Comrade."[2] He controlled all benefits, loans, and opportunities. Madanpur and Chishti share a polling station with a third village. The local Left Front candidate from this constituency belongs to the Forward Bloc. The villages of Madanpur and Chishti were populated almost entirely by Muslims of all castes, along with a smaller population of Doms and Bagdis. Figures from the ballot box of their polling station indicated that more than 90 percent of the adult population from the two villages voted regularly in all elections. Those who did not vote could not because of ill health or physical absence from the village on urgent business in a distant part of the state. Having been in the village during several elections, I came to meet various family members who lived elsewhere but traveled back especially to cast their vote. Amir Ali returned from visiting his daughter's in-laws—after a thirty-six-hour journey by train, bus, and ferry, without a seat—to make it through the doors of the polling station minutes before they closed. His case was not unusual.

On Election Day, one hot May morning in 2001,[3] the village woke earlier than usual and bustled around urgently with an air of suppressed excitement, just as it would before important festivals. Chores were stripped down to the bare necessities of fetching water and milking cattle, with all attention centered on the imminent mile-long journey to the polls and the constant inquiry of "So when are you planning to go for the vote?" The men preferred to go in the early morning coolness to be present when the doors opened, and the women necessarily later, after seeing to children and cooking pots. Keen to look respectable, men swapped the traditional draped clothing of *lungis* and dhotis for their best trousers, and women wore jewelry and makeup and took out their handloom saris (I was chided for not having put on something new). The children were initially bemused because today, unlike other festival days, when they were the center of attention, their preoccupied elders largely ignored them. They soon realized, however, that this meant an entire day of no school, of unsupervised fun and games.

People traveled to the booth in groups of three or four, partly for moral support but also to help pass the time while trying to hitch a ride from passing trucks or while queuing in the sun to vote. The polling station was the little school building in a neighboring village. Adorned with bunting and banners, it could be mistaken from a distance for a shrine or country fair. Outside were rows of chairs for the various parties' agents, who formed a seated guard of honor for any approaching voter, faintly intimidating in their eagerness to check names off their lists. The polling officials were keen to ensure that the day remained trouble free, and armed guards stood around, languid but alert.

For weeks before the election, there had been endless discussion (during quilt making, mat weaving, and tea drinking) about the magical new contraption, the "Electronic Voting Machine" (EVM). The local Communist Party agent had helpfully familiarized his supporters with the curious black box, its buttons lighting up like the eyes of a dark deity, in order to ensure that they would not be too nervous to go to the polling house or too incompetent to use it (pressing two buttons "spoiled the ballot"). This demonstration was followed by much speculation about the "computar," including guesstimates of how many votes it could register per minute.

Those households that had not been given a preview worried that this was because the machine had mind-reading powers and had already ascertained that they were not intending to vote Communist. Rumors spread that it gave you an electric shock if you voted for another party or that a hidden cable allowed officials to monitor which button lit up and thus destroyed the secrecy of the ballot. There was also talk of new special ointments circulating that could remove the black finger mark, enabling the same person to use the machine again and again. Some regretted losing the satisfaction of folding the ballot paper and stuffing it in a sealed box. Others were relieved that they no longer risked humiliation in front of the officials because of their awkwardness with a pencil, reasoning that pressing a button was familiar enough from working the radios and TVs in the village.

Before someone could cast her vote, her left index finger had to be marked with black ink by the polling officer inside the polling station.[4] Such a method is not unique to India. In Bosnia, for example, as Kimberley Coles (2004) discusses, a more high-tech version was used, with silver nitrate–based ink that showed up only under ultraviolet light.[5] There, it was resented as an intrusion into personal space and as an offensive indication that the people could not be trusted (such that it has been long abandoned). In India, it seemed unobjectionably congruent with all the other body decorations that indicate ritual participation, such as henna on women's palms for weddings, markings with paste of *bindis* and *tilaks* on foreheads during ceremonies, the colorful threads of *rakhis* tied by sisters on their brothers' wrists, and the total submersion in the rainbow of Holi. In much the same way, the black vote mark on the finger is worn with pride as a testament to one's participation, like a sacred thread around the wrist after a Hindu ritual or the discoloration on a pious Muslim's forehead caused by years of bowing to the ground in prayer, a coveted stigmata.

Because the vote mark goes away after its function is fulfilled, it can also be seen as belonging to the broad range of ephemeral ritual inscriptions seen throughout India, such as the intricate floor designs of *rangoli*, *kolam*, or *alpona* made with dry colors, rice flour, and grains on festival days. These involve hours of work but are soon washed away or allowed to fade to make way for new ones later. More generally, Indian elections produce their own genres of ephemeral art, in elaborate murals, witty cartoons, and huge cutout figures of politicians that appear on walls everywhere during the campaign but are removed after polling, not to mention all the bunting and banners, pamphlets, mock ballot papers, flags, and such like.

On Election Day, a number of interesting scenes presented themselves to the observer walking around the village. For instance, in Madanpur, to the right of the main village lane stood a bullock cart ready to depart. All that one could see on this heaving, heavily loaded cart were several pairs of feet in plastic slippers dangling from underneath a makeshift curtain covering the cart. In it sat some elite women, no doubt, who maintained purdah and did not travel in public without suitable veiling. Their cover was blown, however, when one of them was suddenly jettisoned from her perch. She hurried home amidst laughter and teasing remarks to change her everyday mill sari into a "proper" handloom one. A casual conclusion to draw from such a scene would be that village women dress up to go to the polls. But longer-term knowledge would reveal several other conclusions. To start with, the presence of the bullock cart, however intrinsic to rural Bengal, was an unusual sight inside a village. It was rarely used to transport people. Women walked or took buses; men and children cycled. The group of ten women who were huddled together was obviously wealthy enough to hire a cart. In this village were women of the Syed caste, who normally did not leave the house. When they did, it was only to retrieve animals that had strayed outside their courtyard or to make a quick dash to the local grocers. They were always barefoot and knew how to sit only on the floor.

For these women to be in their best saris, crisp and billowing with starch, feet in slippers, precariously balanced on an overcrowded bench of the bullock cart, one could surmise that this was no ordinary day. They looked uncomfortable and excited. Meher, the local Comrade's abandoned first wife, voted out of a sense of marital duty, and she hoped that he would notice her commitment. Naseeba was the Comrade's sister, who knew that she would be in trouble with her brother if she were not seen to have made the effort. She was the one who was sent back to change her sari. Two other women were sisters, married to two brothers, Jaker and Shaker, who had long mounted a rival power group to the Comrade. Their party, the Congress, was moribund, but they continued to support it secretly. By traveling together with the other elite women and the Comrade's relatives, they hoped to deflect interest in their rival political loyalties. A fifth woman was Manohara, Akbar's wife. Akbar was an enigmatic and knowledgeable man with twinkling eyes, but he refused to talk politics with me for fear of retaliation from the Comrade. He was an old rival and one who had been punished in the past for his views. Korima's husband was the articulate Mukhtar, who was the village intellectual but who nevertheless kept out of realpolitik. As an intelligent but illiterate woman, Korima understood her husband's explanations about the duty to vote, and she had shown up with her two newly arrived daughters-in-law. Rokiya and her daughter, though elite, were impoverished and now supported the Comrade in the hope of future material benefits. This tableau of women on a bullock cart journeying to the polling station, which would appear unremarkable to a casual observer, was, in truth, the microcosm of a larger world of village politics. The presence of these women was an intricate triangulation of various motivations that drove them to vote.

Crossing over to the twin village of Chishti on the other side of the highway, I came across Tinkari Dom sitting quietly in the courtyard of his house, surrounded by the low mud huts of his son and sons-in-law. His daughter-in-law sat at a distance washing clothes. No one else was in sight. Again, a casual conclusion might have been the lack of enthusiasm for elections among low-caste Hindus. But knowing the family intimately, I was aware that Tinkari was an articulate and politicized individual who had brought up a son to be the same. The large family was close-knit and among the most perceptive and politically committed in the village. On polling day, Tinkari was bitter and depressed because it was on this day more than any others that the enormous influence the Comrade wielded became apparent. What was otherwise implicit became visible as one saw people making the journey to the polling station out of loyalty to the Comrade, fear of him, or anger toward him. The Comrade was an important factor in everyone's participation in the elections.

Tinkari's own impoverished situation, which he normally bore with dignity, seemed unbearable in comparison. Living quite literally in the shadow of the Comrade's sprawling compound, he ruminated on his past. He was the one who had recruited the Comrade as a young man into politics, serving as his mentor, but was soon outmaneuvered by the younger man's skilled strategizing. The daughter-in-law attempted to lighten the mood by telling me about stupid women who were pressing the button on the EVM more than once, thereby spoiling their vote. The casual conclusion would therefore be wide off the mark. Far from being the result of being illiterate and low-caste, Tinkari's reluctance to go to the polls was the consequence of his superior understanding and experience of how politics actually worked. Again, it would be impossible to know this without sustained engagement with the people of this village.

Before I left Tinkari's house, he also told me to watch out for what "the Masters" might say. "They have always been Congress supporters, but they may sing a different tune today," he warned me. There were several "Masters" in Chishti. They were schoolmasters in primary schools and earned an enviable wage of more than Rs 10,000 a month. Surrounded as they were by illiteracy, daily wage earners, and the uncertainties of agriculture, they were among the most envied men in the village. The fifth house on the right belonged to Hanif Master, who told me cheerfully that he had already been to the polling station. Again, the mistaken casual observation would be to note that schoolteachers, by virtue of their education, showed the greatest enthusiasm for elections. Instead, the truth of the matter was that Hanif had just ended a rather public challenge to the Comrade's authority just before the elections. He needed help from the Comrade in acquiring a plot of land adjacent to his house for his son's wedding, which was to be held soon after the elections. His enthusiasm for registering his vote had a pecuniary edge.

Returning to the bus stop on the highway to make my own journey to the polling station, I spotted a family waiting by the roadside, hoping to hitch a ride. Kubera, who ran a tiny cigarette and betel nut kiosk with her husband, had been wanting for months for her daughter and son-in-law to visit her but had failed to persuade them. With the election, she had a useful pretext and threatened them with the consequences of the Comrade's wrath if he found out that they had not been to vote. As they all waited by the side of a melting highway on that blistering May afternoon, she remarked to me that the Party should feed them, too, on Election Day and not just the election workers. "After all," she said with a wink, "we are doing the most important work of all, of pressing the button. Without that, they are nothing." Her statement would have upset any hasty conclusions about the poor Kubera being forced to go to the polling station at any cost by Party workers. She may have been speaking only in jest, but she was serious about the basic message.

Election Day made apparent the relationship between the Party and its supporters. An idea of mutual entitlement has grown on both sides. The Party may have become complacent while in power for nearly three decades, but on Election Day, voters like Kubera offer a harsh reality check: "Without us, the Party is nothing." However short-lived, this sentiment instills a certain humility and nervousness in Party workers' campaigning. Misjudged arrogance could cost them a seat, and they are aware of this. All unfulfilled promises have to be explained away, and more promises made—and made convincingly. This may seem like a charade enacted every time, but as we have seen, the charade is an important performance that redresses power balances, however briefly.

After voting, the hours passed in the relaxed and satisfied conviviality of a holiday in the village. People compared notes on who had gone to the poll when and let passersby know that they themselves had indeed already long been. The excitement of the day, the presence of absent relatives, the peer pressure to participate, the satisfied exhaustion of an important duty successfully discharged, all clearly indicate that elections are regarded and treated as being in substantially the same space as religious festivals and rites of passage celebrations. It seems, then, that we are now getting closer to the heart of why ordinary and marginalized Indians vote in such numbers. Not to vote would be akin to not celebrating your child's wedding— conceptually possible, but so curmudgeonly, eccentric, and antisocial that only a tiny minority would want or dare to do it.

In light of what we have learned about the lived experience of an election, let us revisit the explanations usually offered to explain the role of elections in a democracy. First, from the narrow viewpoint of marginal utility, voting is hardly ever a rational activity because, as studies of American elections have shown, single votes almost never affect the outcomes of elections. This must be still truer of India's vast constituencies, yet unlike in the USA, it does not result in voter apathy (Dubner and Levitt 2005).

Second, in West Bengal at least, the choice of whom to vote for is secondary because the Left Front has ruled for nearly thirty years and is likely to continue for the foreseeable future. Either you vote against it, wasting your vote and hardly improving your material circumstances, or you vote for it, knowing that it has brought some significant improvements to the lives of the poor (for example, land reform) but that these lie well in the past, with little obvious promise for the future.

Third, and more generally, the Indian voter is no more sanguine about politicians and manifestos than anyone else, as became apparent from my discussions in the village around the time of elections. Very few felt any hope of material benefit from casting their vote. They complained that the hopeful candidates urged at campaign meetings, "Vote in our favor. We will look after you," but were not seen again until the next elections. Although basic necessities such as water, electricity, and employment were key issues, the voters knew full well that the funds were being misappropriated or otherwise diverted by local politicos and officials.

The vote is thus not a plausible tool for material improvement. But could it still be a powerful instrument of morality and protest, bringing the satisfaction of "throwing the rascals out"? There is certainly something in this. The Indian voter is a canny rejecter of incumbents; it was estimated that between 1989 and 1999 chances were two out of three that the ruling party in any state would lose elections (Yadav 1999). On the whole, however, even such anti-incumbency feeling cannot explain Indians' enthusiasm for voting—for they are well aware that this usually means merely exchanging one set of rascals for another. In fact, most of my villagers seemed to regard becoming a politician as an intrinsically corrupting process. Ali put it this way: "Poor people should not become leaders because otherwise they will become like rich people. When they say '*gharibi hatao!* [Eradicate poverty!],' do they mean that or '*gharib ko hatao!* [Eradicate the poor!]'? The Chief Minister and all, do they want to get rid of us? It is not a government for the poor people." In this evaluative framework, rich people are evil, and rich people in politics are doubly so.

One can see, therefore, why an instrumentalist view of the urge to vote can start to look a bit threadbare. In response, some commentators, keen to preserve and define the importance of elections, have taken a robustly nonrationalist view of them, the second explanation I recounted at the start of this chapter. Steven Lukes makes a virtue out of necessity by arguing that elections are a way in which "a particular political system reproduces itself" and they "express the symbolic affirmation of the voters' acceptance of the political system and their role within it" (Lukes 1975:304). That is to say, an election is just an elaborate way to embrace the status quo. John Dunn puts the matter less rosily but somewhat similarly, seeing elections as "events which confuse in a very intimate and purposeful way, the largely symbolic identifications of large numbers of people with their effects upon the politically effective conduct of rather small numbers of people" (Dunn 1980:112). According to Dunn, this confusion is beneficial because it makes the electorate feel empowered, albeit briefly and merely symbolically. This is a conception of elections as "ritual." The conception of ritual that it assumes, however, is rather denuded, being equated with the absence of intentionality or instrumentality and thus with something essentially repetitive and automated. Nonetheless, this view's recognition of the symbolic value of what might otherwise be seen as just a dry and statistical event means that it is still a fruitful way to reconsider things in the Indian context, given what we have learned from our ethnographic description above.

At a national level, for instance, it is conspicuous that an administration that often struggles to deliver prosaic matters of infrastructure in an effective and timely way always raises its game for general elections and other mega-scale rituals, such as the Kumbha Mela. The vast township of tents set up for the millions of pilgrims at Kumbha Nagar, the thoughtful establishment of entire bespoke Haj terminals at Indian airports, and the punctual press releases of the Election Commission detailing vital polling information well in advance of the election, all illustrate the civil and military machinery running at unprecedented pitches of perfection.[6] Each of these mass public events comes round periodically according to its own calendar and internal logic, bringing together vast numbers of otherwise unconnected people in participation and faith. Information about the where and when is miraculously diffused among millions who never read a newspaper or listen to the radio, with almanacs, delivery boys, and itinerant peddlers all playing their part.

At the domestic level, most Indians conduct their everyday affairs to the relaxed rhythm of Indian Stretchable Time. Yet these same people suddenly become fiends of precision and punctuality when it comes to holding rituals during the auspicious time slots ascertained from almanacs. Temporary moments of confusion about their conduct seem always to be resolved by the timely arrival, out of the blue, of someone who knows exactly what comes next or by the miraculous appearance of a rare ingredient that is crucial to the ritual.[7]

Before proceeding with this line of argument, it is only fair to note that there has been recent anthropological criticism of the notion of elections as ritual. Kimberly Coles concedes that "an election fits well into many of the characteristics and categories of ritual and ritual-like action: formalism, traditionalism, disciplined invariance and repetition, rule governance, sacral symbolism, and performance" (Coles 2004:553). Nonetheless, she argues that this kind of perspective tends to lead to a neglect of electoral techniques and technologies and their significance, which, if properly considered, make an election look less like a Catholic Mass and more like a scientific laboratory.

Coles's account from Bosnia in chapter 5 of this volume therefore focuses on the detail of electoral laws, polling stations, election officials, and ballots. Building on work by Bruno Latour on laboratories, she sees elections as sites that create knowledge, truth, and neutrality and thus enable democracy, like science, to wield hegemonic authority through its representation as quite distinct from society and subjectivity. The key, then, is to assess how the human agents and technological apparatus interact in the cultural practice of elections. This is a difficult but potentially rewarding agenda for electoral ethnography, and I already edge somewhat in this direction in my discussion of finger marking. More broadly, in discharging its role to defend and foster India's democracy, the Election Commission has certainly created its own set of techniques and practices to suit the country's particular needs, such as facilitating the participation of illiterate voters by requiring each political party to be represented by a symbol in campaign material and on the ballot paper (Jaffrelot 2007). More recently, more than one million electronic voting machines have been deployed as mandatory replacements for paper voting.

Nonetheless, I do not think that Coles's view of the importance of electoral technology necessarily contradicts or undermines the idea of election as ritual. As Michael Herzfeld (1993) has argued, the modern form of bureaucratic rationality looks very much like the ritual systems of religions. Both are exclusive communities whose members' individual sins cannot undermine the ultimate perfection of the ideal they all share. And both post a direct identification between the community of believers and the unity of that ideal: "We may view the continual reaffirmation of this transcendent identity as an effect of some bureaucratic labor and the labor itself is highly ritualistic: forms, symbols, texts, sanctions, obeisance" (Herzfeld 1993:20).

Moreover, the archaeologist David Wengrow (2006) has provided additional historical depth to this rejection of a dichotomy between modern bureaucracy and ancient charisma. Wengrow shows how bureaucratic procedures in ancient Egypt evolved through the gradual extension into the world of the living of the elaborate mortuary rituals that had long controlled the world of the dead. As a result, Egypt's political culture came to be dominated by a strange but intense synthesis of bureaucracy and sacrifice—a mix that Wengrow hints may be closer to the realities of our modern state than we might want to acknowledge.

From this perspective, I am tempted to see a fusion between India's electoral bureaucracy and a ritual not of death, but of birth. As in the United States more than 170 years before, the tryst with destiny of 1947 created in one stroke, and indivisibly, both a new nation and a democracy, and the Election Commission was set up by an act of Parliament immediately after. Ever since, the commission has seen itself as a key guardian, not merely of elections but of the very nation itself, a sacred duty it discharges with great seriousness and diligence. In practical terms, its reach and standardization throughout every corner of the motherland make it one of only a handful of institutions (the army, railways, cricket, movies) that are genuinely pan-Indian and that can serve to bind together the vast and varied country. Consequently, conducting elections in a fair and efficient way helps generate not only faith in the democratic system but also patriotic faith in the idea of India itself.

Again, surveys revealed evidence of this trust in the Election Commission, people's belief that elections were largely free and fair, and an overwhelming support for the commission's decision to switch to electronic voting machines (Lokniti 1999; Rao 2004). The population greatly appreciates the work of the commission, rating it as the most respected public institution (the police are the least) and supporting it through action by availing themselves, in great numbers, of its voting technologies—it would be rude not to! From this perspective, to dwell mainly on the election's festive aspect and collective effervescence in the village, as I did earlier, is to miss what is most important and interesting in the comparison of election and ritual in the Indian context—namely, that so many people seem to share a genuine and thoughtful reverence for the democratic *process* as in some sense "sacred" or "sacrosanct."[8]

This is surprising in view of the rural population's poverty and disillusionment with politicians. One might have expected to hear from them the sort of authoritarian and populist opinions aired among middle-class, urban Indian voters about the pressing need for stability, discipline in public life, and "a strong pair of hands." Instead, strong evidence of rural respect for the lofty ideals of the democratic process emerges strongly from large-scale survey research—and was equally clear in my own ethnographic findings.[9] For example, many of the same people who gave trenchant critiques of politicians nonetheless spoke resolutely of voting as a duty of all responsible citizens. To them, voting contributed to clear-cut and legitimized electoral results, thereby helping achieve political stability and avoid the vast expense of frequently repeated elections. Not bothering to cast a vote was condemned as careless and even criminal. One woman said,

"Even one vote can change the result, so that is an expensive waste." Another woman admitted her lack of political sophistication but was in no doubt about her role and duty: "We don't know why governments break up. We are not concerned with election results. Our job is to vote."[10]

Such directly articulated views also explain why, on Election Day, villagers quietly checked out one another's fingers and made their surprise and disapproval known to those who bore no mark. Any excuse for not voting, perhaps other than severe illness, was met with barely concealed skepticism. Such peer pressure led even natives who had migrated elsewhere to make expensive journeys back to their home constituency.[11] If many saw voting as a duty of citizenship, others put more stress on voting as an *expression* of citizenship. One man who dwelt in a particularly remote corner of the state told me, "If I don't even vote, no one will know I exist!" Another said, "If we don't vote, how can we prove that we are citizens of our country?" For these people, living in semiforgotten corners of the nation, well outside the India that was purportedly "Shining," this opportunity to prove one's membership in the nation and confirm one's status as a citizen was acutely felt. The ability to register one's existence through such a physical presentation of one's body (and vote) at the ballot box was the ultimate validation of one's identity as a citizen, above everything else.

The legal principle of habeas corpus, which Agamben (1998:124) has argued can become "modern democracy's strength and at the same time its inner contradiction," when considered in the context of Indian electoral law, makes voting curiously empowering. Agamben points out that even though the legal principle of habeas corpus was meant to ensure that the accused did not avoid judgment, it also exposed the body to sovereign power: "Corpus is a two-faced being, the bearer both of subjection to sovereign power and of individual liberties" (Agamben 1998:125). In the case of the Indian voter, however, the legal requirement to be present in person to cast a vote is interpreted by my informants, at least, as a rare flowering of their individual liberties in an arid reality of constant subjection. Exercising the right to vote provided one of the very few ways to express one's citizenship and in a more appealing and dignified mode than merely claiming one's rice ration.

The egalitarian mechanics of the poll afforded particular pleasure. People relished the fact that everyone, regardless of caste and class, stood cheek by jowl in the queue to wait his or her turn. And the marking of all fingers, regardless of status, was a similarly satisfying displacement of the administrative thumbprints, which had long stigmatized the illiterate. People also noted that, unlike religious rituals, which require the presence of an officiating imam or priest but not necessarily a congregation, an election could not be held without *them*—a "festival for the people, not for Allah!"

Indeed, *Homo equalis* may exist alongside *Homo hierarchicus* in the conceptual reality of contemporary India, as Andre Beteille (1987) has forcefully and plausibly argued, but in everyday life it is submerged deep beneath chronic social inequality and deprivation. The leveling of the polling station is an almost unique event that brings equality to life, however fleetingly, and dulls the enduring pain of ignominy and oppression, at least for a day. Given this momentary unveiling of a deeper value usually suppressed, it is little wonder that the event has a carnivalesque import and an explosive potential that requires a cessation of all normal activity, as well as close monitoring by security troops and the Election Commission.

Another aspect of this egalitarianism was the frequent description of the vote as the people's weapon (*ostro*). As Noori put it, "Why would anyone want to waste this opportunity? The vote is our weapon. No one knows what is really in my heart, which party I like, and I can express this in secret, on my own, in the booth covered with sacking!" In line with what I noted earlier, however, it is not seen as a weapon to secure better lives but, more realistically, as part of a constant attritional battle to ensure that the treatment of the poor and the marginalized does not worsen. One man neatly put it: "The fact that I can cast my vote is a right. But we have also got our rights through voting. Voting brings more power in our hands, and so if we don't exercise this right, the government becomes autocratic." Using the vote, he implies, compels governments and political parties to display at least a basic minimum of concern and assistance. In a sense, this echoes Amartya Sen's well-known observation that electoral accountability means that famines do not occur in democracies.

SACRED ELECTIONS

My reading of elections as "sacred" is therefore a modification of the election-as-ritual approach. First, it takes the symbolism seriously by paying close attention to what the participants in elections make of its message. The vote is felt to possess both symbolic power, in expressing people's self-respect and self-worth, and instrumental power, in helping to ward off potential attacks by the state upon that self-worth. The vital importance of such power for dignity and survival, the appealing formal equality of the vote's operation, and the sense of dutiful participation as citizen-subjects that it affords generate a deeply felt sense of "something sacred," giving a moral and emotional core to the ritual elements of the election and drawing India's voters irresistibly toward it.

Second, my approach is akin to that of anthropologists, such as Wendy James (2003), who have attempted to de-link "ritual" from religion. James (2003:124) argues that the word *ritual* is weighed down with the "aura of incense" and general religiosity and, more important, has come to be regarded as a disembodied mirror of "society" or "culture." Instead, she suggests that the notion of the "ceremonial" would be a freer and more fruitful term. In her usage, a ceremony is not a reflection of something more solid or an effect of something deeper. In particular, ceremony cannot reflect or represent society because it is intrinsic to what we mean by "society"—*ceremony* assumes sociality in a way that the more abstract *ritual* often does not. In James's (2003:94) imaginative metaphor, ceremony, like dance, portrays "[social] structure in motion," and the anthropologist's task is to come to an understanding of the choreography.

In the context of this chapter, I take the moral of this to be that we cannot simply think of an election as one big ritual that serves a single function (whether of affirmation or of subversion) in respect of "society." Nor should we interpret elections as religious, for all their sharing in that quality of inviolability that religious rituals indeed possess in Indian life. Rather, we should see the ceremony of an election as a congeries of sociocultural "dances" emerging out of the habits, circumstances, and motivations of everyday life. In this vein, anthropologist Jonathan Spencer rejects the notion that elections in Sri Lanka (in the 1980s) were some kind of symbolic ritual dressing that conceals or mystifies the "reality" of political life or necessarily confirms *communitas* or the status quo. Instead, he describes them as "moral dramas" to indicate the ways in which they have "a more lingering impact on people's everyday lives" (Spencer 2007:79). Elections could be the site of genuine dissent with real consequences because "party identification at elections is often justified by appeal to moral criteria: we are good people, they are bad people.... [Also] elections imply division within a community into 'our' side and 'their' side" (Spencer 2007:79).

Equally, it finally became clear to me—after prolonged work in the village—that every actor in the "macro-politics" of Election Day was conducting herself in ways that were inextricably linked to the preceding months and years of the "micro-politics" of the village. In retrospect, Election Day was when the complexity of the village's social life was distilled into moments of structure and clarity and when diffuse tensions and loyalties were made unusually manifest. The election offered potentially powerful snapshots that light up a longer and more diffuse "thick description."

In this chapter, I seek to provide some flavor of this thick description to explore why the disadvantaged in India are those most committed to the idea of democracy and enthusiastic about participating in elections. What we have learned is that even though the material benefits of participating in elections are entirely unpredictable, elections as ceremonies have come to stand for much more. They offer an opportunity for the expression of citizenship and for an understanding of the duties and rights involved in living in a democracy. As a result, they have become as much an end, in themselves, as a means to a better society. (The extraordinary efficiency and incorruptibility of the Election Commission in conducting elections have further added to their importance.)

Elections have come to be considered sacrosanct, in much the same way as rituals are in Indian social life. As discussed above, just as uncompromising punctuality in religious rituals replaces slack attitudes to time in the workplace, elections are conducted in India with an unparalleled degree of probity because of their unique status in public life. To call them "sacred" is not to imply that there is anything religious about them but to signify inviolability.

Durkheim's qualification on the use of the word *religious* is entirely appropriate here:

> We know today that a religion does not necessarily imply symbols
> and rites in the full sense, or temples or priests. All this external
> apparatus is merely its superficial aspect. Essentially, it is nothing
> other than a system of collective beliefs and practices, which
> have a special authority. And it has this special authority derived
> from a moral supremacy because it rises above private goals.
> [Durkheim 1898:23]

Durkheim uses this definition to characterize individualism, which he considers to be the "very religion of humanity" because it is a glorification not of individual qualities, but of the divine humanity he shares with all men. Each individual has a right to this religious aspect because each has within him something of that humanity whose divine character renders it sacred and inviolable to others.

This Durkheimian idea of sacred individualism is crucial (I would argue) to understanding elections as "sacred" expressions of citizenship. At their best, elections facilitate moments of political "anti-structure" and allow for different political imaginaries to be configured. They cast a fleeting shadow over the smug and corrupt, reminding them that *their* end could be nigh, wrought by an electorate that, despite its marginality during the preceding year, enjoys a festive and solemn moment of power and equality that holds out hope and succor for the next. It is a "ritual of thraldom" to democracy and worthy of its sacred ceremonial.

WHY DO PEOPLE VOTE FOR THE LEFT FRONT?

Having considered the reasons for why people vote, the first part of the conundrum, let us now turn to the second question: why do people repeatedly vote for the Left Front?

In April 2006 West Bengal looked disturbingly normal. Although it was only days to the big elections, the public spaces everywhere in the state were bare of the posters, cartoons, and murals that are at the heart of any election campaign in India. This time, there were no buntings or banners of prominent politicians intersecting busy crossroads, no party symbols imprinting themselves in people's minds. It was the first time anybody could remember that the election had not transformed the state into the usual festival of color and sound, of blaring loudspeakers and gaudy pamphlets. In rural areas, too, huts remained unadorned, devoid of paint and murals, and fields lay empty of crowds eager to catch a glimpse of politicians and helicopters. It was so eerily normal that if you did not know that an election was imminent, you would have missed it. Clearly, there was something unusual about the elections of 2006. But a month later, when the results were declared, there was nothing unusual about the results. For the seventh time in a row, the coalition of communist political parties had won its claim to govern the state of West Bengal.

Of course, there are several valid reasons why the LF had been winning elections in West Bengal for more than three decades. In 1977, when the Left Front won its first state-level election, it embarked on far-reaching land reforms. Any sharecropper (*bargadar*) who had worked an area of land for a landlord for more than three years could register his interest in it and be due 50 percent of its produce in return for his labor. The landlord remained responsible for the outlay of capital for seeds, fertilizers, bullocks, and irrigation. The farming decisions now came to be made jointly; indeed, decision making was often dominated by the greater practical experience of the sharecroppers. Their new stake in the land also led them to work harder and invest themselves, and harvests flourished. Meanwhile, casual laborers were recruited into peasant trade unions and enjoyed a new government-prescribed daily minimum wage of Rs 60, which had to be paid to them the moment they showed up for work, ending the old humiliating wait at the end of the day.

Although the implementation of these reforms has been extremely uneven across the state, in areas where they *did* take effect, as in my field site, the results were significant. Together with the introduction of high-yielding varieties of rice, it meant that the majority of even poorer families could eat three meals a day. "No one went hungry anymore," as my informants put it.

But the social effect was even more dramatic, genuinely transforming the feudal character of laboring relations, with the lower castes becoming increasingly self-assured. In my research villages, the Syeds themselves were driven by the new labor costs to sweating in the fields, a heavy symbolic blow, given their traditional abhorrence of the plough and manual labor. The sharecroppers could now look them in the eye when talking. Previously, even riding a bicycle in front of a Syed was considered taboo. The reforms created a mutual dependence, and the growing recognition of this gradually softened the older suspicions and separations. Also, the status of the lower castes benefited from their participation in the farmers' unions and village councils (Panchayats) that the Left Front established.

Its unbroken electoral success since then has rested mainly on grateful support from the rural poor. But the reality of its dominance is subtler than this. Over time, the Left Front has succeeded—largely through the entre-preneurial activities of its local operatives, a "vernacular do-it-yourself hege-mony"—in becoming more of an "all class" party. I shall return to a greater elaboration of this idea later in this section.

The unusually quiet election of 2006 was the response of the Election Commission to growing mutterings and informal charges placed by the opposition parties in West Bengal and in the rest of the country that the real reason for the LF's continued electoral success was its "scientific rigging" of the elections. Not through obviously illegal practices such as "booth cap-turing" or "bogus voting," but through its thousands of cadres across West Bengal, it was implied, the LF subtly and not too subtly pressured voters. To lay such rumors to rest once and for all, the Election Commission decided to put in place stringent measures in the conduct of the 2006 elections so that the process would be totally transparent, allowing no space at all for the processes of "scientific rigging."[12] These included holding the election in five phases over several weeks and bringing in observers and officials from outside the state. All campaigning was banned under these new regula-tions, as were public meetings and public canvassing of votes. The com-plete silence in which the elections were held did, in a curious way, create welcome space to allow for some unbiased thinking among voters, or so my informants reported. When the LF won its largest victories despite such a circumscribed campaign, it not only silenced its critics but also deepened the conundrum of its success further.

Survey figures revealed that in 2006 the LF won a greater seat share than before. Although it lost 5 percent of the vote share among the rural poor and women, in particular, it made this up by gaining among the rural middle and rich peasantry. This led to its growing transformation into more of an "all class" party, an image that the new head of the LF, Buddhadeb Bhattacharya, fighting his first state-level elections for chief minister, welcomed. But the reasons behind this increase among the middle peasantry and, indeed, the continued support of the older supporters still remained unclear. To find some answers, let us turn again to the ethnographic site to see how the support base of such a political party is created, maintained, and expanded. As this chapter demonstrates, only by observing the nondiscursive alongside the discursive and by studying the time in between elections can we find answers to the functioning of democracy.

To do this, however, we need to go back several years, to the winter of 2000, a year when the rice harvest coincided with Ramzan, the holiest month in the Islamic calendar. As stated before, a large proportion of the villagers of Madanpur and Chishti were Muslims, a significant minority of about 18 percent in West Bengal. In the villages, the social elite belonged to the Syed caste, which traced its ancestry to a *pir* (holy man) from Iran. The Syeds were endogamous, considering themselves more pious than other Muslims in the village, and evoked their foreign origins by speaking Urdu among themselves instead of the local Bengali.[13] Most had reasonable-size landholdings (2–10 acres). In contrast, the majority of the villagers (including some Hindus) belonged to lower castes, spoke Bengali, and worked as sharecroppers or hired labor on the Syeds' land. They were the ones who had benefited most from the land reforms, and they were represented by one of their number in the local elected government, the Panchayat.

The main Communist Party representative in the villages had been a Party worker for more than twenty-five years and was also president of the farmers' union for twenty villages. Everyone, regardless of age and gender, called him "the Comrade."[14] His figure was unmistakable, well built and fit, though padded with more fat than your average farmer, a complexion just a shade lighter than those who toiled in the sun every day of the year. Although he dressed like everyone else, his sarong was always less faded and frayed, he usually wore slippers rather than roam barefoot like everyone else in the village, and he had a gold chain around his neck. These slight differences made him stand out, but only just enough to make people take note of him, to recognize that he was someone important. His house suitably sat between the two villages, embodying his place as "gatekeeper" commanding access to news and information. The prestigious roar of his motorbike broadcast his constant comings and goings. A Syed himself from a family in the villages, with a wife and household in each, he was surrounded by people who were both his relatives and his contemporaries among the Syeds, including erstwhile Comrades whom he previously outmaneuvered to reach his current position. His success at their cost also meant that he was the subject of much envy and hostility by his rivals, all of which was, of course, kept from public view. To alienate a man of his absolute power was to invite trouble.

Such a figure was typical of Bengal. The Communist Party of India (Marxist), the leading partner in the multi-party alliance of the Left Front, realized the fragility of vanguard political movements such as the Naxalites, which mobilized the urban intelligentsia to revolutionize peasants in the 1960s and 1970s. Over the years, the Party had built up an intricate network of such Comrades across the state. They were Party members who belonged to the area in which they worked and where they often owned land and businesses that sustained their political activities. They took their orders from the Party, organized political activities in their area, and served as the conduit for the disbursement of funds, loans, and benefits for much of the rural population. The Party headquarters in the capital utilized this capillary network of Comrades and cadres to exercise control in the farthest corners of the state.[15]

The Comrade's primary responsibility was to deliver electoral victory to the Left Front in return for the access to resources he enjoyed. In the best traditions of a vanguard party, he assumed that the mass of villagers made of the lower-caste Muslims and Hindus, whom he called "the poor," would tend to vote for the Left Front *unless* they were "led astray" by alien social elements. His anxiety was that the rest of the Syeds, brooding over their loss of status and money after the land reforms, would seek to exploit the emerging grumbles among the peasantry that the government had not, in fact, done very much new for them in a while. The Comrade's main tactical challenge was therefore to ensure that the Syeds—literate, articulate, landowning, and still possessing influence over tenants—did not unite to spread critiques of the government among the poorer strata. There was, as we know, scope for such a critique; the government's task was by no means complete, even on agricultural reform. The Comrade had to practice a sort of vernacular do-it-yourself hegemony to maintain the complete dominance of the Communists at the local level: no one was allowed to air critiques of the government openly, and no single person was able to build a following of any significance in opposition to the Comrade's. He used the resources of the Party and the government strategically to achieve this and had been largely successful in this. As a result, political rivalry continued to exist but was harder to find. It was certainly not to be found in the activities of any rival political parties, nor, indeed, in overt political activity of any sort. If anything, power play could be glimpsed in innocuous, nonpolitical arenas such as *milads*.

Milads were prayer meetings held during the Muslim holy month of Ramzan. They were scheduled in the evening, after the day's fast was broken, the fifth and final prayer of the day had been said, and all chores completed for the day. Usually, one was held every few days to break up the monotony of the month, giving a chance to the interested to attend as many as possible. They were usually held at someone's house and attended by men and women and a few children who were able to endure the hour-long service. The men usually participated actively in the prayers, chanting the refrains loudly, standing up to offer the final prayers. The women's participation was more muted, sitting as they did, literally on the edges of darkness, in the more physically uncomfortable spaces of the courtyard. These meetings were dominated by men—they were the hosts, active participants, and main players of the evening. Unlike other religious rituals, a milad was not an event for which people dressed up, as they would for a festival; rather, the tone was austere, pious, and participatory. The success of a milad was judged by the strength of the congregation, whether it attracted people from a wide range of economic backgrounds, and the quality of oration by the imam. The latter usually comprised recitations from the Q'uran in Arabic, sometimes with Bengali translations. After the closing collective prayer, sweets were distributed to all present. Sugar was a luxury in these villages, so children and adults alike coveted these modest balls of syrup and milk tinted in bright colors. The host, in a good year, would order enough to have sweets delivered to close kin who could not attend.

The milads were hosted in rotation by the men of the more prosperous, elite Syed households as a sign of piety, but they also gave rise to much interested gossip about which families were able to afford a milad, who distributed a better quality of sweet, who had managed to get the best orators, who could attract the most guests, and, most important, precisely who did or did not come. Because of these connotations of prestige, the Comrade, despite holding to the official Party line of atheism, hosted a milad of his own every year. This began in one of his houses, then moved on to the other in the second village, thereby showing his respect for religion and sharing his favor most widely.

In the Ramzan of December 2000 (a few months before the state-level elections of May 2001), four milads were scheduled for the same evening. This highly unusual circumstance seemed to suggest some element of deliberate competitiveness, for the ability to attract a large number of guests to one's milad was a sign of importance.

One was Hilal's, whose mother's sister was married to the Comrade. Hilal's own political loyalties lay with the Comrade. Hilal's mother's brother was Mustafa, a teacher, and Hilal had asked him to lead the milad. Mustafa Master was the haughtiest and most enigmatic of the several schoolteachers in the village (the Masters, as we learned earlier, are envied for their steady income). His house, located next door to the Comrade's, rivaled it, with extensive brick walls and a large courtyard housing a size-able stock of well-fed cattle. He maintained a studied persona, spoke very little in public, and was mostly seen reading a book or newspaper, through a window of his study that had been carefully positioned to overlook the main village lane. He accepted people's greetings with a slight nod of his head, and his great height, luxuriant hair, and spotless clothes put him in a different league from the rest of the men in the village. All regarded him as being scrupulously honest and a scholar with a deep knowledge of Islam who was fluent in Arabic, Bengali, Urdu, and English. He was widely per-ceived as a potential counterweight to the Comrade, although he kept his allegiances close to his chest.

Hilal's request to lead his milad had put Mustafa in an awkward spot. As Hilal's uncle, Mustafa could not refuse. At the same time, Mustafa would have preferred not to be associated with Hilal publicly because Hilal staunchly supported the Comrade, with whom Mustafa Master was now in dispute. Mustafa Master suspected that Hilal's invitation was a disguised offer of rapprochement with the Comrade. Even if he were to accept the invitation, however, he was not sure that the guests would not stay away to avoid displaying any disloyalty to the Comrade by attending a milad offici-ated by a known rival of the Comrade's. An ill-attended milad would have been unbearable for Mustafa Master's ego.

Hanif Master came to learn of Mustafa's dilemma. He was another teacher and had enjoyed a very active political past, working with the Comrade and even saving him from being killed by a rival mob during an agitation. He was also related to the Comrade through marriage. He, too, desired to be something of a counterweight to the Comrade and was on the lookout for opportunities involving other village heavyweights to build a rival political grouping. Mustafa's dilemma gave him an ideal opening. He offered to schedule a milad of his own at a later time the same evening and promised to bring his audience along to Hilal's if no one showed up, to save the situation. This was not a totally surprising offer. Hanif and Mustafa were friends, though the haughty Mustafa rarely admitted to this. By offering his solution, Hanif hoped to show their bond publicly and, at the same time, to entice Hilal away from the Comrade into a rival "opposition" in the village.

As it happened, things went smoothly at Hilal's, with Mustafa officiating and everyone who had been invited showing up. At Hanif's milad, too, all the lower-caste guests came, as did members of eleven Syed households. Hanif made a great show of largesse, sending sweets to numerous relatives, including some who supported the Comrade and others who were dithering in their allegiances. He pointedly omitted the Comrade himself, however, saying that relatives by marriage did not qualify for this particular prestation.

On the same evening, a third milad had also been scheduled, to be held after the two others, this time at Mustafa Master's own house, in the vast courtyard. So as not to dominate the evening totally, he had graciously asked a third schoolteacher, Hakim Master, to be the orator. The choice was opportune because Hakim had recently withdrawn support from the Comrade and aligned with Hanif and Mustafa. This invitation was intended to cement the new alliance.[16]

Meanwhile, Hakim's estranged brother Abu was officiating at yet another milad, being held at Munsab's house. For Munsab, choosing Abu was the perfect way of thumbing his nose at Hakim, with whom he had recently fallen out. Abu had been pleased to be asked, for he fancied himself to have the best voice for oration, the most rousing style, yet was largely ignored by most hosts because of his lack of political leverage.

The reason all these milads were held on the same evening, at some considerable inconvenience to those involved, was to make apparent, through a thoroughly nonpolitical arena such as a prayer meeting, the newly emerging political alliances in the village. By the end of the evening, the alliance of Mustafa Master, Hakim Master, and Hanif Master, who were opposed to the Comrade, was solidified. On one hand, Hanif's offer of a stand-by audience to save Mustafa's face in the case of a no-show at Hilal's milad, Mustafa's invitation to Hakim to officiate at his own milad on the same night, and the three milads carefully scheduled not to clash with one another were evidence of this. On the other hand, the group loyal to the Comrade, comprising Munsab, Abu, and others, had also felt an urgency to host its own milads on the same evening, thus forcing the audience to choose between their milads and the three held by the rivals.

At one level, such petty machinations are just the stuff of everyday village life. However, in 2000 the converging of three charged events—Ramzan, the forthcoming elections, and the harvest of the High Yielding Variety rice crop—made it a particularly fecund time for political intrigue. Harvests were always a time of heightened tension between landowners and sharecroppers, for it was then that the repercussions of the land reforms were most palpable. Before the reforms, the entire harvest would be brought to the landowner's house, where the sharecroppers were given their tiny shares at the landlord's whim. Now, however, the tables had turned. The sharecroppers could take their share directly from the fields, and the landlord was dependent on the whims of the sharecropper in bringing him his share. If the sharecroppers were on good terms with the landlord, they would deliver his share to his courtyard. If not, they would leave it in the field, to the humiliation of the landlord, who would have to bring in his own harvest manually or pay expensive additional labor costs to others to do the work for him.

This single fact summed up the impact of the Communist-led land reforms succinctly. These were a reminder that sharecroppers no longer had to rely on the largesse of the landowner, that their 50 percent share of the harvest was enough to feed their families twice a day for most of the year, that their labor had a price. Most of all, these were a harsh reminder to the middle classes that they themselves had been transformed into manual farm labor. This proletarianization of a class that had always enjoyed classic middle-class, white-collar (*bhadralok*) sensibilities had made these people the strongest detractors of Left Front rule in West Bengal.

With an eye on the forthcoming elections in the winter of 2000, campaigning had already begun; it was also time for the cadres of the Left Front to harvest the vote for their parties. Much networking, alliance building, and calling in of loyalties were in progress. The milads described above took place in just such a politically charged context. Accompanying the exhaustion and irritability caused by fasting during the busiest time of the agricultural calendar was the heightened stress of establishing one's electoral loyalties within the village. The Syed men, who had solidified their alliance against the Comrade through the milad saga, lent their support to a fledgling opposition party, which was just beginning to take shape in the village. Returning to the village four months later, in April–May 2001 in advance of the elections, I saw the fruits of the carefully planned milads. Mustafa Master, Hakim Master, and Hanif Master, along with new recruit,

Hilal (who no longer supported the Comrade), together backed the activities of a young man called Majhi. An unemployed teacher, Majhi had started up a fledgling cell of Trinamul Congress (a breakaway party from the All India Congress Party) to put up a candidate against the Left Front. Previously, anyone in the village who even mentioned the party Trinamul Congress, led by the volatile and charismatic Mamata Banerjee in Kolkata, was likely to be censured and publicly embarrassed.

But in May 2001, taking advantage of more widespread discussion in the media of a possible defeat of the LF government, Majhi was doing the unthinkable and openly canvassing votes for Trinamul. He was able to do this only because of the support of the three heavyweight Syed hosts of the milad gatherings. This development, along with speculation in the press about Trinamul's chances of winning the elections, emboldened various villagers, including Left Front loyalists, to discuss the new party. Some confided to me that they found its leader, the down-to-earth, matronly Mamata Banerjee, to be an attractive figure in contrast to the remote patricians of the Left Front establishment. They also admired young Majhi's bravery and sympathized with how hard he had to work to make people give him a hearing.

Ultimately, the Left Front was returned to power in the 2001 state-level elections, continuing its unbroken track record of electoral victory. But at the time of the election campaign, it had become clear momentarily how macro-level politics at the level of the state of West Bengal could affect the politics in a small village, and vice versa. It is doubtful that the complicated scheming of the milads in Madanpur and Chishti and the challenge to the Comrade would have happened at all if the media had not so avidly discussed Mamata's chances of winning the elections. Similarly, thousands of small challenges to the hegemonic hold of the LF's dominance, like those in Madanpur and Chishti, had prompted the unprecedented discussion in the media of a state-level Left Front defeat. For the Comrade, it was also a timely reminder of the importance of keeping the Syeds in check, for any fledgling political party that enjoyed their support could become politically viable in the future. Winning the support of the middle peasantry such as the Syeds meant not only gaining the vote share of a hitherto recalcitrant constituency but also quashing any nascent opposition. The Comrade's do-it-yourself hegemony had clearly faltered in the run-up to the 2001 elections, and he needed to make amends before the next one.

As a testimony to the Left Front's resilience and its cadres' efforts, five years later, by April 2006, the scenario had completely changed. In Madanpur and Chishti, despite careful maneuverings in the few years preceding, all opposition to the Left Front lay in disarray. Of the three heavyweights in the milads saga, Hakim Master was dead, and Mustafa and Hanif Masters had retired from their jobs as schoolteachers. Their priorities now lay in consolidating their households and crop yields. They had eaten humble pie and had put aside their differences with the Comrade to curry favor with him in order to further their personal projects. In contrast, the Comrade exuded even more confidence and prosperity than before. He had wrangled some submersible irrigation pumps that ran on state-funded electricity and provided a continuous flow of water to the thirsty rice crops in the fields. This improved output three times more than previous yields. For the first time in years, every acre around the villages lay lushly covered by a bright green paddy. With an eye on the forthcoming elections, the Comrade had made sure that these coveted pumps were given to the rival Syeds first. For the first time since the LF came to power, the middle peasantry felt that they had not lost out completely because of its policies. The Comrade had clearly been "doing it himself" and had picked strategically opportune targets for his largesse this time. At the state level, Mamata Banerjee's career lay in shambles after a series of misconceived moves, disastrous electoral alliances, and lack of party organization. Her chances at the forthcoming elections were not taken seriously anymore, and all attention was focused on the Election Commission's recent directives of holding a silent election.

The fecund agricultural realities twinned with the harsher realpolitik of Trinamul's dismal prospects for the elections meant that the young Majhi, who had entered politics with high ideals and ambition just a few years previously, was already a spent force. He denied having any further interest in politics. From his point of view, building an opposition to the Communists in his village had been an impossible task. The feudal political style of his main supporters (the wealthier middle peasantry) had become mired in personal games of one-upmanships because of the lack of strong party discipline. There was no organization to back him up. This had also made them vulnerable to the maneuvers of the Comrade. The effect of the Comrade's acquisition of the irrigation pumps at this critical juncture and their disbursal to the crucial trouble mongers had been dramatic and immediate. In the elections of May 2006, these erstwhile rivals walked through their lush paddy fields to the polling station to cast their appreciative vote for the Communist candidate. For the first time in decades, the Comrade had achieved the acquiescence of his immediate political rivals. And herein lay at least one of the scenarios to explain the survey finding of the LF's 5 percent gain in vote share among the wealthier rural classes between the elections of 2001 and 2006 in West Bengal.

It has to be recognized that the reasons for the LF's electoral success in West Bengal lay in the informal nature of its capture of social institutions by the Party's cadres. I have dubbed this sort of local-level building of following and influence "vernacular do-it-yourself hegemony." This type of hegemony is so effective—beyond the dreams and understanding even of the Politburo in Calcutta—precisely because the cadres exert influence in creative ways that are pervasive but informal, entirely familiar and therefore seemingly unthreatening. Further, the degree of autonomy afforded to the local Comrade by the Party enables him to adapt his strategy to address the particular political scenario in his local arena. In the case of Madanpur and Chishti, we saw that the reigning in of rival political aspirations and the buying off of its strongest supporters were most urgently required. In other villages across the state, other groups no doubt required other strategies. The flexibility of the cadre system allowed deft political adaptability of strategy that otherwise top-heavy political parties are unable to cater to.

Further, the Comrade is not regarded as a specialist kind of political actor or an alien representative of an oppressive regime, but rather as simply one of the village who has enjoyed—for the moment—more success.[17] As is evident from the example above, the "political" activities of local functionaries, such as the Comrade's, are not so different from the sorts of maneuvers people practice in their own daily social lives. They, too, through the exchange of gossip, currying of favors, and appropriation of information, seek constantly to expand their networks of social capital and ingratiate themselves in one another's lives to be in a position to influence when it suits their interests. Therefore, the Comrade and LF's hegemony did not go entirely uncontested. Even in the face of a powerful Comrade, political maneuverings did not cease, as was demonstrated in the use of the religious milad meetings in December 2000 to build an opposition. The promise of the impending elections in 2001 was seen as an opportunity not to concede permanent ground to the Comrade and to the Left Front in general. The existence of multiparty competition in a democratic system with regularly held elections at the state and national levels meant that the Party was rarely perceived as a looming or monolithic leviathan. The voters of West Bengal were not *Homo sovieticus*, who believed that "everything was forever" (Yurchak 2005). Rather, they practiced, even at the most disaggregate level of village politics, a sort of multiparty competition.

Thus, we have gone some way in solving our original puzzle of why people *repeatedly* vote for the Left Front. An ethnographic approach that pays equal attention to the times between elections and to the elections themselves and takes into its analysis what people do as much as what they *say* they do reveals the following answers. The most entrenched party in a democracy (the LF) was reelected repeatedly precisely because it was the most responsive of all parties. Far from turning complacent by office, it was engaged in endless scrutiny of its own electoral results. By inviting feedback from cadres, it was able to identify sectors of discontent in the electorate that it needed to address before the next election. The methods for doing so were a liberal mix of cynical handouts and ideological programs. A strong Party organization, the Comrades' hegemony, and the triangulation of a thousand individual circumstances and motivations among voters combined to achieve the winning electoral result.[18] The enthusiasm of the voters for elections in such a setting no longer seems surprising. Rather than approach elections as merely an opportunistic moment for bringing in a change of government, either for the sake of change or to punish the corruption of the incumbent, voters in West Bengal seemed to sense how their electoral behavior might influence further policy.

CONCLUSION

Democracy is one of those big words, like *freedom* and *terrorism,* that in common currency is more often used than analyzed. To contribute to analysis, and as an ethnographer of democracy, I have taken my lead from Francois Guizot, who pointed out the following in 1822 in his *History of Civilization in Europe.* "It is by the study of political institutions that most writers...have sought to understand the state of a society, the degree or type of its civilization. It would have been wiser to study first the society itself in order to understand its political institutions" (Guizot 1977[1822]: 12). The young Tocqueville avidly attended Guizot's lectures, and his adoption of the "culture and people first" approach makes his analysis of American democratic institutions fresh and informative still today.

If one were to explore the democratic spirit in West Bengal in this Tocqueville sense, then one would need to study the context, the social matrix in which the political institutions are embedded. Understanding this context requires some classic ethnographical research over an extended time period that covers both everyday and special events and, preferably, includes all phases of the agricultural and ritual calendars. In everyday village life, available to the participant-observer are the endless minutiae of paddy cultivation, brick kiln architecture, kinship diagrams, and an astonishing amount of intrigue and gossip. An ethnographic approach to democracy therefore needs to pay equal attention to the discursive and nondiscursive—alongside studying events relating to kinship, marriage, and religion, for instance—in order to spot those areas of social action that have a political subtext. By interpreting overt political moments such as elections in the light of what we learn in the years intervening between them, we can fully explain electoral results.

Notes

1. In this case, the surveys used are the National Election Studies (NES) surveys, which a Delhi-based research center, Lokniti (Centre for Comparative Democracy) at the Centre for the Study of Developing Societies, has conducted during all parliamentary and state-level elections in India.

2. The names of the two villages have been changed.

3. These scenes are mainly from the Assembly Elections of May 2001, when there was some discussion in the media about a possible challenge to the Left Front's performance from Mamata Banerjee's Trinamul Congress. Some people in the village discussed this, but most were unaware of this news and treated the election like any other election.

4. The instructions given by the Election Commission to polling officers on this subject are detailed and explicit. These specify which of the officers should do the ink marking, how to clean a finger if it looks covered in any suspiciously oily substance, which finger is to be used if the left forefinger is missing, and so on.

5. Coles construes this as marking the body to identify the citizen-subject. When this practice was discontinued in the 2000 elections, Coles heard people warn against multiple voting: "Anyone can pretend to be anyone, without some sort of physical mark!" The main reasons for discontinuing the practice may have had as much to do with budgetary constraints for UV lights, their maintenance, batteries, and ink bottles, but the official line emphasized that elections are an inclusionary rather than exclusionary practice and that the basis of trust should be identificatory rather than physical evidence (Coles 2004:552).

6. A good example of this level of imagination and efficiency was in evidence one year when there was severe flooding in West Bengal during the elections. Rather than throw its hands up in despair, the local administration converted trains into mobile polling stations, arranging for them to stop at various points on the tracks (which, on account of being located on higher ground, were above the water level) so that people could travel by boat across the waterlogged fields to come and cast their vote.

7. A small rite at a brick kiln illustrates my point. It takes about ten days of continuous daylight labor to build a Chinese-style brick kiln. In this time, the bricks are

shaped, baked, and then placed in concentric circles interspersed with charcoal. On the final day, the kiln is lit at sundown. While this is done, a little *puja* is performed with incense sticks and flowers as the person who lights the fire asks for forgiveness for committing the sin of burning Earth. After the fire is lit and the flames spread through the intricate flues of the kiln, sweets are distributed to all the laborers and onlookers. It is a little celebration, but one that is carried out with every element present, with sweets and flowers, even though I had not seen one in the village in the entire time I had spent there. Not only did villagers appear, but also they appeared on time and in the middle of nowhere, where the kiln was located.

8. It is startling and satisfying to learn, too, that this sacrosanct quality of elections, which is a popular grassroots one, is also endorsed by other national institutions. The historian David Gilmartin explores the provenance of the notion of popular sovereignty through electoral law in modern India and quotes a telling response from the Supreme Court to an appeal regarding election malpractice in 1981: "In a democracy such as ours the purity and sanctity of elections, the sacrosanct and sacred nature of the electoral process must be persevered and maintained" (Gilmartin 2007:78). Gilmartin clarifies this quote, in a similar vein to my own clarification of the use of the word *sacred*, that this is not a religious sense but signifying the conceptual space that stands outside both state and society.

9. For a discussion of urban middle-class attitudes, see Harriss 2006.

10. This notion of duty was also akin to the sense of duty that prompts people to pay their condolences at a relative's death: a begrudged obligation that can be inconvenient, but unthinkable not to fulfill. It is worth reminding ourselves here that voter fatigue is a distinct possibility in Bengal. In the span of less than eighteen months, three major elections might be held, for instance, the March 1998 and October 1999 all-India general elections and the May 1998 Panchayat elections.

11. Lest we assume that such commitment to voting under peer pressure or commitment to civic duty is a curiously Indian phenomenon, a comparative example from Switzerland helps prove that this is not the case. Based on a study conducted by Patricia Funk, Dubner and Levitt note: "The Swiss love to vote—on parliamentary elections, on plebiscites, on whatever may arise. But voter participation had begun to slip over the years, so a new option was introduced: the mail-in ballot. Every eligible Swiss citizen began to automatically receive a ballot in the mail, which could then be completed and returned by mail" (Dubner and Levitt 2005:2). The cost of voting in terms of time and inconvenience had been effectively lowered, so an economic model would predict voter turnout to increase substantially. But is that what happened? Not at all, they report. In fact, voter turnout often *decreased*, especially in smaller cantons and in the smaller communities within cantons. But why on earth would *fewer* people vote

when the cost of doing so is lowered? "In Switzerland, as in the U.S., there exists a fairly strong social norm that a good citizen should go to the polls," Funk (2005:2) writes: "As long as poll-voting was the only option, there was an incentive (or pressure) to go to the polls only to be *seen* handing in the vote. The motivation could be hope for social esteem, benefits from being perceived as a cooperator or just the avoidance of informal sanctions. Since in small communities, people know each other better and gossip about who fulfills civic duties and who doesn't, the benefits of norm adherence were particularly high in this type of community" (Dubner and Levitt 2005:2). In other words, Dubner and Levitt conclude, we *do* vote out of self-interest—a conclusion that will satisfy economists—but not necessarily the same self-interest, as indicated by our actual ballot choice. The Swiss study suggests that we may be driven to vote by a financial incentive less than by a social one. It may be that the most valuable payoff of voting is simply that of being *seen* at the polling place by your friends or coworkers.

12. The EC had introduced similar measures in the state of Bihar in the preceding years, where it had been effective, and the national consensus had been entirely positive.

13. My fluency in Urdu, acquired during earlier research in Pakistan, won me instant credibility among the Syeds and others.

14. For a comparative discussion on such "big men," see the work of Mines (1994) and Hansen (2005).

15. For a greater elaboration of how the Communist Party and its cadres work in West Bengal, see Banerjee n.d.

16. Hakim had switched in this way in response to the public beating of his son Raju by Munsab during Moharram six months earlier. Raju had been having an affair with Munsab's daughter Beli, but Munsab's motive was not paternal pride so much as an effort to please the Comrade, for Beli was also the Comrade's paramour! The Comrade himself had retaliated against Raju and his father, Hakim, by building a bathroom and cow shed on the land right next to Hakim's bedroom, cutting off his family's access to the main village lane and forcing them into a roundabout way through the fields.

17. Like Chinese brigade-level comrades, he is a man of the people, "who eats his own rice, not the Party's."

18. The policies advocated by the LF government led by Bhattacharya after the 2006 elections—bringing investment to West Bengal despite severe ideological differences with his colleagues—might be seen as yet another example of this kind of responsiveness and wooing of the disgruntled detractors among the middle classes and others.

4

"Govern Yourselves!"

Democracy and Carnage in Northern Mozambique

Harry G. West

The killings in Muidumbe district began in the second half of the year 2002. In some cases, attacks were witnessed; in others, mauled bodies alone told grisly stories. It was by no means unheard of in the area for a lion to kill a person. But this was different. These lions—by collective reckoning, seven—lingered in and around villages and agricultural camps on the southeastern edge of the Mueda Plateau for months on end, taking victims one after another. Afraid to venture outside their homes, area residents abandoned their fields at the peak of the agricultural season. As the preceding year's stores ran out and the current year's crops rotted in the fields, many went hungry. Women fetched water from sources outside the village only en masse, escorted by men armed with bow and arrow. Bathing became almost impossible. Schools ended classes early so that students could return home while the sun was still high in the sky. Well before dark, makeshift chamber pots were placed inside as villagers made ready for another long night behind barricaded doors and boarded-up windows.

Hopes that the government would resolve the crisis went unmet. Muidumbe district administrator Pedro Seguro later asserted that provincial authorities failed to respond to his requisition for hunting rifles and ammunition. Villagers wondered whether any petition was even made. As far as they remembered, no word to that effect was ever issued from the administrator's office, nor was any other action taken to put an end to the carnage. As the death toll mounted, villagers took matters into their own hands, killing several lions by laying traps in the village or hunting them down with bow and arrow. They also began lynching fellow villagers whom they accused of making, or transforming into, lions to feed upon neighbors and kin. When mobs pulled the accused from their homes, bound and beat them, doused them with petrol, and set them alight, those attempting to intervene became the objects of potentially lethal popular suspicion (Israel n.d.; Limbombo 2003).[1]

For generations, Muedans have suspected a certain few among them capable of making or transforming into lions. Sorcerers, by Muedan definition, perform astonishing acts through which they feed on the well-being of others. According to most people with whom we worked, such phenomena have greatly intensified in recent years, taking on alarming new dimensions. The reason? In a word, democracy. One elder put it succinctly: "In the past, sorcerers were regulated. Today, we have democracy. Anything is possible now. Everything is permitted." In pre-colonial times, individuals accused of sorcery were submitted to ordeals (Dias and Dias 1970:370). The failing of these tests indicated their guilt and often ended their lives. Colonial and post-colonial regimes prohibited anti-sorcery ordeals in Mueda and elsewhere in Mozambique, but these restrictions were interpreted by most as elements of a broader policy also prohibiting the practice of sorcery itself (West 2005). But this, no longer. When I asked the administrator of neighboring Mueda district, Ambrósio Vicente Bulasi, about a recent spate of lion attacks and vigilante justice there, he, too, linked such occurrences, in the present, to democracy. "Democracy," he stated, "means that each one has the right to believe what he believes." Personally, he did not "believe in sorcery": "Of course, people cannot make lions and send them to attack other people. These things arise out of conflicts between families." Nonetheless, democracy dictated that officials such as he remain uninvolved in these affairs. "It is essential not to get drawn into such matters," he told me. "If you try to adjudicate, you wind up taking sides. It is better to have [people] reach a resolution on their own," he concluded. "I tell them that they must sort these things out for themselves." According to residents of Muidumbe, this is precisely what their administrator did when lions besieged their villages in late 2002 and early 2003 (see Israel n.d.).

During a 1998 tour of Africa, US president Bill Clinton declared: "From Kampala to Capetown, from Dakar to Dar es Salaam, Africans are being stirred by new hopes for democracy and peace and prosperity." In support of this, he pointed to the fact that "half of the forty-eight nations in sub-Saharan Africa [had] chose[n] their own governments" (Clinton

1998). By many accounts, Mozambique was a—if not *the*—model for democratization in Africa, having recently emerged from a protracted civil war and successfully staged multiparty national elections (Chan and Venâncio 1998; Manning 2001, 2002). Only a few years later, however, the Democratization Policy Institute declared:

> Despite high hopes following the end of the Cold War, promises of an "African Renaissance" remain largely unfulfilled. Most of the countries chosen by President Clinton as examples of a new Africa are either outright dictatorships, like Rwanda and Eritrea, or quasi-democratic autocracies, like Uganda and Ethiopia. Most African countries that adhere to democratic governance (loosely defined) have shown some slippage, with democratically elected leaders attempting to remain in power by tweaking constitutions. [Democratization Policy Institute 2001]

Meanwhile, observers have reported rising levels of corruption in Maputo—punctuated by the failure of the criminal justice system to detain those responsible for the assassination of whistleblowers—and international observers have expressed grave concerns over irregularities in the 2004 Mozambican general elections (The Carter Center 2005; Clemens 2002; Hanlon 2004). By Western standards, Africa's new democracies, including Mozambique, have had limited success in consolidating regime transition.

But what of African standards? The Cameroonian historian Achille Mbembe has argued that the project of democratization in contemporary Africa depends not on the application of a Western model of power to African realities but, instead, upon the cultivation within Africa of "other languages of power" that express emergent African political ethics. (The same might be said of democratization, political realities, and languages of power in other regions of the world.) These languages, he asserts, "must emerge from the daily life of the people, [and] address everyday fears and nightmares, and the images with which people express or dream them" (Geschiere 1997:7). Elsewhere (West 2005), I have examined sorcery discourse as one such language of power spoken by Muedans; I have also suggested that, in speaking of political realities, Muedans are not limited to this one language. Like most peoples, Muedans draw on multiple languages of power that intertwine in complex fashion in the world they inhabit. The way in which they speak of political realities today has been shaped by historical encounters with various others and the languages of power they have spoken, whether slave traders, Catholic missionaries,

Portuguese colonial administrators, Tanganyikan plantation owners, FRE-
LIMO nationalist guerrillas, or agents of post-independence state socialism. At the broadest level, the language of power contemporary Muedans
speak comprises multiple languages. It is a linguistic mosaic produced and
sustained by speakers who have gained varying degrees of fluency in other
languages and woven them into their own—a system in constant flux. In
accordance with the topic at hand, its speakers draw meaning from different experiential subsystems, geographical reference points, and historical
strata. In the current moment, Muedans have even engaged with the language of power spoken by democratic reformers, adopting or adapting
some terms and concepts from the democracy lexicon while dismissing or
ignoring others.

In this chapter, I argue that the language of power Muedans have spoken in the midst of neoliberal transformation of the Mozambican economy
and polity differs substantially from the language spoken by democratic
reformers, notwithstanding points of convergence, as well as internal variations and dynamic complexities, in both these languages. Recognizing
that, in the face of reform, Muedans have not spoken with one voice, nor
have their ideas and actions derived from some hermetic indigenous logic,
I nonetheless suggest that the language of power Muedans generally speak
reflects and sustains different notions of contemporary political realities.
In the disjuncture between their language and that of democratic reformers, I argue, Muedans have critically engaged with the ongoing process of
democratization. Indeed, I suggest, they have articulated their own vision
of, and for, the working of power in the world they inhabit. Before examining this in detail, I provide an historical overview of democratic reform
in Mozambique.

THE "DEMOCRATIZATION" OF MOZAMBIQUE

The southern African nation of Mozambique was born of guerrilla war
waged against Portuguese colonizers by the Mozambican Liberation Front
(Frente de Libertação de Moçambique, or FRELIMO) from 1964 to 1974.
From rear bases in the newly independent and socialist-oriented Tanzania,
FRELIMO established its central base early in the campaign on the Mueda
Plateau amidst generally supportive Makonde populations. With military
support from China, the Soviet Union, and other Eastern bloc countries,
the Front expelled the Portuguese from substantial portions of the north-
ern Mozambican provinces of Tete, Niassa, and Cabo Delgado (including
most of the Mueda Plateau). In 1974, a military coup in Lisbon toppled
António Salazar's appointed successor, Marcelo Caetano, and set the stage

for FRELIMO to take power in 1975 over an independent Mozambique (Henriksen 1983; Munslow 1983). The party's official adoption of a Marxist-Leninist platform in 1977 consolidated FRELIMO's commitment to socialism (Munslow 1983). In coming years, however, brutal civil war undermined the realization of "socialist modernization" in Mozambique.

The Mozambican National Resistance (Resistência Nacional Moçambicana, or RENAMO) was born in the late 1970s of counterinsurgency operations undertaken by the neighboring Rhodesian regime to harass Zimbabwean nationalist guerrillas based, with Mozambican consent, across the border in central Mozambique. After Zimbabwean independence, the South African apartheid regime extracted, trained, armed, and redeployed RENAMO fighters to "destabilize" a Mozambican state then harboring African National Congress (ANC) activists. By the late 1980s, RENAMO had put down roots in Mozambique—drawing malcontents and conscripts into its ranks—and was operating in all ten Mozambican provinces.

In some areas, the insurgency enjoyed considerable popular support. Not, however, in Mueda. Deeply invested in the historical construction of FRELIMO nationalism, Muedans fended off sporadic attacks and successfully denied the insurgency any foothold on the plateau. Throughout the country, however, nearly one million Mozambicans died, and up to six million were displaced from their homes as rival armies waged war for more than a decade and a half (Africa Watch 1992; Egerö 1987; Finnegan 1992; Hall 1990; Hanlon 1990; Minter 1994; Vines 1991). With the end of the Cold War and then the end of apartheid in the early 1990s, both sides lost external support, making possible a negotiated settlement in October 1992 stipulating that national elections be held in October 1994 (Alden 1995; Alden and Simpson 1993; Chan and Venâncio 1998; Hume 1994; Mazula 1995). FRELIMO prevailed at the ballot box, taking the presidency and a majority of seats in the national assembly (Hanlon 1994), as it would again in 1999 and 2004.

The democratization of Mozambique has consisted of far more than the staging of regular national elections. In the shadow of Soviet perestroika and glasnost and the global ascendance of neoliberalism, the ruling FRELIMO party initiated comprehensive reforms from the late 1980s onward to liberalize the Mozambican economy and polity. In 1986, fiscal austerity measures were unilaterally adopted by the FRELIMO government, making possible an agreement with the IMF the following year for structural adjustment support (Hanlon 1991). In 1989, the FRELIMO party officially abandoned its commitment to Marxism-Leninism. In the ensuing years, government privatized a great many state enterprises (Myers 1994;

Pitcher 2002; West and Myers 1996). A new constitution in 1990 established individual rights of person and property, including freedoms of religion and political expression, fostering foreign and domestic investment and leading rapidly to the emergence of multiple political parties and also a vibrant independent press (Africa Watch 1992). In 1997, government created a framework for state decentralization and for subsequently staged local elections in a number of cities and towns (Alves and Cossa 1997). Simultaneously, government explored means of incorporating civil leaders—including hereditary authorities—into processes of local governance, eventually issuing a decree on the matter in the year 2000 (Buur and Kyed 2003; Hanlon 2000). All of these measures were underwritten by Western donor nations, as well as supported by an array of international organizations.

Although the democratization of Mozambique has comprised these multiple, interconnected, political and economic reform processes, three aspects have been central to the Muedan experience of democracy, namely, elections, state decentralization, and the establishment of individual rights of person, property, and free expression. In the remainder of this chapter, I consider these components in turn, focusing on how Muedans have, through their own language of power, understood and engaged with them rather differently than reformers might have hoped and expected.

ELECTORAL DEMOCRACY, PERPETUAL WAR

Not only is the Mueda Plateau one of the most geographically remote regions in Mozambique, but also it is one of the most politically isolated. The region—often called "the cradle of the revolution"—has, in many ways, remained more loyal to FRELIMO socialism than has the party itself. Indeed, most Muedans took notice of democracy only in 1994. During that event-filled year, UN peacekeepers established camp in the town of Mueda to oversee the demobilization of soldiers. RENAMO set up offices in district seats. UN election observers arrived en masse to coordinate electoral registration and voter education. RENAMO leader Afonso Dhlakama and FRELIMO leader Joaquim Chissano each held campaign rallies on the plateau. Finally, in late October, Muedans voted.

In the context of the modern nation-state, multiparty elections are often the most celebrated component of democracy. Accordingly, great emphasis has been placed on the successful staging of elections in Mozambique. In the aftermath of the first national multiparty elections in 1994, one observer declared: "Peace in Mozambique first and foremost means that the political conflict fought out between FRELIMO and RENAMO in a bloody war has been civilized in the sense that both its theatre and instruments have changed: from the bush to parliament and from weapons to words, respectively" (Weimer 1996:43–44). Above all else, democratic reformers in Mozambique conceived of elections as a means of ending violent conflict and of rationalizing political contestation by rendering contestants and their respective politics directly accountable to the Mozambican people.

From the outset, however, Muedans looked upon elections—and democracy, more generally—rather differently. Many Muedans first heard the word *democracy* spoken on Radio Moçambique and associated with RENAMO leader Afonso Dhlakama, who proclaimed that he had fought for, and won, democracy for the Mozambican people (Manning 2002: 144–145). Muedans subsequently saw the word in print on RENAMO flags and T-shirts appearing in the region during the electoral campaign. To be sure, UN representatives in Mozambique, from Maputo to Mueda, also frequently deployed the term *democracy* in public discourse and in printed matter distributed before elections. Tellingly, most Muedans conceived of the United Nations Operation in Mozambique (UNOMOZ) as a "political party" that, like RENAMO, contested FRELIMO's historical right to govern the nation it had liberated from colonial rule. That many ranking UN military officers were Portuguese, owing to competence in the Mozambican national language, exacerbated suspicions that UNOMOZ constituted a stealth invasion force under the control of the former colonizer.

In the months before elections, UNOMOZ worked to demobilize both combatant armies. Because there were no RENAMO bases on the plateau, however, Muedans bore witness only to the disarmament of FRELIMO troops, whose return as civilians to Muedan villages signaled to them FRELIMO vulnerability or defeat. Meanwhile, UNOMOZ visibly safeguarded the establishment of RENAMO headquarters in Mueda town, where "foreign delegations" frequently appeared to celebrate democracy's arrival in Mozambique by bestowing largesse on those Muedans considered "bandits" and "murderers." In these early days, Muedans conceived of democracy as the ideology of "opposition," the slogan of ignoble enemies, past and present. Democracy's arrival in Mueda signaled the potential undoing of all that FRELIMO—and with it, Muedans—had accomplished since taking up arms in 1964, including the achievement of national sovereignty.

When voter registration began, many Muedans declined participation. When asked why, many told me that they had no use for the identification cards issued by elections officials, for they "already belonged to a political party" (West 2003). When local FRELIMO leaders themselves spoke out in support of democracy and urged Muedans to register for the vote, many worried that FRELIMO was "growing tired."

With the start of the electoral campaign, rival political parties focused attention on potential voters. This was the moment in which, according to democratic reformers, parties would be required to attune themselves to the desires of constituents. What actually happened was rather different from this. Mozambicans everywhere uttered the proverb, "When buffaloes fight, the grass gets trampled." Indeed, the campaign was defined less by "debate" than by contestants' activating networks of patronage and coercion. Voters ultimately "recognized" candidates who most convincingly exercised power in their midst, RENAMO generally winning in regions it had come to control during the war and FRELIMO in regions it had held. The campaign introduced new tensions—sometimes violent—into communities throughout the country, including Muedan villages. At the beginning of the campaign, FRELIMO leaders circulated in the Mueda region, calling upon villagers to remain "vigilant" against the appearance of RENAMO in their midst. This term—which invoked memories of revolutionary wartime campaigns to detect and eliminate "enemies within" the ranks of the FRELIMO insurgency (that is, spies, saboteurs)—accentuated Muedan resentment against, and fear of, RENAMO in the very moment of democratic "consolidation of the peace." Suspected RENAMO sympathizers were identified and beaten. Several times, Muedans attacked RENAMO headquarters in Mueda town, tearing down the RENAMO flag and chasing RENAMO delegates out of town. When RENAMO leader Afonso Dhlakama came to the plateau to stage a rally, Muedans "stoned" him with green (hard, unripened) mangoes and then the helicopter in which he fled. By contrast, FRELIMO leader Joaquim Chissano was met on the Mueda airstrip by throngs of supporters, who carried him on a makeshift throne to his rally in the center of town.[2] Weeks later, Muedans cast their ballots, voting overwhelmingly in favor of Chissano and FRELIMO.[3]

After ballots had been cast and results tabulated, most Muedans with whom we spoke expected talk of democracy to end, for they, and the nation, had recognized "Papa Chissano" as their legitimate leader. To their surprise and indignation, the RENAMO flag continued to fly at party headquarters in district seats on the plateau. RENAMO delegates continued to lay claim to power as they prepared for future elections. To most Muedans, such "provocation" was unprecedented. Under socialism, the one-party state knew no contestants; within the ranks of the highly centralized party, power struggles were quickly—if sometimes violently—resolved. The colonial state, too, had admitted no rivals, within or without. FRELIMO's challenge to Portuguese rule produced protracted, violent conflict, after which only one of the two claimants to power remained in Mozambique, namely, FRELIMO.

The model of singular, uncontested power resonated even more deeply than this among Muedans. To be sure, in pre-colonial times, young men often challenged the authority of their elders—whether on the basis of descent from a founding elder, aptitude for leadership, or courage—giving rise to struggles over settlement headmanships. And such contests sometimes turned violent. In any case, such affairs were considered finished only when all parties recognized a victor or when parties refusing to do so abandoned the settlement (often in the company of their supporters). Until the uncontested authority of one man was recognized, the security of settlement residents vis-à-vis one another and neighboring settlements remained unsure. In contrast to these familiar models for dispute resolution, multiparty democracy, from the Muedan perspective, promised to sustain and even proliferate rival claims to power at the highest levels in the land, with dramatic implications for those living in every province, district, and village in the country. Under democracy, it seemed, no defeat was recognized, and, therefore, no war finished—a political reality to which Muedans have only slowly and partially acclimated themselves.[4]

DEMOCRATIC DECENTRALIZATION, STATE ABANDONMENT

Simultaneous with the staging of national-level multiparty elections, democratic reformers in Mozambique have pursued a policy of democratic decentralization. Just weeks before the 1994 elections, government passed a law (no. 3/94) devolving responsibility for a variety of governmental functions to "municipalities," to be formed of urban and rural districts and administered by elected officials. In 1995, before the law took force, it was declared unconstitutional. A new law (no. 2/97), passed in 1997, established the framework for devolution to democratically elected local governments called "autarchies," to be established only in the thirty-three largest cities and towns in the country (Alves and Cossa 1997; Weimer and Fandrych 1999). Elsewhere, the government would continue to appoint officials, from the district administrator down to the village president and neighborhood secretary.

In parallel, reformers pressed FRELIMO to reverse post-independence policy that had abolished the chieftaincy. FRELIMO justification for banning hereditary authorities from any role in government lay in arguments that such figures had actively collaborated with Portuguese colonial rule (Monteiro 1989). Indeed, colonial administrators had used chiefs at the highest levels as tax collectors, labor recruiters, and agents of law enforcement—tasks for which these individuals received substantial rewards.

FRELIMO therefore proclaimed the need to liberate rural Mozambicans not only from the Portuguese but also from the feudal hierarchies through which colonial rule was consolidated. The party did so by establishing party-based structures of authority that reached deep into every village, displacing hereditary authorities at levels where they had collaborated with the colonial regime (Hanlon 1990). Some Mozambicans celebrated the abolition of the chieftaincy. Others resented it as an attack on local autonomy and custom. Still others manifested ambivalence.

Over the course of the Mozambican civil war, RENAMO insurgents played on mixed sentiments, resuscitating and (re)inventing institutions of hereditary authority among populations in the areas it came to control and using them to extract information, food supplies, labor, and guerrilla conscripts (Alexander 1997). Notwithstanding compulsion in most instances, many communities (particularly in the central part of the country, from which key RENAMO leaders hailed) supported the insurgency, in part because of resentment of various FRELIMO policies, including, but not limited to, the abolition of the chieftaincy (Englund 2002; Geffray 1990). By war's end, democratic reformers had taken notice of this and had begun to advocate renewed recognition of "traditional authorities" by the Mozambican government itself. Reformers sometimes suggested that the institutions of "traditional authority" might serve rural Mozambican communities as forms of "civil society" where successive authoritarian regimes—slave-trading kingdoms (in some places), Portuguese colonialism, the FRELIMO guerrilla (in its "liberated zones"), a centralized socialist state, and the RENAMO insurgency (in some places)—had rendered impossible the emergence and maintenance of other collective social forms (Lubkemann 2001; see also Orvis 2001). Some suggested that, through traditional authorities, the will of the people might be powerfully expressed in the new democratic era (Lundin 1995).

In 1991, the Ford Foundation provided funding for the establishment of a research project on the issue of traditional authority, to be housed within the walls of the Mozambican Ministry of State Administration. In 1995, the United States Agency for International Development (USAID) financed the continuance of the project under the rubric of its broader "Democracy in Mozambique" project (Fry 1997). As project researchers toured the country, holding workshops with ex-chiefs (African American Institute 1997), FRELIMO officials in some places sought to improve relations with these figures, whose potential influence over the rural electorate they deemed significant. Before elections, FRELIMO officials in many parts of the country made substantial overtures to ex-chiefs, particularly where they believed that doing so might swing the balance of support away from RENAMO.

Elsewhere, FRELIMO cadres expressed grave concerns that hereditary authorities were not necessarily qualified to discharge the duties of modern state administration. Perhaps more important, state officials wondered what would become of them if the chiefs who had been displaced by the creation of their positions were once more recognized. Some FRELIMO leaders in Maputo wondered how FRELIMO would hold power if it abandoned loyal cadres in rural areas in favor of traditional authorities, most of whom had been marginalized by FRELIMO rule (West and Kloeck-Jenson 1999). Others, still committed to the socialist project, saw recognition of hereditary authorities as the reestablishment of feudal hierarchies.

Despite promises in the mid-1990s from the minister of state administration that a law officially reinstating hereditary authorities was imminent, no such law was ever passed. Government policy on the matter eventually took the form of a decree (no. 15/2000) issued by the Council of Ministers in the year 2000.[5] The decree mandated local government consultation and cooperation with "community authorities" in relation to various governmental functions, including tax collection, voter registration, policing, judicial proceedings, land distribution, oversight of public education and public health, environmental protection, road construction, and other developmental issues (Buur and Kyed 2003; Hanlon 2000). The decree granted community authorities the right to wear uniforms and to use "symbols of the Republic"; however, it neither stipulated that government was required to heed their counsel nor strictly delineated who they were. Included in the category of potential community authorities were not only traditional authorities but also "village or neighborhood secretaries" (historically, FRELIMO appointees) and "other legitimate leaders" (Buur and Kyed 2003; Santos 2003:83; Hanlon 2000; Meneses et al. 2003:358). According to the decree, such leaders had to be duly "recognized as such by their respective communities" (Hanlon 2000), but the decree specified neither what constituted a community nor the mechanism for recognition (Buur and Kyed 2003).

The Autarchies Law, as well as the Community Authorities Decree, ultimately left it to the discretion of local state officials to craft relationships with traditional authorities in their jurisdictions in accordance with their governing strategies and agendas. In some areas of the country—especially where RENAMO relations with traditional authorities undermined FRELIMO hegemony—local government officials organized ceremonies in which traditional authorities were formally recognized as community authorities (Buur and Kyed 2003; Institutions for Natural Resource Management n.d.), seemingly in attempts to deny RENAMO a point of political contention while rendering these figures more beholden to the ruling party.[6] Some administrators, in fact, began using these duly recognized community authorities as tax collectors, granting them subsidies for their services in accordance with the provisions of the decree (Buur and Kyed 2003).

Recognition of community authorities played out differently in Mueda. There, in pre-colonial times, dispersed settlements had sustained a high degree of autonomy, one from another. Settlement heads had generally exercised authority over very small numbers of people. In order to administer local populations through the intermediary of hereditary authorities, the Portuguese administration had been obliged to construct hierarchies among settlement heads where none had previously existed. Colonial administrators interacted only with the highest-ranking figures in this hierarchy—figures whose authority the vast majority of Muedans considered illegitimate. At independence, FRELIMO orchestrated the construction of communal villages on the plateau, where the former populations of several dozen settlements would live together. Former settlement heads were no longer officially recognized by FRELIMO-appointed village presidents and neighborhood secretaries, but Muedan matrilineages continued to recognize them in clandestine. In the post-socialist era, Muedans openly recognized these lineage heads. However, they demonstrated no interest in resuscitating the hierarchy of chiefs through which the Portuguese had governed in colonial times.

Surprisingly, FRELIMO officials themselves pressed for the recognition of community authorities in Muedan villages. Community authority in Mueda, however, would not look like it did elsewhere in Mozambique. District officials in the plateau region orchestrated processes whereby village presidents—who held FRELIMO-created offices, by FRELIMO appointment—would simply be renamed "community leaders."[7] Like reinstated chiefs elsewhere in the country, these village-presidents-turned-community-leaders were given uniforms to wear and Mozambican flags to plant in their yards, just as colonial-era chiefs had once been given. Elsewhere in the country, debates raged over whether it was appropriate to stage elections to identify legitimate claimants to the title of "community authority"; hereditary authorities themselves often resisted the idea that popular ballot could determine their status. In Mueda, FRELIMO officials decided to stage elections to legitimate office holders in the moment of renaming village presidents as "community authorities." Some polls took the form of referenda, and others, multicandidate contests. In some villages, incumbents prevailed (because villagers had, or felt they had, no choice or because they truly respected incumbents); in others, challengers unseated them.

Notwithstanding FRELIMO high jinks, the process of recognizing community leaders provided Muedans the opportunity to choose those who would govern them at the most proximate level. Ironically, to the extent that the election of community leaders constituted a meaningful form of democratic decentralization, Muedans saw in it peril instead of promise. To be sure, many were displeased with the FRELIMO appointees who had long governed them. As we shall see in the next section, in the years following independence, FRELIMO rule had brought fewer and fewer benefits to the ruled and more and more to the rulers. Before village elections, however, most responded to the idea of *electing* local authorities with a simple question: "Who would rule us then?" Reading such statements as capitulation to FRELIMO authoritarianism would be a mistake, however. Muedans with whom we worked understood the dynamics of governance to be complex, echoing popular understandings elsewhere on the continent. Such understandings warrant close scrutiny.

Many scholars of African history have suggested that, by varied logics, power in Africa has long depended more on "wealth in people" than on "wealth in things" (Bledsoe 1980; Cooper 1979; Guyer 1995; Miers and Kopytoff 1977; Miller 1988; Vansina 1988), more on cultivating social relations than on cultivating lands (Berry 2002). African rulers, they suggest, have long sought to transform material wealth into loyal subjects, for such subjects have been considered both means to the (re)production of power and power's ultimate end. Power in Mueda has, indeed, long been measured in terms of one's ability to attract and sustain subordinates. In precolonial Mueda, warlords depended upon loyal and productive subjects to harvest goods—such as India rubber, gum copal, beeswax, and sesame seed—that could be traded at the coast for arms. With such arms, they not only defended themselves and their people but also mounted raids to capture slaves, many of whom were ultimately absorbed into the group as members with full rights and contributed to its strength like any others. Rulers who abused subordinates or failed to defend them, or to create a mutually beneficial environment in which they might live, faced the prospect that their subjects would abandon them. The Portuguese colonial regime mostly relied (with limited success) on coercive means to capture Mozambican subjects and their productive potential, issuing passbooks in which the required fulfillment of periodic labor contracts was to be recorded. Displeased subjects of colonial rule fled in vast numbers across borders where they found more favorable labor regimes. In the post-independence period, FRELIMO implored rural Mozambicans to produce in their fields in order to produce the nation itself (Machel 1978); the party also rounded up "unproductive" city dwellers and set them to work in reeducation camps (Africa Watch 1992). One after another, these successive regimes struggled through various means to secure "wealth in people."

Muedans with whom we worked were accustomed to the idea that the legitimacy of authority depended in such varied ways upon "cultivating people." They also recognized that the establishment of a prosperous domain was inextricably bound up with the exercise of superior force. Correspondingly, they considered a ruler's power commensurate with his ability to tap resources beyond the reach of others—resources to be deployed in the construction of a mutually beneficial order and in the maintenance of that order, whether by force or by the cultivation of consent. The authority of local officials, as they had experienced it in both socialist and colonial eras, derived from the state, in whose voice and with whose backing local officials spoke. Local power depended upon the resources of the state—indeed, depended upon the state *as* resource.

Such conceptions gave foundation to Muedan anxieties about democratic decentralization and elections at the local level. As long as anyone with whom we worked could remember, the state had appointed local officials who acted in its name. Muedans feared that an official of their own nomination would not speak for the state and therefore would not bring the force of the state to bear in the maintenance of local order and in the resolution of local problems. An official of their own choosing would speak only with their voice—a voice they had no reason to believe the state would hear. Many saw local elections to the post of community leader as an ominous sign. A state that no longer cared who occupied such positions, they reasoned, was a state no longer interested in the domains over which these office holders exercised authority. A state that allowed them to appoint their own officials, they feared, was a state no longer prepared to bestow its largesse in the interest of cultivating consent, a state preparing to abdicate authority over people it no longer considered a source of wealth.

The dynamics of post-socialist reform dramatically confirmed Muedan suspicions. To secure support from the International Monetary Fund (IMF) and Western donor nations, the Mozambican government slashed state budgets from 1986 onward. State enterprises, which had provided a large proportion of employment opportunities nationwide (many of which were not economically viable), began to shut down. The Nguri agricultural scheme in the lowlands immediately southeast of the plateau, where large numbers of Muedans worked, was among these. Shrinking budgets also translated into declining social services. In the Mueda region, teachers abandoned schools and nurses left health clinics as real salaries declined precipitously. Only those schools and clinics enjoying the patronage of a nongovernmental organization (NGO) continued to provide quality services. For all intents and purposes, the state ceased to provide an environment in which Muedans might "produce the wealth of the nation."

In the neoliberal era, the state looked elsewhere for wealth. Government carved up state sector enterprises, auctioning off some of the nation's most valuable assets, or rights thereto, to foreign investors (Alden 2001; Pitcher 2002). High rates of economic growth yielded disappointing employment prospects for Mozambicans because new enterprises tended to hire expert foreign workers and use capital-intensive means of production. Muedans watched from the side of the road as foreign lumber companies trucked massive loads of hardwood from the plateau interior to the coast. As a result of such arrangements, state power was, to an unprecedented extent, delinked from the productivity of the Mozambican people. Needing nothing from the people, the state offered them nothing. Apart from periodic election campaigns, the state betrayed near total lack of interest in "cultivating people" and their productive power.[8] To Muedans, the state's devaluation of its citizenry—of people as wealth—was nowhere more clearly communicated than in the mandate given them under the rubric of democratic decentralization to "govern themselves."

INDIVIDUAL FREEDOM, COLLECTIVE DANGER

Also among the essential elements of democratic reform in Mozambique was the ratification of a new constitution for the republic (1990), giving foundation to a wide range of civil liberties. Article 74 of the new constitution established rights to freedom of political expression. The freedom to "pursue religious aims freely" was laid down in article 78. Article 86 delineated the right to ownership of property. Whereas the rights of the Mozambican people as a whole had been elevated over those of the individual in the socialist era, democratic reformers argued that, to secure prosperity in post-war Mozambique, it was essential to lift socialist-era constraints on individual creativity and entrepreneurship. The early 1990s witnessed the formation of more than a dozen political parties, the growth and proliferation of religious communities, and the emergence of a robust independent media. Businesses, large and small, appeared on the economic landscape. Investors, including nationals and foreigners, canvassed cities, towns, and rural districts throughout the country for investment opportunities. By the end of the decade, Mozambique was able to claim some of the highest annual economic-growth rates on the African continent (Fauvet 2000).

Notwithstanding dramatic political and economic transformations, marked continuities were also observable. The faces of power remained familiar. Such continuities were, in part, the product of the very processes defining transition. For example, state officials controlled and often personally benefited from state enterprise divestiture. Calls for bids—many of which were issued before the passage of legislation officially mandating and giving structure to divestiture—were often posted in inconspicuous places, such as bulletin boards on state officials' office walls. Through what the Mozambican attorney general later sarcastically referred to as "silent privatizations" (Harrison 1999), officials at various levels privatized assets unto themselves, their cronies, and clients from whom they might extract rents (Myers 1994; West and Myers 1996).[9] Through such means, national-level military leaders from the plateau region took possession of military warehouses, garages, and machine shops in Mueda. Agricultural officials staked claims to large plots of land in the Nguri State Farm irrigation scheme.

Advocates of privatization generally suggested that, through market mechanisms, these valuable assets would eventually pass into the hands of those most capable of exploiting them, contributing to sustained economic growth and greater national prosperity. Indeed, those who first took possession of state assets often sold them at considerable profit to more capable investors. In other cases, they kept controlling interest over such assets, seeking manager-investors who might provide essential expertise in exchange for a share of the wealth to be generated by their exploitation.

Included among advocates of democratic reform were those who criticized such forms of opportunism. Participants in donor-sponsored workshops on the topic of corruption railed against the use of public office for the pursuit of private gain. People spoke openly in the independent media about the criminalization of the Mozambican state (Hanlon 2004). Mozambican officials themselves were among the most vociferous critics of corruption, some speaking out in earnest and some to cover their own behavior. Ironically, public furor over rising rates of corruption provided grist for the mill of neoliberal condemnation of the Mozambican state and reinforced donor and NGO tendencies to bypass the state in order to "work directly" with intended beneficiaries, further weakening the project of state governance.

Muedans, too, looked critically upon the behavior of the national elite. They, however, expressed criticism in a different language. The standards by which they condemned the powerful among them derived from various historical moments and models of power. Indeed, Muedan experiences with and expectations of power, in some ways, licensed privilege. In pre-colonial days, Muedans told us, settlement heads never went hungry. These figures of authority enjoyed the best and the most of everything available. According to Muedan parlance, they not only "ate well" but also "ate" their subordinates. Youngsters, when successful in the hunt, offered these elders the choicest cuts of meat. Men returning from coastal trade expeditions were obliged to give these elders the goods they had procured. The most powerful of these elders even "ate" potential rivals by forcing their neigh-bors to join their own settlements, thereby augmenting the number of peo-ple paying them tribute and defending them against potential attackers. Through feeding their own appetites, these elders expanded the social bodies of which they were heads. At the same time, they fed these social bodies and the individuals of which they were composed. Successful settle-ment heads spurred their subjects to produce the wealth of the group, which they used to ensure the well-being of those upon whom they depended. They demanded that subjects fill their plates but also used their plates to feed their subjects. The satisfaction of their expansive appetites thus gave foundation to their subordinates' sustenance.

The power of the settlement head was diminished under a colonial administration that required subjects to fill the state plate instead. Only those used by the Portuguese as administrative intermediaries "ate well." When FRELIMO initiated its guerrilla campaign in the plateau region, party "chairmen" displaced hereditary authorities altogether. But, like their predecessors, these figures of authority mobilized subordinates to fill the plate from which all were fed (Negrão 1984). Following independence, the FRELIMO-orchestrated project of collective production was reproduced on a national scale. Faced with the prospect of total economic collapse in the wake of the mass exodus of Portuguese colonials following indepen-dence, FRELIMO "intervened" in the management of abandoned planta-tions, farms, factories, and machine shops and eventually nationalized many of these properties (Hanlon 1990). The party coordinated produc-tion and, through the management of trade and the setting of prices, appropriated and redistributed the nation's produce. Like settlement heads before them, FRELIMO leaders fed their subjects from the plate their subjects were required to fill. Of course, state officials never went hun-gry. Although the wealth of the nation purportedly belonged to the people, these officials enjoyed it most directly. Goods were sometimes scarce, but ranking officials had first dibs. Vehicles belonged to the state, but party bosses generally rode in them. To most Muedans, this was not particularly surprising.

The behavior of the post-socialist elite was another matter altogether. They ate well, according to Muedans, but failed to feed others. With profits generated in the exploitation of former state enterprises or with rents garnered from foreign investors to whom they served as godfathers, elites tightened their hold on power even as the state weakened. On the plateau and elsewhere, they built new homes surrounded by walls. They sent their children abroad to be educated. They manipulated and controlled banks and donor-funded credit schemes to acquire fleets of cars, trucks, and tractors with which they often provided "services" at a charge, consolidating control over local economic hierarchies. As we have seen, the enterprises and transactions over which they presided generated few jobs. All but the closest of family members were denied access to the plates they filled high to satisfy seemingly insatiable appetites.

From pre-colonial days, Muedans have associated insatiable appetites with sorcery. Whereas the fruits of one's own labor can satisfy the ordinary appetite, the sorcerer is sated only by feeding on the well-being—indeed, the very life substance, the flesh—of others. This, it is said, sorcerers undertake in clandestine, through the use of a medicinal substance called *shikupi*, which renders them invisible to ordinary people. Such illicit consumption, as well as the social carnage (literally, meat derived from slaughter) to which it gives rise, challenges the prerogatives of legitimate authority to measure appetites against one another and to nourish the social body as a whole. According to Muedans, legitimate authorities have met this challenge since pre-colonial times by following sorcerers into the invisible realm of sorcery, wherein they monitor sorcerers' activities and quash their appetites. The exercise of legitimate authority constitutes a form of sorcery, according to Muedan conceptions. Muedans have long distinguished between the "sorcery of self-advancement" or "sorcery of self-enrichment" (*uwavi wa kushunga*) practiced by common sorcerers and the "sorcery of self-defense" (*uwavi wa kulishungila*) practiced by responsible authority figures in behalf of the larger group. They have also recognized the fine line between these two forms of sorcery. In the socialist era, they were generally convinced that FRELIMO leaders practiced uwavi wa kulishungila. In the era of democracy, by contrast, most suspected that authorities practiced uwavi wa kushunga. Post-socialist elites were suspected of transforming kin into *mandandosha* (zombie slave laborers) to tend their fields, work in their factories, or guard their houses, cars, and other possessions. "How else could they get so rich?!" Muedans often asked rhetorically. "How else could they protect themselves?! How else could they protect their wealth?!"[10]

The idea that present-day elites act as maleficent instead of beneficent sorcerers arose from and reinforced Muedan understandings of the new regime of tolerance for political and religious expression as well. In the socialist era, FRELIMO authorities in Mueda had prohibited sorcery accusations, proclaiming belief in sorcery to be a reactionary form of "obscurantism" that jeopardized the emergence and consolidation of class consciousness and solidarity. Muedans, however, interpreted socialist-era condemnations of sorcery beliefs and practices as the enforcement of a ban on self-serving forms of sorcery—in other words, as the FRELIMO enactment of a beneficent form of (counter)sorcery. In the new democratic era, as we have seen, FRELIMO officials demonstrated "respect" for individual "beliefs" through tolerance of sorcery discourse. Muedans interpreted such tolerance as official acceptance of—even collusion with—maleficent forms of sorcery. Indeed, state tolerance of sorcery discourse confirmed popular suspicions regarding the elite's practice of sorcery of self-enrichment. Tellingly, Muedans sometimes referred to the new, more liberal regime as one of *uwavi wa shilikali* (government sorcery).

New constitutional freedoms of expression contributed to an environment in which Muedans heard daily evidence of sorcery's rise. Radio Moçambique reported incidents of sorcery. New independent churches—along with traditional healers plying their trade openly after years in clandestine—called attention to sorcery in the act of treating its ills. But to Muedans, freedom of expression not only meant that one could speak *of* sorcery but also meant that *sorcerers* could *speak*. Muedans referred euphemistically to sorcery when they lamented, "With democracy, anything can be said, and anything can be done." Where state officials refused to intervene as responsible figures of authority in sorcery-related disputes, sorcery ran wild at all levels of society, Muedans told me. Under cover of democracy, it was said, sorcerers formed political parties of their own. Their motto, "Each one for himself!" echoed new constitutional rights in a sinister register. In the shadow of suspicion and resentment of the new elite, accusations flew among villagers themselves. As the wealthy and powerful ate their fill, ordinary Muedans went hungry or worse still, many feared, satisfied their hunger by feeding on their neighbors and kin.

DEMOCRACY, CARNAGE

The same language of power through which Muedans had engaged with democratic reform over the preceding decade and a half gave shape to their understandings of and responses to the grizzly attacks taking place in Muidumbe in late 2002 and early 2003. That provincial authorities took nearly a year after the maulings to provide arms and ammunition with which to kill the menacing lions only confirmed suspicions that the FRE-LIMO state was weak and that local officials did not have its ear.[11] Even more disturbing to Muedans was that district administrator Pedro Seguro never publicly condemned the sorcerers they knew to be responsible for the attacks. They assumed Seguro—a man of great authority—capable of seeing into the invisible realm of sorcery and practicing (counter)sorcery therein. But as the death toll mounted, Seguro remained "silent."[12]

Where provincial- and district-level authorities failed to resolve the crisis, village authorities did what they could. Hunting parties were organized, and, in time, six lions were caught in traps or killed with bow and arrow.[13] Meanwhile, the community leaders in some villages summoned councils of elders in attempts to discern who was responsible for the killings. "When the situation got bad," Namakandi community leader Pedro Agostinho told Radio Moçambique reporter Óscar Limbombo, "we put out word that if anyone knew who was making these lions, they had better say so" (Limbombo 2003). Some community leaders made public pronouncements that the attacks must cease. Through such acts, these village authorities attempted to play the part of beneficent sorcerers. But in the wake of democratic decentralization—meaning, in this case, elections confirming the community leaders' "legitimacy" at the ballot box—villagers perceived these figures as representatives not of some greater power who governed them all but rather only of those who had voted for them (generally, their matrilineage). As such, community leaders were deemed able to quash sorcery attacks within their own matrilineages but not on the grander scale on which these attacks were apparently taking place. Tellingly, the proclamations and accusations of some community leaders only fanned the flames of intermatrilineage suspicion and hostility. In the villages of Litapata and Mandava, community leaders themselves incited villagers to lynch their neighbors (Israel n.d.; Limbombo 2003).

District administrator Seguro expressed frustration that he was able to respond to vigilante killings only after crimes were committed and frenzied mobs dispersed (Limbombo 2003). Villagers blamed him more for failing to prevent the precipitating incidents—the attacks of sorcerers qua lions. Rumors circulated that Seguro himself was behind the attacks (see also

Israel n.d.). Others suggested that Seguro had "sold the district" for "three sacks of money" to "three whites" (reportedly including an Italian dental technician working at the Nang'ololo Catholic mission health clinic), meaning that he had granted permission to these foreigners (and, by most accounts, their local sorcerer colleagues) to attack people within a domain nominally under his protection.[14] That Seguro was both the ranking state official and the leading businessman in the district was interpreted by many residents as evidence that he practiced sorcery of self-advancement rather than sorcery of self-defense in behalf of his constituents. He was, by all accounts, the richest man in the district. Whereas reformers saw in Seguro an energetic entrepreneur bringing development to the district, villagers generally saw in him a man of expansive appetite who fed only himself. In Muidumbe, as in his previous posts, his personal "development" projects cannibalized the infrastructure of the collapsed collective project of social-ist modernization, creating jobs for only a few close family members (his wife, for example, ran a "restaurant" in the town marketplace that captured meticais spent by visitors to the district on official business). While Seguro "ate well" in late 2002 and early 2003, those under his charge went hungry (for fear of harvesting their meager crops) and, in some cases, were devoured by fellow villagers or literally eaten alive by lions. By the middle of 2003, lions had claimed the lives of forty-six men, women, and children and gravely injured another six. Eighteen villagers had been lynched.

In mid-2003, provincial authorities finally convened and provisioned a hunting party, headed by a man named Fernando Alves, and dispatched it to Muidumbe. Alves killed the fifth lion, after which villagers killed two more, bringing to an end the carnage that had beset the district for more than a year. Alves was a man of local legend long before he killed what Muidumbe residents identified as the most vicious of the pride that had stalked them. The son of mulatto parents, Alves lived in Pemba in the *bairro do cimento* (the "concrete neighborhood," composed mostly of houses built by Portuguese occupants in the colonial period) and earned a living as a self-employed mechanic. Like his father, he was an avid big-game hunter. According to Makonde trackers employed by Alves, he was adept at recov-ering *lyungo*, the life substance Makonde say a predatory animal, such as a lion, vomits in the moments immediately before dying. Alves himself attrib-uted his success as a hunter to his ability to find and ingest lyungo. Thus, the man who put an end to the carnage in Muidumbe came from outside the district as the bearer of superior force but acted in defense of the well-being of ordinary Muedans in a language they recognized.

That Muedans conceived of and engaged with events defining their world in the post-socialist era in a language of their own did not mean that they failed to recognize or to understand democracy's emergence in their midst. Indeed, I would argue, the language of power Muedans spoke in the course of these events and processes afforded them profound insights and allowed them to formulate a nuanced critique of democracy as they experienced it. Whereas neoliberal reformers suggested that democracy would rationalize political competition, render power more accountable to the people, and open greater space for individual contribution to a prosperous post-war environment, Muedans experienced democracy as a regime that promoted irresolvable conflict in their midst and provided cover for dominant political actors to forego the responsibilities of authority and to feed themselves at the expense of others. Muedan perspectives on democracy have resonated with the critical assessments offered in recent years by various commentators of deepening corruption and electoral fraud in Mozambique. Their skepticism regarding the true objectives of democratization has been validated by ongoing donor support (notwithstanding these disconcerting phenomena) so long as Mozambique has continued to adhere to IMF provisions and to sustain a friendly climate for foreign investment and trade.

Muedan conceptions of and reactions to democracy *do not* constitute a failure of understanding. *Neither* do they support the idea that Africa and Africans are ill suited for democracy. I would argue that, by critically engaging with democratization in a language that differs profoundly from the one spoken by democratic reformers, Muedans have, ironically, enacted democracy. After all, if democracy is conceived of as "government of the people, by the people, and for the people," following Lincoln's famous formulation, then democracy necessarily resides within the languages and terminologies used by "the people" to assess power's workings in their midst. Accordingly, regardless of constitutional reform, the staging of elections, and the devolution of power to the local level, any regime failing to create a beneficial order, by the people's definition, can scarcely call itself a democracy. If democracy resides in the understandings, experiences, and expressions of the people, then Muedans have enacted it—to the best of their abilities, albeit with limited success even by their own evaluations— through critical assessment of what reformers have called democracy, through expression of "the will of the people" in an altogether different language.[15]

Alas, democratic reformers rarely entertain such possibilities. In the run-up to the 1994 elections, the international community invested considerable resources in civic education programs designed to teach

Mozambicans about democracy. If the meanings and methods of democracy depend, by definition, upon the political subjects in question, then such initiatives betray unfounded conceit and also render democracy's actualization more difficult. One can only imagine what might have come of investing such considerable resources in attempts to discern what the Mozambican people had to teach policymakers about viable and desirable forms of governance. The notion reinforces the idea underlying this volume, namely, that anthropologists—through the dialogical methods of extended fieldwork and ethnographic writing—potentially have much to contribute to facilitating and strengthening democracy as variably defined by people in diverse locales around the globe.

Acknowledgments

This chapter draws on field research conducted in the Mueda Plateau region between 1993 and 2004. Marcos Agostinho Mandumbwe, Eusébio Tissa Kairo, and Felista Elias Mkaima participated in various phases of research. Funding was provided by the Fulbright-Hays Program, the United States Institute of Peace, the Wenner-Gren Foundation, the Economic and Social Research Council of the United Kingdom, and the British Academy. This was first presented as an essay at the School of American Research (now the School for Advanced Research, SAR) advanced seminar "Toward an Anthropology of Democracy," March 5–10, 2005, in Santa Fe, where David Nugent provided insightful commentary. It was subsequently presented at the Anthropology Seminar in the Instituto de Ciências Sociais da Universidade de Lisboa, April 15, 2005.

Notes

1. This account draws on Limbombo 2003, as well as a number of interviews conducted by the author in April 2004 in Muidumbe and in Pemba (the provincial capital). A more extensive account is provided by Paolo Israel (n.d.), an Italian anthropologist conducting doctoral research in the area at the time of these events. Israel also generously contributed valuable information (including alternative accounts) and commentary on a draft version of this chapter. According to Israel's account, most lion attacks occurred in lowland villages and in camps in the Messalo river valley where sugarcane is harvested and made into alcohol. Intensive fear of lion attack was limited to these places.

2. Muedans also dressed Chissano as a *humu* (ritual elder). Elsewhere (West 1997), I argue that this constituted an ambivalent gesture whereby they "recognized" his power but also demanded that he enact it responsibly, to the benefit of his subjects.

3. FRELIMO won 25,207 of the 30,023 valid ballots in Mueda district, 18,084 of 21,065 in Muidumbe district, and 13,164 of 17,540 in Nangade district (Mazula 1995:496).

4. I have argued that Muedans conceive of politics as "an unending contest with ever-changing rules—one in which no victory [is] final, and no defeat complete" (West 2005:265). What I argue here is that, instead of placing hopes in a *system of rules and regulations* that might broker and temper such contests (as democratic reformers urged them to), Muedans expect powerful actors to assert victory and to impose an order of their own making. Also, Muedans assume that any regime thus established must constantly, assertively, even preemptively, protect itself against any challenge to its established order.

5. Such a decree requires no legislative discussion or approval, has no legal force, and can easily be rescinded at any time.

6. Meneses and others (2003:370, 380) report several cases in which FRELIMO recognition of traditional authorities led to RENAMO's condemning such figures as "sellouts."

7. Local FRELIMO officials loosely based their initiative on Diploma Ministerial no. 107-A/2000 (the Community Authorities Decree Regulations), which stated that where the legitimacy of a "traditional chief" and "neighborhood secretary" were simultaneously recognized, the community was obliged to identify which of the two entities enjoyed precedence as "community authority" in the representation of the community vis-à-vis local government. In the process of recognizing village presidents as "community leaders," local FRELIMO officials did not explicitly present Muedans with the option of choosing a traditional chief to fill the post. The use of the term *community leaders* instead of *community authorities* further reflects the looseness of local application of the decree.

8. During election campaigns, both parties momentarily cultivated people, often through doling out jobs in the temporary but lucrative elections industry (undermining concerted donor attempts to professionalize the electoral bureaucracy).

9. Some, including once staunch socialists, declared the need to ensure the emergence of a strong national bourgeoisie, as opposed to allowing the wealth of the nation to fall into the hands of foreign investors.

10. As David Nugent pointed out in his commentary on this essay at SAR, the idea of the self-governing individual is essential to most variants of Western democracy, but it is an idea that Muedans find threatening. Most are unable to achieve it and are left vulnerable to those who do.

11. Israel (n.d.) reports that arms were sent to the district but that local hunters

feared using them against sorcerers and, in some cases, used them instead for hunting game.

12. According to Israel (n.d.), Seguro openly declared that the lions were "bush lions" (that is, not sorcery lions), but his "refusal" to identify and condemn the makers of these lions was widely interpreted as complicity. Suspicions were exacerbated by the fact that suspected sorcerers sometimes took refuge in the district seat under Seguro's protection.

13. There are conflicting accounts here as well. Israel (n.d.) reports that the only local hunting parties were vigilante groups hunting suspected sorcerers and that local hunters killed lions only before the maulings began or after the principal man-eating lion was killed by a hunter sent from Pemba (described below).

14. Israel (n.d.) reports that because he traveled to the lowlands to investigate rumors of the existence of a gang of assassins masquerading as lions, he himself was one of the suspected foreigners but that he and the mission dental technician alone were rumored to be working with Seguro, "the Supreme Leader of Lions." Many local residents closely associated Israel with Seguro because the administrator had granted Israel permission to build a small house in Seguro's yard. According to Israel, the "three sacs of money" were the bags of field gear he brought with him to Seguro's compound (personal communication, August 24 and September 2, 2005).

15. In Santa Fe, David Nugent and Kay Warren provided stimulating commentary on this point.

5

International Presence

The Passive Work in Democracy Promotion

Kimberley Coles

Charles came to Bosnia-Herzegovina to help in its post-war democratization.[1] He, along with thousands of other Americans and Europeans, was part of an international election-monitoring effort, a practice that has gained global currency and strength in the past twenty-five years as a cornerstone of democracy promotion activities (see Carothers 1997; Lean 2004). Charles, a British man in his mid-sixties, had visited Bosnia, East Timor, west Africa, Palestine, Afghanistan, and Kosovo as an international election monitor. His employers were normally the United Nations (UN), the European Union (EU), or the UK Foreign Office but could also include NGOs (nongovernmental organizations) such as the Carter Center and the National Democratic Institute and IGOs (international governmental organizations) such as the Organization of American States (OAS) and the Organization for Security and Co-operation in Europe (OSCE). International agencies like these and foreign ministries throughout North America and Europe now regularly fund volunteers (sometimes paying them a salary and sometimes not, but always providing per diem, insurance, and travel costs) to observe, supervise, and implement elections in new democracies, including those transitioning from socialism or experiencing political and social unrest. In Bosnia's case, four years (1992–1995) of war, genocide, destruction, and displacement set the stage for tumultuous democratic and electoral performances and laid the groundwork for the presence of international election supervisors in its post-war elections (1996–2000).[2] This chapter scrutinizes democracy promotion by closely, and ethnographically, examining what election supervision looked like on the ground in post-war Bosnia-Herzegovina. What work does Charles do as he helps democratize countries and citizens? How is democracy promotion practiced by the people who come as its representatives, verifiers, and proselytizers?

One method to answer these questions would be to detail what election supervisors do when they are supervising polling stations, registration centers, and ballot counting practices. International polling supervisors in Bosnia-Herzegovina, for example, set up polling booths, pointed out deviations from established rules, delivered ballots and other sensitive electoral documents, and rectified mistakes made by the local polling staff. They could also suspend voting. Their work in monitoring elections and promoting democracy involved enacting the election or, at a minimum, assisting in its enactment.

Another method—the one followed here—involves paying close attention to the experience of being an international election supervisor. Doing so gives a more nuanced picture of this increasingly important stratagem of foreign policy, but it also uncovers new paradoxes and questions about the purported effectiveness of election monitoring. That is, ethnographic research in Bosnia evidences that the experiences of many international election supervisors were at odds with the importance given to their role by the election administration and the foreign governments funding their involvement. For example, democracy promotion activities (that is, election observation and technical assistance) are now a cornerstone of the European Union's foreign policy aims and development goals (Commission of the European Communities 2000). After years of ad hoc and low-visibility electoral assistance, in the early 2000s it moved toward a common, systematic, and purposeful European standard and approach. The EU now funds approximately five to eight election-monitoring missions each year (averaging two to six months in duration) with the intent of legitimizing electoral processes, enhancing public confidence in election processes, and deterring fraud (Commission of the European Communities 2000). Similarly, the OSCE funds observation, supervision, and assistance activities (electoral and nonelectoral) in new democracies under the theoretical proposition that democracy and peace are highly correlated (see USIP 2001, but analytically see Gowa 1999; Ray 1997; Russett 1993). More often than not, however, Charles and others like him in post-war Bosnia-Herzegovina questioned the necessity and efficacy of their election monitoring, expressing jadedness about the utility of their work or offering alternative accounts of the purported work they were doing. Guy, a Belgian colleague, confided over coffee, "I don't really have a job here....I had one for maybe three of the sixteen months I have been here, but mostly someone else is doing the work or could be. Really, I'm part of a foreign policy strategy to bolster the number of internationals in-country. More internationals will make the election more smooth."

How are we to make sense of the apparent contradiction between the political importance given to international election monitors in democracy promotion parlance, budgets, and foreign policy strategies and the actual election monitors' on-the-ground experiences and perceptions that de-emphasize or refute that very same importance? The disjunction between foreign policy rhetoric and experience raises dilemmas about how democracy is promoted, as well as other kinds of work that democracy promotion obscures yet relies upon or fosters. What is actually being promoted across the globe under the umbrella of "democracy"?

BOSNIA-HERZEGOVINA AND INTERNATIONAL INTERVENTIONS

Yugoslavia began to disintegrate violently in 1990, ten years after the death of its authoritarian socialist leader Josep Broz Tito. Prolonged economic crisis and rising nationalism eventually led to the secession of republics away from Yugoslavia, first Slovenia and Croatia, then Bosnia-Herzegovina and Macedonia. Each independence movement and moment was marked by ethnonationalist rhetoric and armed conflict. Slovenia fought a seven-day war with Yugoslavia, but Croatia and Bosnia were less lucky. Bosnia suffered almost four years of war with both Croatia and the rump Yugoslavia. Both sought to claim territory within the republic of Bosnia-Herzegovina and incorporate their ethnic compatriots into their own nation-state's borders. In December 1995, the Dayton Peace Accord was signed, after forty-three months and more than 250,000 deaths, including the (in)famous Srebrenica massacre, in which eight thousand men were executed as a UN "safe area" fell to Serb paramilitary forces, and a one-hundred-day siege of Sarajevo, including the shelling of the Sarajevo Market.

The wars in Bosnia-Herzegovina brought the term *ethnic cleansing* into popular parlance as armed forces swept through villages and towns with the intent of killing, imprisoning, or removing all but the favored ethnicity. Ultimately, some 2 million people (out of a population of 4.4 million) would be displaced from their homes, either moving to another part of

Bosnia or fleeing the country as refugees. The wars are also, unfortunately, notable for the use of rape camps. An estimated twenty thousand women endured sexual assaults in the form of torture and rape, not by dissident soldiers but through a systematic assault planned by the military (Salzman 1998; see also Stigylmayer 1994). Rape camps were used as instruments of terror and "weapons of war." Although the World War II–era International Military Tribunal at Nuremberg established rape as a crime against humanity, the International Criminal Tribunal for the former Yugoslavia (located at The Hague) was the first to successfully prosecute mass rape as a crime against humanity.

International organizations provided humanitarian aid during the war, but the "international community" blossomed after the peace treaty. No longer were they helping residents survive; they were beginning to help people live. Under the auspices of a High Representative (a foreign diplomat), international governmental and nongovernmental organizations began to reshape the country and society into new forms. Projects spanned the spectrum of social domains, from rebuilding roads and water supply lines to conflict mediation radio shows. These projects were implemented by employees of IGOs and NGOs. Although local Bosnian support staff was always involved, the majority of aid workers were European or North American citizens.

In Bosnia, they were known within aid circles as *internationals.* Internationals were essentially short-term residents in Bosnia, often having six-month renewable contracts. A human resources manager for one of the IGOs reported to me that her figures showed that the average international worked in Bosnia for about two years before moving on to other jobs in other countries (either returning home or staying on the international aid circuit). International election workers were one subset of internationals, in-country for as short as ten days and, for administrative posts, as long as two, six, eight, or ten months. (A few head positions were more permanent in nature.) Notable, then, is the short duration in which even those with relatively long-term positions had to get to know Bosnia-Herzegovina, its people, and its political debates. Although some election internationals became repeat visitors, the election project (like many others in post-war Bosnia-Herzegovina) was marked by implementing personnel with superficial knowledge of Bosnia and of elections, what I have elsewhere termed *gloss* (Coles 2007; see also Gilbert 2005, 2006; Helms 2003a, 2003b, on the interplay of power and knowledge in Bosnia's relief programs). Few election personnel had professional experience in electoral matters; rather, they were retired army colonels, high school teachers, college graduates looking for careers, lawyers, civil society activists, and homemakers.[3]

In many respects, my research into the meanings and practices of democracy promotion and electoral supervision mirrors the paths that other internationals took on their route to Bosnia. The work presented here is based on eighteen months of fieldwork fragmented over four years and five election periods (1997–2000). I was sometimes in Bosnia for two weeks, sometimes eleven months, as I ethnographically researched the international election effort. Unlike the typical international paths, I was reviewing and analyzing my collected data during the times I was not resident in Bosnia. Fieldwork included interviews, participant-observation, and document collection at various electoral sites (for example, polling stations; field, regional, and main election offices; and subdepartments such as election supervision, public information, and election appeals). A large portion of my research incorporated becoming an election international myself. To that end, I participated in five elections in a variety of positions, including polling supervisor, election trainer, and chief of administration for the supervision department. These positions gave me a technical and bureaucratic insight and breadth not possible through interviews and observations alone. It also, of course, afforded coveted rapport and access that would not have been possible even in a realm governed, at least in rhetoric, by claims of transparency.

ELECTION SUPERVISION REDUX

Recently embraced, election monitoring contributes to the dissemination and strengthening of basic standards of election administration and advances competitive and regular elections as an international norm (Carothers 1997:20). Carothers argues that the effectiveness of monitors primarily lies in detecting and deterring fraud and in encouraging wary citizens and politicians to participate; monitors are normally more watchdogs and reporters than responsible members of the polling station staff. Their ability to catch fraud is actually weak, Carothers claims, but officials may abandon plans out of fear of being caught. Election supervision in Bosnia-Herzegovina was a more conscious and direct effort at solidifying democratic elections, because supervisors did have formal responsibilities; they were much more than watchful bystanders. In Bosnia, the international election supervisor was a key cog in .running and ensuring free and fair elections. Carothers also notes that even though monitoring benefits elections by detecting and preventing fraud and strengthening standards, it is plagued by the problems of unqualified observers, an overemphasis on Election Day, and poor application of standards. His critique raises similar dilemmas as Charles's about the work of observers and supervisors during the election period. What is actually going on? How is democracy promoted? What are the mechanisms that deter fraud, encourage participation, strengthen standards, and normalize the idea of competitive elections?

Election supervisors—these international, Good Samaritan, democracy-watching volunteers—served as "the eyes and ears" (and sometimes the hands) of the international community. International supervisors were meant to ensure that the Bosnian elections were conducted in a "free and fair manner" and that the established rules and regulations of the election were followed. Supervisors were mostly engaged with polling activities, but also registration, counting, and auditing were often under a supervisory mandate. Upon arrival at a field office, each polling supervisor was assigned a polling station to watch and oversee on Election Day. The polling station committee members were the ones who checked voter IDs, handed out ballots, and the like. Polling supervisors watched over the efforts and actions of the local polling station committees, the voters, and other observers. Although the local polling station chairpersons were nominally in charge, polling supervisors also had substantial authority over and responsibility for the events taking place in the polling stations. Over the five years of internationally administered elections in Bosnia-Herzegovina (1996 through 2000), international supervisors engaged in tasks such as setting up polling stations, observing or performing ballot counting, pointing out deviations from established rules, overseeing the distribution and receipt of electoral materials, verifying data entry of raw-number ballot counts, rectifying incorrect procedures taken by voters or staff, and suspending voting. In many cases, supervisors were responsible for electoral integrity, as seen by their sole handling of "sensitive material" and having to sign or co-sign electoral documents, such as ballot delivery receipts and accounting forms.[4]

Amid these responsibilities and duties, international workers like Charles often expressed frustration about their lack of "real work" or the uselessness and meaninglessness of their overt supervisory election work. Instead, they emphasized certain functionalities of their existence and the overall power of their simple presence in Bosnia-Herzegovina. The meanings and utility of this alternative rationale for their presence were diverse: what international workers thought they were doing ranged from pedagogy to demonstrating compassion. Regardless, no explicit action was required on their part, only their existence. In this chapter, I argue that the presence of international election supervisors was not just a logistical means and pragmatic strategy of technical democracy assistance, but also social practice of the transformative ideology of international intervention itself, including democracy promotion. Beyond the bustle of election preparation activity was another important aspect of international intervention: just being there. This mode of intervention is marked simply by the existence of international bodies.

If we add the idea of what I term *presence* to the analysis of democracy promotion and election monitoring, then Charles's complaints and Carothers's critique take on new meaning. That is, what international workers do, or do not do, may not matter much: another aspect of their "real work" was "just being there." In the following three sections, I analyze the work done (or thought to be done) by passively just being there. The transformative potential of passivity can be seen in supervisors' self-perceptions, other electoral staff's perceptions of them, and technical and bureaucratic decisions and processes. Their existential presence, beyond actively ensuring free and fair elections, was, in itself, a governance strategy aimed at controlling and transforming the conduct of Bosnia-Herzegovina and Bosnians, as well as Bosnian democracy.

To understand the practices of international presence, we must broaden conceptions of international presence past a limited understanding of it as simply a necessary condition for the design and implementation of humanitarian and transformative projects. It must also be understood as a strategy and a materialization of intent. For example, democratization projects, largely thought up and actualized by internationals, attempted, among other things, to inculcate the Bosnia-Herzegovinan population with "new" values and behaviors based on specific, value-laden understandings of a liberal order.

Importantly though, this existential presence did not always do what internationals thought it did, claimed it did, or wanted it to do. Nonetheless, it made up part of the tool kit of international intervention strategies. My purpose here is not to comment on the successes or failures of international presence, nor its material effects, but rather to trace the contours of internationals' own practices of presence. Social and political transformations toward formal democracy have occurred and will continue to occur because of the processes and practices proselytized and set in motion. Equally, however, they will not occur as planned, for those targeted for reform respond with complicity, resistance, and accommodation (as seen in past colonial, missionary, and development encounters, as well as within post-socialist transitions). Side effects and unintended outcomes may take on inadvertent importance (Ferguson 1999). In order to understand transformation schemes, such as transitions to neoliberalism or liberalism, it is necessary to understand how they are conducted, not just their effects (Verdery 1996, 2003). How, exactly, is it that democratization efforts work and are thought to work, regardless of their actual success or failure in democratizing a country, a people, or a political system?

I have separated presence in Bosnia-Herzegovina into three conceptual modes: sheer, mere, and peer. These three modes are the latent undercurrent of a model of transformation that international agencies claimed as the proper course for post-war, post-socialist Bosnia-Herzegovina. *Sheer presence* refers to the quantity of international personnel resident in Bosnia-Herzegovina. It represents the force and the reach of the "international community" through its multiple bodies. *Mere presence*, also having its source in the body of the international, contrasts with the explicitly professional tasks of the international. Concurrent with their (other) job duties, international workers played an important role in passively "just being there." Last, *peer presence* has implicit and explicit pedagogical implications. Here, I do not mean specific training programs given to Bosnians on advocacy or fiscal responsibility. Rather, certain international workers consciously and unconsciously attempted to demonstrate proper behavior and professionalism in their interactions with Bosnian colleagues and society in the hopes that Bosnians would learn from their example, eventually becoming their democratic peers. Democracy promotion activities, then, rely only partly on the technical and active deployment of monitors to encourage participation, deter fraud, strengthen standards, and normalize elections. Instead, democratic presence does much of that work.

SHEER PRESENCE

Sheer presence describes the overwhelming number and scope of internationals, international organizations, and international funding in Bosnia-Herzegovina, the magnitude of it all. At its high mark, the international population was equal to approximately 2 percent of the post-war Bosnian populace of 3.5 million residents: seventy thousand internationals. Military forces constituted a significant portion of the international presence: approximately 70–90 percent. The civilian international population was never insignificant, however. In 2001 the three main organizations—the UN, Office of the High Representative (OHR), and OSCE—alone employed almost three thousand internationals.[5] During my fieldwork, international staff at those three agencies, approximately 180 IGOs, twenty-eight diplomatic missions or embassies, governmental agencies such as USAID or EC Monitoring Mission, and numerous business consultants probably ranged between five thousand and eight thousand.[6] In Sarajevo alone, fifteen thousand foreign citizens were present every day (Papić 2001:10).

The election project, although short-term in nature, involved the largest civilian presence. The international "population" peaked during election periods with the arrival of hundreds of medium- and short-term international election staff. On Election Day 1998, with an overall budget of US$39 million, almost three thousand internationals worked for the election department. The polling supervisors made up the bulk of election personnel (for example, 2,625 polling supervisors in 1998), but the election department also included international election officers at each field office, senior election officers at each regional center, and a range of other supervisors (international long-term supervisors, international counting supervisors, international field assistants, municipal election commission international supervisors).[7] The local support staff (interpreters and drivers) for internationals almost tripled election-related personnel. In most field offices, an extra building had to be rented in order to house the election department.

Election staff in the main electoral administrative office housed more than one hundred people in branches such as Voter Registration, Political Party Services, Out-of-Country Voting, Election Supervision, Joint Operations Center (that is, security and operations), Election Services, Election Information and Civic Education, Professional Development, Database and Program Development, Quality Assurance, Director General/Legal Counsel, and Deputy Head of Mission. Other agencies were also extensively involved during the election period: Swiss Support Unit, the UN International Police Task Force, the European Community Monitoring Mission. The Swiss unit, supporting the OSCE in transportation and medical care, delivered 150 tons of material: training kits; polling station posters, ballots, and furniture; voter information material during the April 2000 election period (personal communication, Swiss Support Unit, June 2000). The international military forces (the Stabilization Force [SFOR]) were also heavily involved in elections, mostly in the communications and security realms. SFOR liaison officers spent several days and nights parked outside regional election offices during the election period, monitoring the radio channels and providing security for the huge influx of international civilian personnel.

Elections, according to one electoral administrator, had to deal with jealousy from other departments because of the attention they demanded and received. In the words of another international working in logistics, "Anything Elections want, they get. If they want one hundred mobile phones, they can have them, tomorrow. All of our resources are at their disposal. Democracy is the international community's top priority for Bosnia."

She was not necessarily pleased with the leverage that elections wielded, but she was following high-level orders and policy. The election project was an immense, complex, multi-sited undertaking with an incredible amount of diplomatic, logistical, and financial support.

The sheer number of internationals served as a constant visible reminder of the might of the "international community." Internationals were the bodily representation and manifestation of the political, military, and economic power used by international organizations and individuals to force issues, to frame the terms of reconstruction, and to implement policies. Bosnians and internationals alike sometimes criticized the power of the "international community." Bosnian critics, often leaders or members of nationalist political parties, referenced the international presence as an "occupying force." Many internationals would readily admit the colonial or missionary tenor of the international interventions. Indeed, it was hard to miss. The missionary emphasis was more explicit, noted, and accepted by internationals, however. An American election worker, Martha, candidly explained during an interview that she was proselytizing: "Democracy is my Bible." Internationals more often than not, though, refuted the colonial tenor. They would explain that the goals of international intervention in Bosnia-Herzegovina and those of colonialism were different. As one aid worker put it during a formal interview, the "international community" in Bosnia-Herzegovina explicitly sought independence and national sovereignty for Bosnia-Herzegovina, not to use it as an economic resource as colonial powers had in controlling India, Congo, Latin America, and Vietnam. Internationals candidly criticized the "international community," its hierarchical structure and paternalistic behavior, but few felt that intervention itself was problematic (in a similar vein, see Ferguson 1994 on critiques of development). The same could be said for international liberal (that is, democratizing) interventions: criticism was couched in terms of the intervention being flawed in its implementation, not in its essence. Internationals and international projects proselytized the graces that would be bestowed on converts to and adherents of democracy, privatization, and the rule of law and transparency. Internationals who spoke to me specifically on this theme (that is, the colonial/missionary nature of the international interventions) attempted to balance what they thought was a needed and necessary change to sociopolitical life, as well as their role in helping bring it about, with (to varying degrees) their discomfort with a system that hierarchically placed them above Bosnians and into separate social, political, economic, and legal existences.

Sheer presence manifests itself through what I term "social visibility."

By *social visibility*, I mean the implicit and explicit show of international concern, resources, actions, and being. To international workers, the magnitude and scale of the international presence represented the importance placed on Bosnia (and on "fixing" Bosnia), as if to say, "After all, look at the dedication of so many resources to it!" The electoral effort was exemplary on all fronts of social visibility and in the symbolism of numbers: personnel, money, resources, and advertising. Thousands of workers spent their per diem cash (90 USD/day, or 150–180 DM/day) on food and drink, rent, and curios. Although few supervisors spent all of their per diem each day (that is, I never met any who even came close to spending that much each day), most spent around 25 DM/day on lodging and perhaps that same amount on food each day. At the time, the average monthly salary for a Bosnian was less than 150 DM (UN Development Program 1998:32). In the international community as a whole, expenditures by internationals (not their organizations) totaled 2.5 billion DM per year (Papić 2001:9). By contrast, the Bosnian GDP in 1998 was 6.9 billion DM. "This influx is creating a completely artificial virtual picture of Sarajevo, a picture of normal life, a European city, without any basis in the reality of the [Bosnia-Herzegovina] economy and the city itself" (Papić 2001:10).

The same could be said of the temporary effect of electoral sheer presence. Institutional money was funneled into Bosnian pockets as drivers, interpreters, assistants, and professionals were temporarily employed. These temporary local staff earned more than the monthly average, at least for a few weeks. Short-term accommodations had to be found for the influx of supervisors, often in local homes rather than in hotels or hostels.[8] Hired vehicles sported temporary OSCE signs in their windows. International electoral presence saturated city streets: it was nearly impossible for supervisors stationed in even medium-size towns to walk into a bar or café without seeing other supervisors. Bootleg CD shops in small towns were cleared out of inventory as supervisors sampled musical genres at the price of 5 DM per CD. Electoral advertising filled the airwaves. International electoral advertising included billboards, radio jingles, television spots, and magazine ads, as well as the less typical placements on sugar packets, beer mats, and grocery bags. A press officer with a mandate for electoral advertising told me that he had had to negotiate with press officers from other international organizations for billboard space; there were not enough billboards in Bosnia for all the messages they wanted to get out! Although ads for non-election programs often promoted the actions of the internationals, such as SFOR's "Ovdje za Mir [Here for Peace]" public relations campaign, election media asked them to think about corruption, announced election dates, marketed democracy as progress and the road out of war-damaged lives, and urged tolerance. A mechanism of governance, electoral advertising worked at transforming Bosnians into new, democratic subjects, subjects with new patterns of behavior and new concerns.

Sheer presence, whether in people, resources, or money, and the consequences of accommodating that volume of people and currency costituted a mechanism of international governance and of Bosnia-Herzegovinan democracy through social visibility. Visible numbers were meant to symbolize international commitment to and caring for Bosnia-Herzegovina. The numbers, a strategy for transformation, were part of a larger mechanism seeking changes in systems of governance.

MERE PRESENCE

International electoral staff from a variety of job classifications commented on the redundancy of their positions. Some, realizing that they had little work, struggled to find "work" and give meaning to their existence and activities. I commonly heard complaints that there was little work to be done, that jobs had to be self-created, and that there was a constant struggle to justify one's existence. These sentiments actually grew over the period of my fieldwork. As institutional reforms were put in place that gave more direct responsibilities and tasks to national officials and employees, internationals across elections (and across the aid community as a whole) increasingly found that a large part of their job was to oversee and verify the work of others. Within election supervision, however, the change was not so stark because a large part of the job description was always about oversight. As early as 1997 and 1998, it was possible to hear supervisors complain about their redundancy.

Although many bemoaned their lack of "work," it was also common to hear about ambiguous, unfocused, and unnecessary tasks. Many municipal election commission supervisors complained to me along these lines:[9] "I believe that with more planning and scheduling, [we] could have effectively performed our duties in a much shorter time frame—three or four weeks—instead of six. We felt we had to create a role. Our sense was that there was little planning, [that] it was all made up as we went along."

In particular, most reported that they were often given "busy work" to keep them occupied. Out of frustration with tedious nothingness or trivialities, some attempted to expand the scope of their work (sometimes to the extreme annoyance of their immediate supervisors) or to take on more responsibility. However, as in any bureaucracy, it was professionally prudent to avoid stepping on people's toes (that is, turf wars). In some cases, superiors soundly squashed attempts to expand the scope of the supervisors. In other field offices, officers welcomed the assistance but still gave them meaningless tasks ("to get them out of [our] hair"). It was also common for supervisors to enjoy their unexpected free time—touring the countryside, taking coffee, socializing. This led, for some, to mild feelings of guilt over not being professionally engaged during "work hours." This sense of guilt, however, failed to take into account the "alternative work" that their international body was performing.

Under the logics of international intervention, there were concurrent, subtler purposes given to internationals, purposes that required "work" not as typically imagined but achieved by the mere presence of an international. The passive work done by an international was not, as some might critique, "a waste of resources," but highly significant and productive. This alternative work can be teased out of comments made by internationals, despite their complaints. The complaints arose, I argue, because democracy promotion rarely appeared like "real work," even to the supervisors, in that little action or skill was necessary.

Regardless, at least three utilities were granted to an international's mere presence, including acting as a catalyst, evoking goodwill and postwar reconciliation, and implicitly enforcing rules and proper conduct. Each utility was reckoned to function through the body of the international, rather than through her skill or mastery. First, international bodies were thought to be more effective tools in prodding reluctant Bosnian election officials to comply with international demands. During interviews with national (that is, Bosnian) election officers (EOs) in 2000, I was repeatedly told that internationals were useful tools to deploy. Although all EOs felt capable of doing the job themselves and some felt that their international counterparts—the international election advisers (IEAs)—were redundant or that they did not know why they "had" one, EOs still admitted to an "international usefulness," saying that "the authority of the international is easier [to establish]."[10] One EO, faced with an offer of another colleague, exclaimed, "I'd rather have an IEA than another national EO!"

IEA was an international position created in 1999 when the (international) election officer position was "nationalized"; at least on the first pass, the ex-EOs became IEAs. IEAs were considered more able to pressure, convince, and force Bosnian election officials to "do their jobs," "implement the tasks given to them," and "follow given procedures and regulations." Because the international body was felt to carry with it an essence able to promote productivity on the part of Bosnian officials, it remained present despite "nationalization." Bosnian officials unanimously felt that, at a minimum, an international would always be more successful than a national at forcing an issue to completion or resolution. Several EOs told me that when a topic or task given to the (local) election commissions became particularly contentious and was not going to be done correctly or at all, they would send in their international counterpart. In some cases, any international colleague would suffice because he or she, too, embodied the weight and authority of the "international community." The international, as tool, held within his or her body the authority of the "international community."

The utility of international mere presence as a catalyst manifested clearly during a trip I took to the Vrata Grad Municipal Election Commission (MEC) with Igor, a Bosnian election officer. I had arranged to interview Igor as part of my research schedule; he graciously invited me to observe his day, correctly assuming that I would be interested in more than just an interview. Vrata Grad was in an area that, before the war, had substantial populations of each ethnicity. During the war, it suffered from multiple waves of ethnic cleansing and was now almost entirely Croat. Bosniacs (that is, Bosnian Muslims, an ethnic category instead of a religious one) and Serbs were beginning to return to their homes and land, but nervously and in trickles.

On this day, Igor's task was to push the ethnically mixed MEC to agree on the formation of the municipality's six polling station committees. They had been discussing this for some weeks with no progress, and the deadline for choosing committees had already passed. The MEC had not only failed to choose individuals but also was still debating the ethnic composition of the polling station committees. The ethnically mixed commission was notoriously uncooperative. The chairperson, a Croat, had previously proposed an ethnic distribution of four Croats, one Serb, and one Bosniac for the six-person polling station committee, based on current demographics. The Serb and Bosniac members had been willing to approve the previously proposed 4-1-1 distribution, if two (of six) committees had non-Croat chairpersons. This was summarily refused by the Croat member. The original proposal was unacceptable to the Bosniac and Serb members of the commission, so the issue was unresolved. Igor was dreading the meeting and spent the ninety-minute drive to Vrata Grad telling me how uncooperative and unpleasant the MEC was.

Our meeting was remarkably short. With little fanfare or discussion, they agreed upon a distribution of 3-2-1, with a Croat chair always. Igor had been prepared to threaten them with arbitration by the country-wide Provisional Election Commission, which would have likely resulted in a

2-2-2 distribution. He said that they knew about this ultimatum and therefore were ready to make some compromises. But he was surprised by how smooth and quick the negotiations were and explained this as the result entirely of my mere presence as an international and an academic researcher: "They knew you were studying elections and them and were embarrassed to not be able to reach an agreement. Your presence helped." When I protested, he shook his head in disagreement, saying that without my presence he would have been there for hours with them, bickering over it. In this example and others like it, such as the "effectiveness" of the IEAs described earlier, the ability of an international to provoke a decision rests neither in that individual's conflict management and mediation skills nor in his or her professional expertise (although the people present may possess both), but in the individual's bodily presence. In this case, I had no official authority or coercive power; I was not even employed by the election department.

Second, supervisors resoundingly believed that their relationships, contacts, camaraderie, interactions, and exchanges with local Bosnians had positive and transformative effects. In response to survey questions asking what polling supervisors felt was the most gratifying and most important part of their job or time in Bosnia-Herzegovina, polling supervisors answered that the most positive element was their role as a goodwill ambassador.[11] That is, whether or not they prevented electoral fraud, they thought that one of their major contributions to democracy promotion in Bosnia-Herzegovina was their mere presence as a congenial foreigner:

> It showed local people that the international community cares about them, and I assisted in continuing to build the bridge between local people and the international community.
>
> Our job encompassed far more than just registration. Our presence brought an insight of the outside world to the locals.
>
> Yes, not so much because of the supervision I performed, but more because of the contacts and relationships that were developed with the locals. I really believe that these were valuable and significant.

Supervisors downplayed their technical assistance efforts—the primary rationale for their job position—instead, judging their usefulness to lie in their empathy and interpersonal skills. One American, Mara, fluent in Serbo-Croatian and with extensive aid experience in Bosniac areas, rarely mentioned her official work with the Municipal Election Commission in a journal she kept on my request. Rather, she focused on the context in which she found herself, the stories of the people she met, and her interactions with her colleagues and friends. There was little information on what she "did" as a supervisor. Multiple times, however, she commented that "touching the lives" of Bosnians was her most useful and productive task. She believed that she contributed to the social reconciliation of the country as she brought people together again, acting as a facilitator and mediator. She described visiting a Muslim area where she had worked in previous years: "Neither of my [Bosnian Serb] colleagues had been to Jezero Pelo before and didn't have the highest opinion of the place. But after being there and meeting all of my [Bosniac] friends, they are very impressed and now look forward to going there. I'm very glad about this. Perhaps, of all the things I will do here, that is the most important." In her view, the technical assistance given to the MEC was auxiliary, if not offensive, because she considered the MEC experienced and competent. She saw herself as merely an assistant. Most of her references to the election work commented on the controlling nature of the bureaucracy, its inflexibility and incompetence. Instead, her election journal is a testament to the tragic stories of all Bosnians and her individual attempts at bringing about reconciliation and recovery:

> One of my best memories that I will take home with me is that of Suzana's younger daughter teaching [Bosnian Serb] Zdravko how to pray Muslim style! Meanwhile, Suzana and Danko compared their understanding of the Bible and the Koran and found them similar. They said that perhaps the war could have been averted (at least, in Bosnia) had everyone been encouraged to practice and then share their religions. We'll never know, of course, but it is an interesting theory based on the basic premise of "Love your neighbor" and "Killing is a sin."

Although most supervisors did not have the linguistic skills, historical and political knowledge, or opportunity to have Mara's in-depth interactions with Bosnians, most still emphasized the importance of bringing forth opportunities of reconciliation: "[I was only useful] in the counting process. Otherwise, I was only an ambassador trying to be nice and improve relations between my country and this one." Supervisors believed that their role extended past the polling station and into the community, both the internal Bosnian community and the community of nations.

Third, according to supervisors and following the dominant rationale for election monitors given by foreign ministries, they felt that they deterred voter and committee fraud, added legitimacy and objectivity to the process, and gave confidence and confirmation to the local Bosnian staff. When asked how supervisors did this work, answers fell back on the effects of mere presence:

> [Supervisors were] important as a political symbol. Our presence prevented the worst fraudulent practices.

> [Local] staff feel more confident in this post-war time when a foreign and objective monitor is staying with them [during] all periods of this very important issue for the future of Bosnia.

Supervisors believed that they carried an authority rooted in detachment from the particular politics of Bosnia-Herzegovina. Rather than rooted in impartiality and externality, however, their (perceived) authority was based on a commitment to bureaucratic and technical rationality. That is, supervisors generally believed in following the rules. Like law, rules were conceptualized as apolitical and impartial, as affecting persons equally despite evidence otherwise. Supervisors' distance from the creation of the rules and often from the political situation and debates allowed them to continue believing in the overlapping nature of "neutrality" and "rules." Their role was to enforce compliance of established rules and to ignore or avoid the politics behind, and potential effects of, the rules. Their bodily presence served to coerce and legitimate "proper" electoral behavior, behavior conscious of universality before the law if not under the law.

This presence had to be international; only the purely foreign bodies were considered (by internationals and Bosnians alike) to have the utilities described. The power of international bodies came to the fore during situations in which a Bosnian body was swapped for an international one. Body swapping took place in at least two situations: when nationalization efforts "converted" international positions into national positions and when diasporic Bosnians or those with Bosnian heritage held international positions. The latter situation blows apart the dichotomy between the rhetoric of the placeless and universal "international." The category *international* occludes tremendous diversity and power relations within the international community—individual and national biographies and histories did matter (Coles 2007). Indeed, the dichotomy between national and international reinforces and reifies a problematic simplification of and reduction to "international." Within the power hierarchies of internationals, those who had Bosnian heritage were at the bottom and were widely considered to be masquerading as internationals, or as not truly international.

Some were "binationals," born to Bosnian parents in, for example, Germany, where they were raised. An Australian-Croat working in a "national" position said that Bosnians usually assumed that she would be biased toward her ethnicity. But she was not convinced that it would be any different if she worked as an international. With the intent of preempting criticisms of bias, a Croat-Canadian international mostly socialized with international colleagues and did not talk about her background. These two binationals were one generation removed from Bosnia. Those raised in Bosnia but with dual nationality were especially problematic for more "pure" internationals. An Italian-Serb raised in Bosnia-Herzegovina was discredited in his "international" position; his colleagues saw him as an impostor. A Norwegian election supervisor was found out to be a Bosniac emigrant after she confessed great discomfort and reluctance at being stationed in Bijeljina, a town in Republika Srpska. Her supervisor roommates suggested that she was not yet sufficiently removed from Bosnia to count as an international. They reported that she feared for her safety and would not leave their temporary residence except to go to the election office. In their eyes, she was still a national, despite her ability to pass as an international through her new citizenship.

Throughout my fieldwork, debate continued voraciously about whether a "national" could adequately do an international job, even as international positions were "nationalized." One manager chastised his staff:

> I believe the root of the problem is contained in "problem 1" cited in your memo; that is, "being one of the ethnic groups jeopardizes the integrity of the job being done." This is arrant [sic] nonsense, and I will hear none of it. This is no more true of Bosnians than of internationals. Our hiring policy is that we hire nationals for all positions, regardless of ethnic identity. Please make this extremely clear to all, and those who do not accept it should find jobs elsewhere in the mission or in the world. We are here to fix this problem, not institutionalize it.

This memo was resoundingly not implemented, and it was still policy two years later that some jobs were marked as "international" and others as "national." Bosnians were often the most anxious about job conversions, fearing that ethnic or personal nepotism would guide all decisions. The main fear on the part of internationals was that the work would simply not get done because the national bodies were not vested with enough authority.

Mere presence, like sheer presence, is a strategy of international interventions—used to prod Bosnians toward governmental, social, and liberal cooperation and compliance. The passive utility of mere presence inter-acted with more action-centered practices yet was considered a transfor-mative agent in its own right.

PEER PRESENCE

Over drinks, Edith, an American in her late twenties, related a long story about her managerial role during the registration of voters. Her job was to oversee and ensure the proper functioning of the office. She was not tasked with the functions themselves, but rather to supervise them. Throughout the eight weeks, in fits of boredom and frustration with the staff, she would sit down to partake in the checking of forms or recording the arrival of pack-ages. In part, she was looking for something to keep herself occupied, but Edith explained that she was also explicitly trying to show the staff that the work could be done faster and more efficiently than they were doing it. She went as far as posting productivity reports per day and comparing her com-pletion rate with the average rate of the Bosnian workers. Her strategy was not subtle. Here and in locales across Bosnia-Herzegovina, internationals engaged in explicit demonstrations on the proper way to comport oneself "professionally." Others debated what counted as professional. Was it profes-sional, an anguished colleague asked me, to hire someone who desperately needed a job instead of the most qualified candidate? She wanted to do the right thing but feared that it might entail showing Bosnians how "business" ought to work. Internation-als, through peer presence, attempted to demon-strate what needed to be done in order for Bosnians to become liberal, neoliberal, and modern peers.

Internationals involved in election work believed that they were dem-onstrating professional and democratic behavior through their commit-ment to the electoral rules and regulations and in their administrative and bureaucratic techniques.[12] Supervisors and other election staff did not always agree with the rules, but they almost always obeyed the rules and reg-ulations. In this, I argue, they believed that they were "demonstrating" how to be democratic. This demonstration included a commitment to rules and an emphasis on administration and bureaucracy, but also on "democratic values" such as tolerance and inclusiveness. Internationals explicitly stated this pedagogical impulse in their responses to questionnaires asking about the importance of their supervisory role:

> Yes, I think it was important that the registration had been super-vised. It's the best training the national teams can receive…to do it themselves with somebody who watches and explains.

> [My] strict adherence to the rules provided confidence in the
> integrity of the registration election process.

Polling supervisors consciously negotiated the demands of electoral regulations and the necessity of following the rules as a pedagogical device, even
though many of them recognized the arbitrary nature of the regulations.

Many supervisors specifically mentioned the need to "get democracy
right" for their committees and insisted that the polling station committees
also get it right, but many of the practices of peer presence are embedded
in other activities as well. An Italian who had come to the United States as
a young teenager told me, "Our presence trains them, sometimes through
observation, sometimes by actual training. Both inside and outside work,
people see the international community and how we work and behave."
Mastering technical democracy—the accurate filling out of forms, the
checking of voter identification per the rules and regulations, the equal
treatment of voters—was important for a smooth election, but it was equally
important to supervisors that Bosnians see how essential smooth elections
are and how much effort is required to achieve them. The demonstration
of democracy was not thought of as a professional and skilled task as much
as something that happened alongside the technical work.

Peer presence also affects national newcomers to the "international
community." In the Bosnian case, many supervisors from eastern European
countries felt the counterweight pressure of being peers—the responsibility of being a role model of successful post-socialism. (This also points to
the hierarchies within the community of internationals. Bulgarians were
not well regarded by superiors, mostly for their poorer language skills, partly
for their uneven "success" in being an appropriate peer.) This was structural,
as well as individual. In 1998, for example, the US government footed the bill
for 63 percent of the eastern European supervisory presence as part of its
foreign aid commitment (which included these six hundred supervisors
and four hundred American ones). The financial backing of newcomers to
liberalism and neoliberalism as promoters and verifiers of democracy was,
according to a colleague in the American embassy in Vienna, considered
to be "good training exercise" for the newly democratic.

"DOING NOTHING" MATTERS: INTERNATIONAL
BODIES AND DEMOCRACY PROMOTION

Despite Charles's complaint that he had no purpose—that he was
"doing nothing" as an international election supervisor—it is clear that
supervisors and other international election monitors had incredible pur-

pose, just not the one that they necessarily thought they should have or that they could explicitly link to democracy promotion. Charles and his electoral colleagues talked a lot about the alternative work they performed. Supervisors' self-perceptions, the perceptions of other electoral staff, and international bureaucratic decision making demonstrated that democracy promotion was, in large part, about *being there*. The presence of an international body was seen to be an agent of transition as much as, or more than, the explicit work with which internationals were tasked. The inert power residing in their international body also made their "actual" tasks easier or even possible. For those who travel the globe in the name of democracy, the substance of democracy is not necessarily in the "checklist," but in the body. That is, they are only partially confirming specific techniques and requisites of democracy. Their existential presence is thought to be a transformative agent in the service of democracy. The passive work of democracy promotion assists free and fair elections through visibility and symbolism of scale, investments and interpretations of bodily authority, and implicit demonstrations of being.

No longer are elections solely national affairs. Rather, all elections around the globe are heavily implicated by international circulating discourses—most often Nugent's (chapter 2) normative democracy. Election monitoring as a foreign policy practice serves to consolidate and codify further the aesthetics and practices of this normative democracy through the circulation of transnational actors who beseech newcomers to join the democratic club and become like them. The close ethnographic analysis of how this is done demonstrates that the technical mastery of democratic elections is only one small part of the democracy promotion package. Sheer, mere, and peer presence also act as transformative mechanisms for globalized democratic interventions—subtler, but no less particular or power-laden, strategies of political and social change.

Acknowledgments

Selected portions of this essay are excerpted from Kimberley Coles, Democratic Designs: International Intervention and Electoral Practices in Postwar Bosnia-Herzegovina. Copyright © 2007 University of Michigan. Used by permission of the publisher, University of Michigan Press.

Notes

1. All names, locations, and job positions have been altered to protect anonymity.

2. Under the authority of the Dayton Peace Accords, signed in December 1995, the OSCE was to organize and implement elections within six to nine months of the peace treaty. This mandate was subsequently renewed throughout the years, such that the OSCE organized six elections between 1996 and 2000. In August 2001 the Bosnian legislatures passed an election law, and a Bosnian election commission (with international consultants) organized later elections.

3. Recruitment of supervisors was the responsibility of the sending country. The election administration office simply received names of supervisors to expect, and then they arrived. Countries were supplied with job descriptions that specified the supervisors' tasks and duties and listed mandatory and desirable skills. For example, in 1997 candidates for registration supervisors were asked to have, among other things, experience with a field-based organization of civic education or public information programs, four years of professional experience, cultural sensitivity, English language proficiency, computer literacy, and, preferably, experience with election procedures. Countries differed in how they chose to recruit (through their foreign offices, for example, or via a third party, typically an NGO) and how closely they kept to the requirements of the position.

4. In three of the five post-war elections during this research, polling supervisors signed the final result forms, thus carrying formal responsibility for the conduct of the election in their specific polling stations. During these three elections (in 1997 and 1998), each polling station was supervised full-time by a polling supervisor. For the latter two elections (in 2000), supervision moved to "partial supervision," with each polling supervisor responsible for four to six polling stations. Because they were required to travel around in a polling station circuit, spending fifteen or twenty minutes at each location each visit, supervisors were no longer required to certify the results with their signature or to carry forms, ballots, and other materials back to storage centers.

5. Year 2001 statistics counted 2,000 UN IPTF policemen, 340 other UN international employees, 220 OHR internationals (secondees, consultants, interns), and 180 OSCE internationally seconded members (OHR 2000; OSCE 2001; SFOR 2001; UN 2001; UN Development Program 1998).

6. Estimates are based on data from the International Council of Voluntary Agencies (ICVA).

7. Polling supervisors were present each election, but not all elections had all the other types of supervisors.

8. Logistics personnel commented that it was not always easy to find accommodations in towns without hotels and with housing shortages due to destruction or refugee influxes.

9. The quotes are from an anonymous survey I gave to all municipal election commission supervisors at the end of their contract period.

10. The EO job, at one time classified as an international position, was nationalized in 1999. Internationals remained in the election department at the field-office level but were recategorized as international election advisers (IEAs). At the time, most EOs simply transferred to IEA positions. In turn, their (national) assistants became EOs. The explicit labeling of certain positions as "international" suggests an increased authority given to the designation.

11. This is not to pass over the comments of a certain minority who responded that the best part of the job was "handing in equipment on the last day of registration" or that "it was not something gratifying."

12. Whether they were demonstrating professional and democratic behavior is another question altogether. Certainly, some internationals did not exhibit professional or democratic behavior (even if there is agreement on what that entails). Furthermore, Bosnians were not silent; they criticized errors and problems, as well as international policies.

6

Participatory Democracy, Transparency, and Good Governance in Ecuador

Why Have Social Movement Organizations at All?

Julia Paley

About three hours north of Ecuador's capital city, Quito, along the Pan-American Highway high in the Andes, a road stretches off to the left. It cuts through agricultural fields occasionally bisected by entrances to rural communities,[1] then proceeds downward over a bridge spanning a river and ravine. As the road ascends, set vividly against the hills are large billboards announcing the international accolades won by this place. "Cotacachi, City for Peace, with Citizen Participation and Transparency" says one,[2] attributed to the "International Prize of UNESCO, 2002." "Example of Participatory Democracy and Decentralization" says the other, referencing the United Nations and Habitat's "International Prize DUBAI 2000 of the Arab Emirates."

The signs are a tribute to work by the government of Auki Tituaña Males, a Cuban-trained economist and an indigenous resident of urban Cotacachi. Elected in 1996 through the political movement Pachakutik, affiliated with the national indigenous organization, the Confederation of Indigenous Nationalities of Ecuador (CONAIE), Tituaña came into office along with the first wave of mayors forming "alternative local governments" in Ecuador. In keeping with CONAIE's effort to establish popular parliaments, Tituaña created the Assembly of County Unity (hereafter, the

Assembly), in which representatives of organizations come together for making policy recommendations and creating agendas for the year's work. Through these participatory strategies, along with others, he formed the county's development plan (Municipalidad de Cotacachi 1997). In 2001 he established a participatory budgeting procedure in which priorities for municipal expenditures are decided by organized citizens in budgeting workshops. As the billboards at Cotacachi's entrance attest, these activities have garnered international recognition and attracted an inflow of external funding that has enabled it to fare much better than other municipalities amid a national economic crisis (Cameron 2003). High levels of international support have, to this point, been sustained.

As the road extends past the billboards along a winding route, visible high in the distance is a giant, red, geometric sculpture of the sun—an appeal to pre-Columbian symbolism that expresses an element of indigenous identity and pride under the present municipal leadership. The sculpture comes fully into view as the road reaches the Plaza del Sol (Plaza of the Sun), an open-air space used for concerts. There, Andean musicians, some of them world-famous and recently returned from international tours, perform in their home territory. By the plaza, a long row of flags recognizes the many countries whose donations have flowed into the county. The building at the Plaza del Sol houses a temporary health clinic where Cuban doctors provide treatment to residents and is the site of a new library formed by Peace Corps volunteers. These are just two instances of the international representatives and nongovernmental organizations (NGOs) permeating many aspects of municipal governance and citizens' organizations.

Farther along the road, after it forks to the right, sits the main plaza, bordered by the municipal building, the main Catholic church, and the Assembly building. In the Assembly offices, staff coordinate activities and plans, often through "intersectoral" committees on environmental management and management of natural resources, organization and municipal modernization, tourism, education, production, and health. Specific projects contracted through NGOs fund the staff's salaries. A board near the Assembly building's entrance gives a snapshot of the week's activities: meetings of committees on the environment, health, education; sessions of leadership schools—some for women only, some for men and women; conferences; assemblies; events.

Across the park sits the municipality, where displays in the lobby showcase the local government's achievements and plans—three-dimensional depictions in miniature of renovations to the market (a USAID-funded project) and planned highway construction; wide posters giving a step-by-step explanation of the participatory budgeting process; newspaper clippings of media-covered events; and an endlessly playing set of professionally made videos, one on religion and culture, another on participatory democracy and transparency. Like the billboards at the entrance to Cotacachi, these displays are part of the ongoing publicity about the county's achievements—a publicity that is cemented through the mayor's international travels and the frequent influx of visitors (mayors from other Andean countries or emissaries from provinces in southern Ecuador, for example) seeking to learn about Cotacachi as a model of participatory democracy.

WHY ARE STRONG SOCIAL MOVEMENT ORGANIZATIONS NECESSARY?

This chapter responds to a question posed in January 2005 at the United Nations Development Program conference in Paris. After I gave my presentation on participatory democracy in Ecuador, an attendee asked why I insist on the continued importance of social movement organizations. After all, they may come and go. They may display elements of corruption, clientalism, and lack of representativity. Is not the most reliable strategy the formation of enduring procedures for transparent governance?

This question is an excellent one to bring to bear on the case of Cotacachi, which is (at least, in theory) a near perfect example of what he was calling for. As implied in the descriptive tour above, the municipality invites participation by organized citizens; residents decide most of the county's budget; broad working groups tackle important themes such as the environment, health, and education; the mayor gives an annual public accounting (*rendición de cuentas*) of budgetary income and outlays and explains how promises for public works and programs were met; a systematic planning process guides expenditures; an explicit discourse of "interculturality" highlights cross-ethnic interaction, and prominent symbolic displays celebrate the culture of the most subordinated group; a citizen oversight committee monitors government propriety; and a commitment to honesty is exemplified by the fact that the salary of every municipal employee, in rank order from highest to lowest pay, is available on the website for all to see (Municipalidad de Cotacachi n.d.a). Given these conditions, are strong, independent social movement organizations necessary?

I argue that the existence of strong social movement organizations is vital even in the face of apparently participatory and transparent governance. I suggest that, far from being suitably replaced by a transparent and responsive local government, strong social movement organizations are crucial: to hold politicians accountable to the demands of "base" communities, to generate proposals to guide governance, to establish transnational networks as counterparts to governing systems that transcend local boundaries, to produce new leaders, to bring proposals to participatory assemblies, and to outlast a possible dismantling of the formal citizen-participation structure.[3]

To address this issue, the chapter proceeds as follows. First, it introduces the Union of Peasant and Indigenous Organizations of Cotacachi (UNORCAC), the county's primary rural indigenous social organization, and traces UNORCAC's organizational history. Next, it explains the collective decision-making structure, the Assembly of County Unity. Then, it reports ethnographically on UNORCAC's internal debates and deliberations about holding mayoral candidates accountable. Finally, the chapter returns to the question of why social movement organizations are of value in the context of participatory democracy.

RURAL INDIGENOUS ORGANIZATION: FROM STRUGGLES FOR CULTURAL RIGHTS, TO DEMANDS FOR SERVICE PROVISION, TO CAPTURE OF THE MAYORALITY

UNORCAC was founded in 1977, two years before the end of military rule. As organizational leaders tell the history and as books recount it, the founding of this organization, as well as its precursors, took place in response to acute oppression and scarcity.[4] Rural communities lacked roads, community centers, drinking water, electricity, and, for the most part, schools in a population in which 80 percent of indigenous people were illiterate. Residents of these areas also experienced exploitation and abuse, particularly before the agrarian reform of 1974: police routinely beat and imprisoned peasants; the Church exacted payments and took (without compensation) the best portions of crops; hacienda owners required of inhabitants two or three days a week of unpaid labor in exchange for use of the land for grazing animals, gathering wood, or collecting water (for other purposes, they extended credits that put residents perpetually in debt); authorities used forced Indian labor for public building works projects in urban areas, with no such infrastructure even planned for rural zones. These racist abuses are captured by two widely recounted images: mestizo landowners routinely snatching Indian peasants' ponchos or hats off them and demanding unpaid work in exchange for return of the clothes, and Indians moving off a sidewalk to allow white Cotacachi residents to pass. Under these conditions, interethnic relations entailed a naturalized subordination of Indians and existed amid an intensely unequal land distribution, organized through the large haciendas on which indigenous people worked. In Cotacachi in 1974, "1.1% of land owners controlled nearly 60% of the land and 92% of the peasants controlled 23% of the land" (Guerrero and Ospina 2004:96; Ortiz 2004:208).

Amid these conditions, indigenous intellectuals in Cotacachi and neighboring Otavalo, who had benefited from access to expanding education systems in the 1970s and had received training as teachers, organized themselves into a discussion group (Baez et al. 1999:59). Working jointly, they created the provincial-level Federation of Indigenous Communities of Imbabura (FICI). In a formative decision that would have repercussions years later, leaders from Cotacachi and Otavalo soon split, with the former dedicated more to indigenous cultural issues and the latter emphasizing economic issues, such as access to land (Garcia Bravo 2002). Having consolidated a federation of fourteen communities, those from Cotacachi created the Federation of Communities of Cotacachi County, which in 1980 (when it became legally recognized by the government) changed its name to UNORCAC. Commitment to the organization escalated after a particularly violent incident in November 1977; a community leader suffered torture while under arrest and later died from the effects of police abuse. This death galvanized motivation for the organizing. It also led to the search for national support, resulting in affiliation with an organization that years later came to be known as the National Federation of Peasant, Indigenous, and Black Organizations (FENOCIN).

We can see, in this early period, dynamics that would shape organizational relations for years to come. Cotacachi's peasant leaders' predilection for cultural issues, articulated in their efforts to "struggle for the defense of indigenous cultural values" (García Bravo 2002:290), foreshadowed a weak fight for land reform and labor rights. To this day, a sharply unequal distribution of land and low salaries for workers have generated high levels of out-migration, stark poverty rates (nearly 80 percent of Cotacachi's population lives in poverty), and poor prospects for economic development in Cotacachi—conditions that even a highly participatory local government can barely begin to address. The commitment to cultural issues also helped generate support in 1996 for an indigenous mayor and participation in the Pachakutik political movement, even where these decisions required crossing organizational boundaries.

Perhaps one of the most ironic outcomes of this situation is UNORCAC's national-level affiliation: the guidance and support it received nationally was less ethnic than class based. The provincial organization FICI, which had first met in one of Cotacachi's rural communities but from which Cotacachi's leaders soon separated, became a provincial member of the highland indigenous organization, the Conferation of the Kichwa Peoples of Ecuador (ECUARUNARI). In 1986 ECUARUNARI would become a founding component of the national confederation CONAIE, an organization in which ethnic identity predominates. In contrast, the Federation of Communities of Cotacachi County decided in late 1977 to affiliate with FENOC (National Federation of Peasant Organizations), which claimed a specifically class-based instead of ethnic orientation. This was very much in keeping with the union movement and leftist politics of the time. Only in 1988, two years after the formation of CONAIE, would the organization change its name to FENOC-I and later FENOCIN, adding the words *Indigenous* and *Black* (*Negro*) sequentially. Even this signified less an ethnic specificity than an interethnic unity on issues that affected them all. Within the affiliation, ideological differences persisted. Although FENOCIN advocated for agricultural and land reform and the Federation of Communities of Cotacachi County's leadership pronounced their support, the Federation of Communities did not primarily pursue land reform (García Bravo 2002:291).

UNORCAC's form of political action has changed over time with transforming national and local circumstances. In its first years, the organization was oriented toward combating discrimination, exploitation, and abuse, particularly the racism embedded in the hacienda and church systems. These efforts included a struggle for "civil rights: respect for personal integrity, equality before the law, dignified and just treatment for indigenous people, respect for their cultural forms, the right of association and expression, with the same rights as the mestizos" (Ortiz 2004:79). At the same time, FENOC linked the organization to the national peasant movement and organized labor, which in the 1970s reached a peak of mobilization manifested in national strikes. In addition to framing struggles in terms of economic and class-based claims, its organizational styles privileged conflictual action over incorporation into existing institutionality. An example of this conflictual approach occurred when the Federation of Communities of Cotacachi County occupied the municipal building by force to demand the creation of public works.

At this juncture, it is important to reflect on the presence of the term *participation* in the discourse of the era. The phrase in use among class-based collective actors at the time, *popular participation*, framed the term *participation* in a very different way than would its incorporation into the idea of "participatory democracy" in the 1990s. In an era of continent-wide currents of liberation theology, popular education, and dependency theory, organizations were engaged in conflict with the state (manifested in Ecuador in national, provincial, and municipal governments) and resisted representation in or incorporation into institutions of formal government (Ortiz 2004:70). "Popular participation" foregrounded *lo popular*, the contestatory poor and working people's politics that stood outside dominant forces, aiming to win concessions from them while asserting the people's own power. The permutation of the word *participation* in the context of 1990s participatory democracy is explained later in the chapter.

The conflicts of the 1970s, moreover, took place in a national context of state-led modernization that was dismantling traditional relations of servitude, enacting land reform (through the 1974 Agricultural Reform Law), and opening a labor market. Because these changes occurred during and through a military regime, however, they simultaneously entailed repression of organizations and reinforcement of unequal power relations. In Cotacachi, the intersection of state-led and movement-led efforts resulted, by and large, in changed racial and employment relations (indigenous people became free laborers who could, at will, leave and take jobs in areas such as crafts work, construction, and agriculture), but without significant land reform. Rather, in the coming years the haciendas would be "modernized" to accommodate agribusiness, most notably, plantations for growing roses for export, with Cotacachi residents working long hours for little pay. Following Auki Tituaña's arrival as mayor in 1996, as before with other forms of municipal rule, these unequal land and economic interests would remain outside the purview of local government. The plantation owners would not bother launching an attempt to undermine participatory democracy precisely because they remained unaffected by it, with their economic interests, political networks, and forms of control (if any) directed toward and emanating from Quito.

The year 1979 brought the end of the military government. In 1981, for the first time in Ecuadorian history, illiterate citizens were allowed to vote. Seeking to take advantage of these political openings, UNORCAC leaders visited each of the member communities in an effort to overcome a history of indigenous people's voting according to the wishes of bosses, landowners, and clergy. In its place, they began a discussion about launching the organization's own candidates and analyzing which of the existing political parties to support. Through this process, UNORCAC founder and president Alberto Andrango was elected to the town council, becoming its first indigenous member. UNORCAC has placed one or two representatives on the municipal council in every election since. Until 1996, UNORCAC entered the electoral scene in alliance with existing leftist or class-oriented political parties, first the Broad Left Front (Frente Amplio de Izquierda, FADI) and later the Socialist Party, which to this day has close links with FENOCIN.

This first instance of electoral politics in 1979 initiated a change of approach to political action. From external conflictual action, the organization transitioned to a moment of working partially within the governing institutionality, albeit with but one representative in an otherwise exclusionary municipality. UNORCAC also shifted its focus from a primary insistence on cultural rights to an effort to increase public services to rural areas.

Although UNORCAC had placed one representative in the council, the organization was commonly called a *municipio chiquito*—a small municipality unto itself. This is largely because the municipality pursued its own development agenda through independent relationships to external sources of funding. In an interview with me, a former mayor of Cotacachi described social conditions of indigenous communities in these terms: "The majority of the indigenous people don't have food, don't have work. The women are the most self-sacrificing in the family, the children malnourished, the education bad. Migration, alcoholism."

When I asked him what he did to address this situation when he was mayor, he replied, "I didn't do anything because they…put themselves in charge of solving the problems through UNORCAC. Because UNORCAC existed, there wasn't a need for the municipality to concern itself with [the Indians]." He went on to say that the municipality took responsibility only for providing three basic services: drinking water, electricity, and the construction of schools. (Electricity was just coming to some areas of the county in 2005, and lack of potable water remained a major concern for many rural indigenous communities.)

The former mayor's comments highlight the irony in UNORCAC's chosen role. In contracting directly with external financing organizations and nongovernmental organizations, UNORCAC has strengthened its political leverage because of the economic power it wields and political relationships it cultivates. In fact, this dynamic makes UNORCAC, at least potentially, a major force in relation to the Assembly and municipality. At the same time, by engaging in the kind of work that a municipality would do, it deflects responsibility from elected government.

The transformation of social movement organizations into agents of development is, in part, a product of the low credibility that official elected governments have had in Ecuador. National, provincial, and municipal governments in the 1980s and 1990s and into the 2000s have been notorious for corruption, and power has long concentrated among segments of economic and political elites. The government's poor credibility has also been shaped by its inability to meet rising expectations in the population, due to poor financial management and lack of economic resources. These failings especially manifested themselves in the political instability of the late 1990s: in the eleven years between 1995 and 2007, Ecuador had eight presidents. The perceived bankruptcy, both ethical and economic, of the national government exists to such a degree that international agencies such as the World Bank and Inter-American Development Bank, which, in principle, work precisely with national governments, have at times chosen to circumvent state ministries to work directly with community organizations and local institutions.

Amid these processes, UNORCAC's role in local development increased throughout the 1980s and 1990s. Over time, the organization took on literacy campaigns, micro-credit financing, reforestation, and infrastructure projects through relationships with nongovernmental organizations and national funding initiatives. All the while, it continued to fight for public services in rural areas, such as public schooling (particularly bilingual education), drinking water, and electricity.

The dependence on funding from external organizations has further resulted in contracting and expelling personnel on the cycle of project grants and subjecting (mainly indigenous) employees to a dramatic inequality of salaries in relation to formally credentialed (mainly mestizo or foreign) technicians of the NGOs. This has perpetuated the frustrated educational aspirations and limited professional development of rural indigenous peoples. Ironically, one of the organization's major demands was bilingual and bicultural education, and the development of a group of intellectuals, through formal education, was one of the dynamics that brought the organization into being. This dependency has bureaucratized and subjected to an officialistic accounting logic an organization that arose from the struggles of rural indigenous communities.

In the 1990s the organization took note that funders' priorities were driving the kinds of projects being developed, thereby dislocating decision making from the concerns of rural communities to funders' interests. In response, UNORCAC created a strategic plan (with help from NGOs) that established a set of working areas; now funders must fit their projects into UNORCAC's themes. Nonetheless, those project contracts continue to be worked out by a set of organizational leaders in relation with the NGOs, many times without thorough involvement of or communication with the "bases" or indigenous communities (García Bravo 2002), thus affecting the kind of representativity the organization enacts. In short, the development agenda transforms the cultural atmosphere and the types of political action that UNORCAC takes.

This role of creating and implementing development agendas and building economic resources parallel to the municipality continued. UNORCAC faced a changed political landscape, however, when the 1995 law of political party reform permitted independents to run for office for the first time in Ecuadorian history. The law was, in fact, initiated by the political right in an effort to enable non-affiliated candidates to run for election. The indigenous movement then appropriated the law to use to its own advantage. At this juncture, CONAIE promoted the creation of the political movement Pachakutik/Nuevo País to run candidates directly for office without recourse to electoral alliances with established political parties. Organizationally independent of CONAIE and incorporating other organizations, Pachakutik attracted both mestizo and indigenous adherents. Beginning with the elections of 1996, it succeeded in getting elected a range of public officials—from representatives to the national congress, to council people in provincial and municipal governments, to mayors and provincial governors. Auki Tituaña, to this day (2008) mayor of Cotacachi, is among the most famous of them.

PARTICIPATORY STRUCTURES IN MUNICIPAL GOVERNANCE

When Auki Tituaña took office in 1996, he installed a version of participatory democracy that has as its centerpiece the Assembly of County Unity. Organizations, including youth, women, neighborhood groups, and others, convene to engage in a process of planning and decision making about the county's future. Through a participatory budgeting process, organizations identify priorities for expenditures. As described on Cotacachi's municipal website, the Assembly is "a space for citizen expression to socialize, work together, [and] plan in a participatory way the future of the county, whose decisions are based in the principles of: solidarity and tolerance for the existing pluricultural and multi-ethnic diversity, without distinction of gender or generation" (Municipalidad de Cotacachi n.d.b).

The Assembly holds its main meeting once a year, when commissions report on their work and set agendas for the year ahead. The mayor presents a public accounting (rendición de cuentas) of budgetary income and outlays and describes how promises for public works and programs were met. In addition to its annual meeting, the Assembly functions year-round through numerous task forces. Broad working groups, called intersectoral committees, tackle major issues such as the environment and natural resources, health, education and culture, tourism, production, and municipal governance. These mechanisms constitute Cotacachi's version of participatory democracy.

SECOND THOUGHTS, RETROSPECTIVE APPRAISALS: WHAT DOES UNORCAC GAIN BY HAVING AN INDIGENOUS MAYOR AND A PARTICIPATORY ASSEMBLY?

"Our fundamental objective wasn't only to win positions in these last elections at a local, provincial, and national level. Our fundamental objective was searching for a way to consolidate our organizations."

—*Luis Macas, current president of CONAIE, in an interview with journalists in 1996, just after he had been elected among the first indigenous members of the national congress [SAIIC 1996 (printed in English)].*

I am sitting in the meeting room of Jambi Mascaric, the building that UNORCAC has inherited from Doctors without Borders. Bordered by a tall iron gate recently painted green and a small open area, the building houses offices, a large open meeting room, and a downstairs dining area. While the meetings go on upstairs, women who are important leaders (for example, UNORCAC's vice president and UNORCAC's elected representative on the municipal council) spend hours preparing meals and serving them to visiting delegations and working groups. It is March 2004, a few weeks before UNORCAC's major assembly in which delegates from all forty-three rural communities, as well as the constituent group from the sub-tropical zone Intag, will gather to determine UNORCAC's candidates for mayor, municipal council, and *juntas parroquiales* (groupings of communities within a common parish) in preparation for the October elections.

This particular meeting, preparatory to UNORCAC's assembly, is designed to be an internal analysis of the position UNORCAC should take in the upcoming mayoral election. The week before, a similar meeting had been facilitated by a FENOCIN staff person whose purpose was to lead the organization in a statement of its priorities and goals and to contextualize UNORCAC's situation within the dynamics of national politics. His most central point, articulated repeatedly, was that the criterion for every decision should be whether a particular option contributes to building the organization. Implied, therefore, was this challenge: does having Auki Tituaña as mayor strengthen or weaken UNORCAC? An UNORCAC member raised a related point: There should similarly be an evaluation of UNORCAC's municipal council representatives. They have been unconditionally loyal to Tituaña. Does this help or hurt UNORCAC?

This week, with the FENOCIN representative absent, the discussion is more internal, more fluid, and more specific to the particularities of the situation. UNORCAC's directorate and other organizational leaders contemplate their options and analyses with respect to Auki Tituaña. The feelings are decidedly mixed. A set of critiques and defenses emerge about Tituaña, ranging from "He hasn't done anything in the communities," to observations that he has made certain contributions but has accomplished them through circumventing the representative organizational structure of UNORCAC by going directly to communities, to recountings of the public works and public services the mayor has produced. These divergent opinions about his leadership remain impassioned and unresolved. What does emerge in the course of discussion is a suggestion that offers a path to take the organization forward and solve some of the dilemmas being posed. The group agrees that what is needed is a way of making any mayoral candidate, whoever it may be, responsive and responsible to the demands of UNORCAC.

Proceeding along this route would require UNORCAC to go through a collective process of developing proposals. These proposals would then be set in writing in a statement for each of the candidates to sign, signifying his commitment to enacting them once in office. The signed document would be both a prerequisite for obtaining UNORCAC's support and a way to hold the official to his word during his administration. With that, the meeting ends. Proposals are too complex to be developed in one meeting (the hour is late, no one has eaten, everyone has responsibilities at home). In any case, UNORCAC's assembly is just a few weeks away. There, the indisputable main order of business will be to come up with candidates and decide whether to support Auki Tituaña.

What is significant about this incident is that the formulation of proposals, much less the step of obtaining a commitment from mayoral candidates, never occurs. Nor is there an evaluation or decision-making procedure about whether UNORCAC's representatives on the municipal council should support the mayor in everything he does. In the organization-wide assemblies that follow, individuals, from the national president of FENOCIN to presidents of *cabildos* (the most local of councils, one in each of the forty-three communities), make passionate and sometimes inflammatory statements for and against Tituaña, and Tituaña himself responds. (He was present at the assembly—apparently without being invited, but also without being asked to leave.) Also at play is a discussion of whether UNORCAC can field a mayoral candidate from within its own organization, for example, Pedro de la Cruz (president of FENOCIN; he becomes unavailable as soon as he is reelected to that post) or founder and past president Alberto Andrango. A call is made for a second assembly, to improve attendance and therefore representation of all the communities, even though a quorum of communities is present. A second assembly would also allow the presidents of each of the cabildos to consult with their community members about other possible candidates.

UNORCAC leadership and members convene at the organization's second assembly for the official vote. Support for the other candidates is insufficient, though some suggest that Alberto Andrango run for provincial office. UNORCAC as a whole decides to support Tituaña, which means that virtually all voters in all constituent communities will follow the organization's collectively made decision and give Tituaña their vote. In subsequent weeks, the few high-profile individuals who dislike Tituaña with unremitting passion defect to support not an UNORCAC candidate (none is running), but the other political party, the Democratic Left (Izquierda Democrática). Its candidate is widely reputed to have made racist remarks about Cotacachi's having gone long enough with an Indian running the municipality.

The campaign season that follows reveals a strong urban mestizo backing of the Democratic Left candidate, with support also from portions of the subtropical zone Intag. Tituaña puts together a list of council candidates in coordination with UNORCAC and under the auspices of Pachakutik. With much fanfare and energetic UNORCAC support, Tituaña triumphs in the elections, gaining a third four-year term. Pachakutik also emerges with a majority of council seats (four out of seven), enabling the mayor to consolidate his project not only through the Assembly but also through the elected council, of which UNORCAC's representatives form a part.

I relate this set of incidents taking place over an eight-month period because it reveals much about the relationship between UNORCAC and the indigenous mayor it supports. On the one hand, UNORCAC backs Tituaña. After the organization makes a collective decision to support Tituaña for mayor, constituent communities and voters—with few exceptions—conform to this decision in a show of unity. On the other hand, there are important currents of dissent and discontent. Although this is an indigenous mayor, not all the members see him as an asset. Indeed, even some of those who worked tirelessly for his electoral victory express their misgivings. Why do these two tendencies coexist?

Part of UNORCAC's ambivalence stems from its relation to the Assembly of County Unity, a centerpiece of Auki Tituaña's version of participatory democracy. Cotacachi's Assembly of County Unity is constituted through organizations, rather than through individual citizens. To participate, constituents must organize and send representatives. The process has caused an upsurge in the generation of groups and has created the need for and existence of a set of leadership schools to instill organizational culture and leadership qualities. One of the complications in the way the Assembly is composed, therefore, is that organizations are being initiated through local governance instead of surging from social struggles independent of it. Another dimension is that the newer groups have a shallow historical trajectory and poor grounding in grassroots relationships.

For this reason, UNORCAC is unique in Cotacachi. Formed in 1977, as of 2004 it had twenty-seven years of experience behind it. Moreover, it represents all forty-three communities in the rural zone through a systematic membership of cabildos, the decision-making bodies comprising all residents in each community. Having a broad set of relationships with external funders, it also manages important relationships and funds and has ample experience with development projects. One source commented that the organization's contracted technicians were even more qualified than those working for the municipality. For UNORCAC to act through the Assembly of County Unity, therefore, is to curtail its own power. Although UNORCAC represents thousands of organized citizens (potentially enough for significant social mobilization), within the Assembly of County Unity it has the same number of votes as do the urban sectors, which have far less of a connection to a base. UNORCAC further ends up having less voice in Assembly decisions than do urban sectors because the cultural atmosphere can be mestizo dominated, making rural indigenous people, especially native Kichwa speakers, far less likely to speak out in those circumstances.

Here is a description of the situation by the president (in 2004) of UNORCAC:

> Without UNORCAC...the Assembly [wouldn't exist]. Specifically, the [urban] neighborhoods...are not politically organized....The same with the artisan organizations, the organizations of women...they are not established, nor born from an organization with vision, with force of struggle. In contrast, UNORCAC is the force of struggle. The organization is not something that, all of a sudden, after a [funded] project, comes into being.... [UNORCAC] lives for the communities.
>
> The communities are permanently organized, so...it [would be] very [unlikely] for UNORCAC to fall rapidly into disorganization.

Institutionally, UNORCAC gives strength to the Assembly of County Unity, which requires the existence of organized groups. But the Assembly of County Unity does not give strength to UNORCAC. It erodes UNORCAC's strength, calling on the organization to make space for the strengthening of newer organizations of other sectors rather than focusing only on rural people's needs.

UNORCAC leaders, moreover, critique the notion of "participation" advanced through the Assembly's structure. Said one member of UNORCAC's directorate in an interview:

> Citizen participation is in style. It's in style because, beginning in 1996, they continued speaking of the participation of the actors within the county in the making of decisions. But we say that, in our way, we have [had] participation since much earlier.... UNORCAC...today [celebrates] twenty-seven years since its founding....I don't think that the leadership, for as much good-will as it has, would have been at this level at which we find our-selves [without participation]. [Without participation,] who knows? UNORCAC might not have lasted five nor six nor ten years. But...we are achieving solid bases, and we continue strengthening those solid bases.

His point is that the leadership of UNORCAC is rooted in communities, which is what produces the organization's endurance.

When I asked him, "Before 1996, did you use the word *participation* to describe what you do?" he replied:

> The word wouldn't have made sense. What does the term *partici-pation* mean? It is nothing but a term. For us, the *minga* [collective work] is participation...this minga, this assembly, this meeting, this uprising. If we speak of an "uprising for the revindication of our rights," it is a [type of] participation. That is to say, the forms of participation have always existed. What happens is that the term is applied at this time...*participation* is a recent note. This is why I said that UNORCAC has been achieving participation since much earlier.

What is important, though, is the *kind* of participation. He made the fol-lowing contrast: "For us, participation is much more real—we understand participation [as rooted in] the intention of the bases, of the families that live in the communities. In 1996, in contrast, a much more technical form of participation comes into being." In these comments, the UNORCAC leader is contrasting the kind of participation UNORCAC has cultivated over time through connections with base organizations to the kind of "technical" participation induced in other sectors through the process of the Assembly.

UNORCAC's independent ability to shape policy and hold the municipality accountable, however, is submerged within a set of personal loyalties, institutional cooperation, and ethnic identity that make cooperation far more the norm than contestation and perpetuate a sense of ambivalence and mixed fortunes in having an indigenous mayor who does not emanate from, nor build, the organization.

The analysis in this chapter suggests that the Assembly, as it currently operates, dilutes rather than builds UNORCAC's strength, subordinating it to mestizos in the urban neighborhoods, who are given disproportionate voice (in terms of cultural style of political discussion and in terms of their weight in the decisions) when they have less connection with a social "base." At the same time, the Assembly gains credibility through UNORCAC because of the organization's history of organizational strength and its representational structure. The fortification UNORCAC provides to the Assembly strengthens the mayor and municipality, enabling them to garner international awards and external funding.

Yet UNORCAC weakens when the mayor short-circuits it by communicating in Kichwa with rural communities and directly promising them public works. Ironically, for UNORCAC, holding an indigenous, inclusive mayor accountable may be more difficult than holding to task a mestizo, exclusionary mayor, against whom the organization can exert pressure (Ortiz 2004:208). UNORCAC has specifically found it difficult to hold Tituaña accountable amid dynamics of personal loyalty, fictive kin relations, room for manipulation of the organization, and commitment to unconditionally supporting someone with a similar ethnic identity. As expressed in the quote by Luis Macas at the beginning of this section, the national-level indigenous organization CONAIE struggles with a similar problem in regard to the political movement Pachakutik, through which candidates run for office. In both cases, the major issue is whether the indigenous movement or the rural organization can formulate proposals to direct the politicians and establish mechanisms with which to hold them accountable—a project that each organization, in its own way, has been limited in its ability to accomplish.[5] Gaining spaces of official governance has posed risks to, and arguably weakened, the indigenous movement and rural indigenous organization.

WHY STRONG SOCIAL MOVEMENT ORGANIZATIONS ARE IMPORTANT: PRESENTING SOME ANSWERS

At the beginning of this chapter, I posed the questions of whether and why social movement organizations are important to sustain after they have helped create the conditions for transparent governance. In proposing that such organizations are crucial for accountability in democratic governance, my intent is not to romanticize social movements and their organizations (the divisions, dilemmas, and problems of UNORCAC have been noted above).[6] Nonetheless, I argue that there need to be strong social movement organizations for a variety of reasons.

First, the movement and its organizations must exist to hold politicians accountable to the needs and demands of people in "base" communities. Without an organized public to direct a rendición de cuentas to and without a set of social consequences (such as pressure and mobilization) for deviation from the agenda, there is much latitude for governing officials to respond to other agendas, such as seeking higher office, jockeying for power, and responding to the agendas of funding agencies. Intimately linked to this first point is a second: the vital importance for social movement organizations rooted in communities to set forth proposals that can guide governance and to which officials can be held accountable. Both of these are vital in a formal electoral system in which there is only a limited number of candidates. The classic consequence for a politician not responding to a constituency is to be elected out of office (or, in the case of some countries, to be thrown out of office by force). However, an alternative candidate may not fulfill social demands any better than the first, as the indigenous movement discovered when it deposed President Mahuad only to have him replaced by a man who perpetuated his policies. Hence, the need for strong proposal-making social movement organizations.

Third, local governments (and, increasingly, national governments) are sharply limited in what they can accomplish in a time of global economics and transnational governing and financial structures (such as the World Trade Organization and International Monetary Fund). Parallel to the globalization of capital, therefore, social movement organizations need to be able to transcend boundaries, creating connections and sharing ideas with other organizations, moving political power and pressure beyond the confines of a given locale.[7] In the case of Cotacachi, land holdings are sharply unequal, and salaries notoriously low. These phenomena are largely beyond the influence of the local government, as participatory as it may be. Addressing these requires connection with a broader social movement and organization.

Fourth, social movement organizations are a crucial space in which to produce a new generation of leaders who can become candidates for mayor, council, and governor, as well as organizational leadership. The founders of UNORCAC came of age through expanding (though by no means universal) educational opportunities and social movement experience. Gaining experience within a social movement organization's struggle for rights and against injustice is a very different set of life experiences than being trained through an administration's quest for technical competence: it produces different kinds of visions, commitments, and connections to rural communities and broader social movement activity.

Another set of reasons is related to the character of Tituaña's particular version of participatory democracy and the structure of the Assembly itself (therefore, the particularities of this phenomenon would vary in counties with different institutional structures, but the overall point would likely stand). As currently structured, Cotacachi's Assembly is a space for making proposals—it has no binding control over the mayor. To the contrary, the mayor makes final decisions in consultation with the council (but, in his second term, Tituaña often sidestepped the municipal council as well). Because the Assembly is a weaker arena of action than a social movement organization, which can, in principle, exert pressure on politicians, the weakening of UNORCAC as an independent social actor means a concentration of power in the mayor.

Even within the ambit of the Assembly, the social movement organization has to be strong to be effective. UNORCAC's leadership has noted that the organization has not been able to take advantage of the space created by the Assembly, because UNORCAC is weak in formulating proposals, unprepared in knowing the ins and outs of issues being debated, and limited in asserting leadership and speaking in a mestizo-dominated cultural arena.

Finally, social movement organizations are crucial for longevity of struggles for civil, human, and cultural rights. In the case of Cotacachi, the Assembly—the local instance of civil society participation—could be dismantled or radically transformed by a mayor not of Tituaña's political movement or persuasion. Indeed, although there is no legislation making the Assembly illegal, there is also no legislation making it required. If the process of "participatory democracy" were to weaken UNORCAC or relegate it not only to a parallel development agency but also to a mere constituent of the Assembly and then the Assembly were to disappear, then this would undermine the prospects of long-term advancement for indigenous organizations, the presumed goal of Tituaña and CONAIE.

Ironically, the Cotacachi model is based on the production of and reliance on social organizations as collective actors. Individual citizens do not compose the Assembly—organizations do. Yet the forms of action available to these organizations in this ambit—what those forms of action can achieve and what kinds of individual and collective subjects they construct—is the crucial question.

What are the implications of all this for an anthropology of democracy? Democracy has classically been recognizable through the existence of elections, as well as the active operation of competing political parties, rotating of different figures through political offices, and other instances of institutional procedure. However, if democracy is conceptualized as a situation in which representatives or leaders are in close communication with their constituents—faithfully and accurately representing the desires and demands, then engagement by social movement organizations in electoral politics might diminish that connection and actually weaken democratic representation. These unintended and sometimes counterproductive effects are important areas of analysis both for ethnographers able to spot their dynamics and for social movements aiming to shape them.

More recently, actors of a wide variety, from international financial organizations, to nongovernmental organizations, to governments, to academics interested in civil society and social capital, have set their sights and their hopes on the democratic potential of citizen participation, particularly as implemented through local governments. This chapter suggests that, even in the most successful and highly touted cases, these local participatory democracies also have their limits and must be judged in relation to the aspirations and organizational capacities of social movement organizations.

The strength of independent grassroots organization may be crucial for any kind of reformulation of democratic practice. The anthropologist needs to highlight and compare the local definitions and practices labeled "democracy" to be able to gain insight into the degree to which these modes of political practice are achieving goals as the people define them, rather than assume a universal template for what democracy is or should be.

Acknowledgments

This chapter was researched with funding from the Fulbright Commission and the Wenner-Gren Foundation and is based upon work supported by the National Science Foundation under grant no. 0620452. Additional funding came from the University of Michigan through the Rackham Graduate School and the Office of the Vice Provost for Research. The chapter benefited from discussion in the advanced seminar "Toward an Anthropology of Democracy" at the School of American Research (which also received funding from the Wenner-Gren Foundation), where Mukulika Banerjee, Carol Greenhouse, David Nugent, Jennifer Schirmer, Kay Warren, and Harry West provided valuable feedback. I thank Keith Brown, Catherine Lutz, and Kay Warren for inviting me to join a panel, organized through Brown University's Watson Institute for International Studies, at the United Nations Development Program conference in Paris, France. Portions of this chapter were presented at a Department of Anthropology colloquium at the University of Chicago, where participants gave insightful feedback. This chapter benefited greatly from the work of two research assistants, Viviana Quintero and Janneth Teran. Rafael Boglio Martinez and Katherine Fultz also provided valuable assistance. My deepest appreciation goes to the leadership of UNORCAC, Cotacachi's mayor Auki Tituaña Males, the leadership of Cotacachi's Asamblea de Unidad Cantonal, and other residents of Cotacachi, who shared their ideas and welcomed me to their events and meetings. I thank María Elena García, David Gow, Bret Gustafson, Rebecca Hardin, Ayako Kano, Eduardo Kohn, Chris Krupa, Bruce Mannheim, Christi Merrill, Nadine Naber, Damani Partridge, Elizabeth Roberts, Miriam Ticktin, and Gordon Whitman for their feedback.

Notes

1. There is a compelling literature problematizing and contextualizing the term *community* (Creed 2006; Joseph 2002). I employ it here as a direct translation of the Spanish word *comunidad*, used routinely to refer to Cotacachi's rural locales.

2. Translations from Spanish to English are my own.

3. For literature on municipal governance in the Andes, see, among others, Albó 2002; Cameron 2003; Gustafson 2002; Grupo Democracia 1999; Korovkin 2001; Postero 2004; Radcliffe, Andolina, and Laurie 2002; Red Interamericana 1998; and Van Cott 2006.

4. In preparing this section, I benefited from the historical overview in Ortiz 2004. Other relevant works include Clark and Becker 2007; Pallares 2002; Rhoades 2006; and Van Cott 2005.

5. For more on accountability, see Paley 2004.

6. Analyses of the major national organizations CONAIE, FENOCIN, and FEINE (Council of Evangelical Indigenous Peoples and Organizations of Ecuador) would only serve to emphasize the point.

7. For the literature on transnational connections of indigenous movements, see, among others, Brysk 2000 and Radcliffe 2001.

7

Literacy, Bureaucratic Domination, and Democracy

Akhil Gupta

The Indian state may appear no different from other modern bureaucracies in the importance it gives to writing. What makes this emphasis, which borders on an obsession, so significant in the Indian context, however, is that bureaucrats, at least at lower levels, often have to deal with a population of clients who are largely illiterate. The consequences of insisting on writing in a social context in which literacy is highly stratified have seldom been appreciated in the scholarly literature on states.[1] In such a context, the power of the state is intimately tied to the power of the written word.

The organization of this chapter is as follows: the next section deals with the relationship between the written and the oral in government bureaucracies, and the final section looks at strategies employed by subaltern groups to undermine or challenge bureaucratic writing. My fieldwork, conceptualized as an ethnography of the state, compared the functioning of the Block office, which coordinated the implementation of approximately thirty development programs for an area comprising roughly a hundred villages (a Block), with the functioning of the Integrated Child Development Services Program (ICDS), an initiative aimed at maternal and child health and welfare. I did fieldwork in these two offices in the Mandi subdistrict of Uttar Pradesh (UP) for one year, between 1991 and 1992. The Block office, housed in a small cluster of buildings just outside the town, had twenty employees and was headed by a Block Development Officer (BDO).

The goal of the ICDS program was to provide supplementary nutrition for pregnant women and young children and education, immunizations, and preventive medicine for poor and lower-caste children. The ICDS structure of command at the Block level was as follows: A Child Development Project Officer (CDPO) was the head of the office and was responsible for overseeing the work of the four Supervisors (Mukhya Sevika), the eighty-six Anganwadi Workers in the Block, and their eighty-six Helpers. The Anganwadi Workers were responsible for the day-to-day functioning of the crèches, or centers, in villages. The centers were supposed to operate every day from 9 a.m. to 1 p.m. In Mandi, all the Helpers, Anganwadi Workers, and Supervisors, as well as the CDPO, were women; the rest of the office staff were men.

THE WRITTEN AND THE ORAL

For Indian bureaucrats, a vast gap separates the written from the oral, with the former clearly being given pride of place. Oral complaints have no bureaucratic or judicial standing; by contrast, written complaints are treated with the utmost seriousness. From the perspective of the Block staff, the most important goal was to avoid having a written complaint submitted against them.

During the course of my fieldwork, the Uttar Pradesh state government instituted a new program called the Kisan Seva Kendra (Farmers' Service Center) in an effort to improve the government's image in rural areas. It ordered all the officials whose jurisdiction overlapped for a group of eight to ten villages to come together at a fixed place once a week from 9:30 a.m. to 5 p.m. The idea behind this program was that if villagers had problems requiring action on the part of two or more officials, they would be able to obtain signatures and authorizations in one spot. Because officials rarely went to the villages where they were supposed to work, it was frustrating and time-consuming for villagers to track down individual officials in the town, especially because many officials worked out of their homes.

On one of my many visits to the Kisan Seva Kendra, I came across a heated debate between a villager and the officials present. After it was over, the man said that he wanted to register a complaint against the functioning of the Gram Panchayat (Village Council). "What is your complaint?" asked one of the officials. He replied that the Village Council did not hold meetings, that council members were not informed when such meetings did take place, and that there was no public forum where beneficiaries were selected for programs like the Indira Awaas Yojana (a house-building scheme for indigent people) and other government schemes. The Secretary of his village told him that the Village Council had indeed met. He then recited the dates and said that if the man did not know those dates, it was not the council's fault. He also said that he had noted down the date at which a meeting had been held to select beneficiaries. But the man insisted that his complaint be noted down in the register where they recorded villagers' complaints.

One of the officials interjected and said that they could act on his complaint only if he submitted it in writing. Another official stated the same thing: "Submit it in the form of a petition [*Ek prastaav ke roop may day dee-jeeay*]." "Why do I need to give it in writing?" insisted the man. "Isn't the purpose of this meeting that people can submit their complaints verbally?" The officials held firm. Soon after, he left, saying, "I don't want to disturb your meeting any more than necessary. I just wanted to bring this to your attention. Please go on with your meeting." After he left, none of the officials made any effort to note down what he had said.

It was clear that the man complaining was educated and that he was a member of the Village Council, although on the side opposed to the current headman. But even someone well-informed like him, who knew that the Kisan Seva Kendra was set up to listen to villagers' complaints, thought that it was largely an internal meeting of officials instead of a context to invite villagers to submit problems and complaints. When he apologized for disturbing their meeting, none of the officials corrected him by saying that their purpose in being there was to serve the public and act on complaints such as his. They resisted noting down his complaint, knowing full well that he would be unlikely to submit it in writing. I later asked the Secretary how it was possible for someone on the Village Council not to find out when a council meeting would convene. He explained to me that a quorum for a Village Council meeting was considered met when a third of the members were present (that would mean three of the nine elected members). Usually, the headman called three or four people from his faction on the council to his house for a Village Council "meeting." "If you pass these people talking inside the headman's house, you would not know that it is a Village Council meeting," volunteered the Secretary helpfully. This is why the man was under the erroneous impression that no Village Council meetings had been called! The Secretary had undercut the man's complaint by giving him the exact dates at which such meetings had taken place. These dates had been recorded, were official, and could be used to refute any allegation such as the one raised by the man about the head-man's failure to call council meetings to select beneficiaries for government programs.

The preceding decennial census had put the literacy rate for Mandi Block at a mere 29 percent, and this did not imply the ability to read a letter or to write a petition, but merely to sign one's name. In the context of low rates of rural literacy, this devaluation of the oral might be seen as a straightforward sign of the domination exercised by bureaucratic elites over the rural population. But two factors militate against such a simple reading of power relations. The first is that we need to situate such restricted literacy in a historical context in which rural peoples have long been accustomed to dealing with state officials. Scribes and other literate intermediaries were widely employed, thereby reducing the importance we might be tempted to give to the imbalance between literate state officials and the largely illiterate population.[2] Second, we must not forget that, in the democratic context of post-colonial India, bureaucrats are answerable to elected officials, some of whom are, themselves, illiterate. Therefore, the continuing distrust of the oral in bureaucratic procedure is, in some ways, surprising and in need of explanation, rather than a practice we can take for granted. At the very least, we might expect that *new* bureaucratic initiatives, as opposed to long-standing practices, make room for oral inputs from rural peoples, particularly from those lower-caste people whose rates of literacy are even lower than the average and who have been the clients and target of an emergent populist politics.

One argument in favor of the written is that it is better at preserving and recording events and actions; the oral is transitory and potentially more open to corruption and contradiction. For example, a written complaint can be passed up the hierarchy "verbatim," whereas an orally transmitted complaint is likely to have errors of transmission, as each person who passes it upward unconsciously changes or embellishes it to suit his or her own purpose. But written complaints can be "lost": a file can be accidentally or deliberately misplaced. Similarly, the veracity of a complaint can be called into question because of a minor "factual" error: a wrong date or a missing or misstated fact. Small inconsistencies are better tolerated in oral testimony than in written. In Indian bureaucracies, written documents are not always chosen as a preferred medium for their ability to preserve the truth of the official record. Tarlo (2003:74) demonstrates this convincingly in her discussion of paper truths, "whose status as truths was intrinsically linked to their symbolic value as official papers."[3]

We can also easily imagine a situation in which oral testimonies at the interface of bureaucracies and rural peoples are converted to written documents when such documents are required for purposes *internal* to bureaucracies. This is already done in procedures such as the First Information Report (FIR) collected by the police whenever a person comes to report a crime or attack. Something similar in other offices would allow a villager's oral testimony to be converted into a written document: the scribe would move into the government office, and his or her job would be to record oral complaints and petitions.[4] However, the example of the man who wanted to register a complaint at the Kisan Seva Kendra demonstrates that the opposite situation prevails in most bureaucratic offices. Not only are bureaucrats reluctant to "write down" oral testimony, but also they insist that the person who has a complaint first submit it in writing before they are even willing to consider acting on it. The substance of the complaint is therefore bracketed: however plausible or true such a complaint might be, if it is not in the right form, it cannot be admitted.

Why do written documents now appear to have this property of better preserving original intent and of providing stability of meaning as the document is transmitted from one hand to another? Such a position is by no means either universal or self-evident. In other situations of restricted literacy, the oral is sometimes considered more reliable and less prone to error than are written documents. In "modern" courts all over the world, oral testimony by key witnesses still serves as the most important procedure for discerning the truth of the evidence, often supplying the suspense in real-life cases and in the genre of the detective thriller. This may appear surprising, given the importance of writing to court procedure and the significance of "documentation," which now refers exclusively to written materials. It is ironic, although not surprising, that even oral testimony, elicited under strict rules, is transcribed verbatim by a court stenographer.[5] What are we to make of the continuing centrality of oral testimony in a bureaucracy densely entangled in a forest of paper?

Clearly, the question of reliability is the most important one, in terms of evidence and also transmission.[6] In Messick's fascinating study of the transmission of the *sharia'* in Yemen (1993), he points to the contrast often made in Islamic "tradition" and "jurisprudence" between writing and oral instruction.[7] Writing is considered an unreliable and error-prone form of disseminating the sharia', as compared with oral transmission from teacher to pupil. The reason follows Socratic thought in that it sees, contrary to modern Western prejudice,[8] the written word as that which makes the text more vulnerable to interpretive play and distortion (Messick 1993:24–26). In the oral transmission of a text, the speaker guarantees the reliability of the text: she can be interrogated, and meanings that are unclear or ambiguous can be clarified (Messick 1993:27). By contrast, a written text offers no such possibility; it is "open" to misinterpretation by people who do not understand it (Plato 1995:80–81).

At first glance, such a position privileging the oral might appear archaic today, but we express our solidarity with Socrates every time we schedule a personal meeting rather than convey messages by email. I have often heard people justify such a preference by saying that the potential to be misunderstood is greater in email.[9] Take the role of the job talk or the personal lecture in the academic world in the contemporary United States. Given that publishing is so important in research universities, we would expect that a careful evaluation of the written work should be the clearest indication of the "quality" of a job applicant. However, the quality of a person's mind is often judged by how she or he responds to questions in the job talk. Even with advanced students (or especially with them), students who are quite capable of interpreting texts on their own, the importance placed on the oral transmission of knowledge in a small graduate seminar underlines the continuing centrality of the oral in an institutional context that supposedly privileges the written word over everything else.

Why have bureaucracies, and state bureaucracies in particular, become so dependent on writing? Several answers have been proposed, but what is clear is that the portability of written communication in the form of scrolls or sheets of paper is a huge advantage in its dissemination. Issues of security and authenticity, however, have continued to be a big problem; documents, precisely because of their portability, are easily stolen or replaced with forged ones. To ensure the security of transmission, effective modes of transporting the inscriptions of bureaucracies developed quickly in the form of postal services (Goody 1986:96). Even today, the importance given to the security of the mail is evident in that, in most countries, the state can imprison a person for tampering with or opening someone else's mail. Other practices, such as notarizing important correspondence and sending copies of a letter to different offices, also help prevent fraud. However, the world of official documents is always shadowed by the counterfeit. As we shall see below, the *authenticity* of documents has continued to trouble bureaucracies up to the present.

Even historians of writing have expressed doubts as to the continuing salience and centrality of the written word. Clanchy (1979:8) surmises that the technology of writing "may be entering its final century" with the reassertion of oral modes of communication encapsulated in televisual technologies and emerging inventions that make visual telephonic communication affordable. Media critics were already proclaiming that radio and the gramophone had introduced a "new age of orality" and that the "age of print" simply represented an interval between two epochs of orality, one before print and an emerging one that would follow it (Kittler 1999:xii). Such views have a strongly teleological cast, progressing from orality toward a world of print and literacy and, from there, to a new epoch of orality. The shift from one era to the other is marked by displacement. Therefore, we have the concept of "oral residues" in literate cultures. For instance, Clanchy (1979:2) observes that reading aloud, an oral mode of communication, *persisted* for a long time after the advent of literacy. The natural progression implicit in such a statement would see literacy not existing alongside, but replacing, oral communication.

If we reverse this assumption and see that, in civilizations such as India and China, conditions of restricted literacy have been the rule, instead of the exceptional states of complete illiteracy and total literacy, then the coexistence of written and oral modes of communication, and especially transmission across these genres, is unsurprising. More important, perhaps, is that the economy of exchange between the written and the oral may operate on different principles. Kaviraj argues that, in "traditional" India, the class of people who jealously guarded their privilege of reading and writing—the Brahmins—nevertheless relied heavily on memory and oral recitation for the transmission and preservation of knowledge. This has more to do with a knowledge tradition in which speech and intonation are closely linked to transcendental knowledge and in which the theory of speech is far better elaborated than is an epistemology of writing (Kaviraj 1992:28–29).[10]

This is true even of this second epoch of orality in the West. Witness, for example, the morning programs on US television; one of their regular features is a glance at the headlines of leading newspapers. Rather than see the written in opposition to the oral, we need to pay attention, historically and in the present, to modes of intertextuality. What we may be witnessing is not so much the displacement of the written by the oral, but a new relation of exchange between their respective economies.

One example from my own fieldwork might help make this point more clearly. The (literate) bureaucrats who had gathered for the Kisan Seva Kendra, mentioned above, were debating a fine point about what uses could be made of the money allocated for this new program. For instance, if they were required to be in a village all day long, could the money be used to buy chairs so that they could sit down comfortably? The Secretary replied that the scheme contained no provision for purchasing equipment or for building a space where they could gather. Having said this, he took out a long, cyclostyled sheet of paper from his bag and said, "You can read it for yourself." This was passed around, and, at the request of some officials, a land records official agreed to read it aloud for the benefit of everyone present. The Government Order (GO) was signed by the Chief Secretary of the provincial UP state government. It gave detailed instructions as to who was to attend the Kisan Seva Kendra, what its function was supposed to be, and how that function was to be achieved. It listed all the people who were to be present. The directive ordered the officials not to waste time but to ensure that the day was spent productively. All the officials were required to attend from 9:30 a.m. to 5 p.m. The order also proposed that a suitable place be found for the centers to operate and advised that a board be put up at that site. If a problem could not be solved at the center, the order suggested that the officials present refer the matter to departments higher up the bureaucratic hierarchy.

Several interesting aspects underlie this oral performance. The officials who had gathered at the Kisan Seva Kendra came from different departments of the bureaucracy. The Government Order, which required them to attend, had been sent to the heads of their respective departments, who had presumably read it and told them what they had to do. Apart from the Secretary, none of them had actually seen the Government Order. That was one level at which the written had already been translated into the oral. When the Secretary produced the order, it could have been passed from one person to the next, each of whom could have read it silently, for they were all literate and probably well versed in bureaucratic prose. But there was a call for reading it aloud, not merely because such an act speeded up the transmission of the text and therefore was more efficient, but also because oral communication allowed for commentary, discussion, and debate. They could interrupt the person reading, interject comments, voice criticism, and debate various points. Reading aloud created a community of subalternity shaped by the Government Order: it was highly unlikely that all these lower-level officials from various branches of the bureaucracy would have ever found themselves in the same space. What brought them together, uniting them in this (uneasy) space of companionship, was an order from above that all of them roundly criticized as a "waste of time."

These examples from the Kisan Seva Kendra also demonstrate the *directionality* of the flow of different forms of communication. Both written and oral communications, as well as translations from one to the other, traveled easily from higher levels of authority to lower ones. It was much more difficult for something in writing to go up the hierarchy, from lower-level bureaucrats but especially from rural peoples. This had much more to do with the fear of getting involved with the state than simply with unfamiliarity with writing, although familiarity with writing also usually implied a greater knowledge of the world of bureaucracy, which might contribute to a greater willingness to engage the state. State officials like Asha Agarwal, the head of the ICDS program in Mandi Block, were frustrated when they received oral complaints from villagers about day care centers that were not functioning. Such complaints were useless because officials could not act on the basis of oral complaints. When Asha tried to persuade villagers to give her a written complaint, they almost never followed through. "The problem," Asha told me, "is that with government work, unless you have something in writing, you cannot build a case and take any action."

Clanchy (1979:2) argues that trust in writing develops over time and is the result of a "growing familiarity with documents." Here, again, we encounter a progressivist narrative of total literacy. If we view restricted literacy as a transitional phase from total illiteracy to a condition of universal literacy, then (and perhaps only then) such a formulation makes sense. However, if restricted literacy is seen as the "normal" condition for most people in the history of humankind, then "familiarity with documents" clearly has little correlation with people's trust or distrust of writing. People in rural north India have long been familiar with documents such as deeds of land ownership. Here, the attitude toward writing is determined not by people's relationship to writing but by their relationship with the state.

WEAPONS OF THE WEAK?

If state officials employ writing as an instrument of domination, what strategies do subaltern peoples use to combat or resist such domination? Next, I investigate three themes that link writing, democracy, and liberation. In the first part, I examine the possibilities and limits of an approach that emphasizes the emancipatory promise of literacy. It is often presumed that the best way for subaltern groups to oppose the domination exercised by literate elites is to become literate, to use the master's tools. The second part of this section is not just about writing in a narrow sense, but about the broader connections and disjunctures between democratic participation and literacy. Here, I explore the ambivalences and contradictions of domination based on literacy in a political situation in which illiterate people are, for the most part, enthusiastic participants in democratic processes. In other words, what are the conflicts engendered by the discrepancy between a high degree of political literacy and a low level of functional literacy? The third and final part looks at the production and circulation of illegitimate forms of writing that mimic and copy official bureaucratic writing. The term *duplicate* in rural Uttar Pradesh connotes both "copy" and "counterfeit." Duplicate writing is to be found wherever state documents are necessary and requires a theory of the counterfeit that sees it as not merely a response to domination, but as coeval with state writing.

Writing Back

I have mentioned already that the procedures of the Indian state, like those of modern states in general, privilege writing and devalue oral forms of communication. The latter were treated with suspicion, as not being reliable and trustworthy, whereas written communication was perceived to be stable in its expression and meaning. Given the importance of writing in state procedures, literacy is essential if subaltern peoples are to prevent exploitation at the hands of bureaucratic elites. Therefore, becoming literate is one very important strategy of empowerment for poor, semiliterate, and illiterate populations. Almost all the illiterate people I knew in rural Uttar Pradesh were acutely aware of how much they were disadvantaged by not knowing how to read and write and were fully committed to preventing their children from sharing such a fate. For the same reason, lower-class and lower-caste people who were literate and who had perhaps even attained a school education were much more comfortable in dealing with state officials and better at safeguarding their own interests against such officials. Given this fact, it is ironic that states often mount (adult) literacy campaigns in order to "protect" the poor from exploitation by moneylenders and other rapacious groups. State elites almost never consider that an important use of literacy might be to empower the poor against the state.[11]

The irony here is that the use of writing for exploitation enables literacy to become a tool of liberation. But the liberating potential of literacy is not confined to particular situations such as this. In fact, a widespread belief exists (among literate people?) that literacy is essential to subaltern empowerment. So much is this taken for granted that literacy campaigns have often been the first major actions undertaken by popular socialist revolutionary governments, such as those in Cuba and China. Efforts to achieve "full" literacy share a teleological narrative about civilizations, in which there is a historical evolution from near-complete illiteracy to complete literacy. Even in the West, such a narrative came to fruition only with the imposition of compulsory schooling in the early nineteenth century (Boyd and King 1995). Historians have often interpreted the degree of literacy of a society as "an essential mark of civilization" (Clanchy 1979:7).

But such a view assumes that situations of "restricted literacy" (a term in which the teleology of complete literacy is already present) are somehow anomalous and that movement toward complete and full literacy is the "natural" progression of societies. In the modern world, one might say that the assumption of full literacy shapes everything from the design of road signs to that of computers. Even when icons are employed, they are accompanied by letters, and written signs very often are used exclusively when icons would have been more effective.

If we resist such a teleology and recognize that, in the past two thousand years, the vast majority of people in the world lived in situations in which only a small group of individuals knew how to read and write (Goody 1986:4–5), then the narrative of "literacy as liberation" becomes problematic. So widely held and so naturalized has this relationship become that it seems almost reactionary to argue that literacy is not essential to liberation and empowerment. Yet I argue that there are at least three good reasons to resist this comfortable assumption.

The first reason has to do with the unraveling of the binary encoding of literacy. It is difficult to establish definitively whether someone with low levels of proficiency in reading and writing is literate or illiterate; as a population, it is almost never the case that the population is fully literate or completely illiterate. Combined, these two problems demonstrate that the idea of a "fully literate population" is a mirage masking situations that may be closer to "restricted literacy" and propagating an ideology by which countries in the North continue to assert their "fully modern" status vis-à-vis the global South. Rather, we should think of literacy as a gradient, both for an individual and for a population (Collins and Blot 2003). For the individual, we have to ask not *whether* someone is literate, but his or her *degree* of functional literacy: Is someone who knows how to read and sign his or her name literate? How about an individual who can write but cannot do basic mathematics? In an advanced capitalist nation-state, is an individual who cannot compose a letter or memo literate? What about someone who does not know how to operate a bank-teller machine or a computer? In Paulo Freire's pioneering work, *Pedagogy of the Oppressed* (1968), he emphasized how much literacy depends on political context. Teaching someone to read and write is not what leads to liberation, but how he or she is taught and what uses are made of that literacy. In Freire's understanding of literacy, the pedagogical and the political are inextricably linked. A fully literate population, in this view, would also be one mobilized against oppression and exploitation.

This brings me to the second point that bears on the relationship between literacy and resistance. Literacy in the form of "being lettered" is not, by itself, a guarantee that subaltern peoples will be able to improve their life situation, either by being better able to fight oppression or by finding avenues for upward mobility. It might be true that literacy enables both these consequences, at least for some people, so that a small proportion of newly literate subalterns are affected, but the ability to read and write may also have the opposite consequence. The ability to read, especially, can lead to new possibilities of co-optation and incorporation into hegemonic projects. Literary forms as disparate as the novel, the newspaper, and the popular magazine are then able to interpellate subaltern subjects into hegemonic projects. Clanchy (1979:8) recognizes this when he says that there is "little sociological evidence to suggest that a minimal ability to read and write has released proletariats in modern societies from mental confinement." Such an understanding is caught up in a telos in which literacy is seen as having "opened up" worlds of possibilities for upper-class people. This often provides the pedagogic justification for fiction: reading fiction, it is said, broadens one's mental horizons.[12] Without the class prejudices implicit in Clanchy's statement, one can only note that, in the United States, nonfiction consistently outsells fiction in the best-seller lists.

My third and final reason for resisting the easy equation of literacy with liberation follows from a new emphasis on the oral in the (post)modern world. In the standard narrative, as societies become modern, they move from illiteracy to partial literacy to full literacy. In this rendering, as societies move to full literacy, writing achieves dominance over orality. Communication theorists are now positing a new epoch of orality in which telephones, televisual media, and soundscapes are becoming more important culturally and socially than the written word. This is the "lesson" sometimes deduced from the decline of newspaper subscriptions and from the survey data showing that, in the contemporary United States, more people get their news from television than from newspapers. Following the conventions of popular history, the rise or revaluation of the oral is accompanied by prophecies of an epoch of orality *replacing* a now superannuated epoch of writing. Clanchy (1979:8) appears to subscribe to such a view when he writes that the technology of writing "may be entering its final century."

If, on the contrary, we view the history of literacy as not one in which written modes have replaced oral ones, but in which the two have comfortably coexisted for at least two millennia (see, for instance, Messick 1993:21–30), then we should not expect that the new forms of orality will necessarily replace the written word, but that they will create a new configuration of the communicative field. However, there are profound *political* implications of this new epoch of orality for societies in which only a small proportion of people is literate. The spectacle and the performative achieve a new prominence when technologies for disseminating oral performance (television, radio, sound recording) become dominant.

A critical difference exists, however, between the technology of oral transmission in the presence of a speaker and the televisual or telephonic transmission of that person's speech. Therefore, in thinking about the political consequences of orality, we should distinguish between various technologies of orality, just as we need to make a distinction between hand-written letters and email. "Orality" when the speaker is present in the same space is not the same thing as when she or he is present on the television screen: what matters here is not the presence or absence of orality as the mediation of the voice. The new age of orality is not a return to a previous situation, or even simply an extension of it, but constitutes a completely different situation, in which politics cannot be equated with modes of oral communication mediated by face-to-face presence. That said, it is also clear that these new technologies of oral communication offer a new way for politicians to reach, and create, their (formally illiterate) constituents, which, in turn, has profound implications for the nature of democracy.

Literacy and Democratic Citizenship

If literacy is taken as a precondition for empowerment in general, it is considered even more essential in republican forms of government. Can a democratic politics survive without literate citizens? How can illiterates exercise a responsible vote? These questions loomed large for Indian leaders at the time of independence from British colonial rule. Under colonialism, even in the context of the limited opportunities for "self-rule," the franchise had been far from universal.[13] Nor were there good examples to draw from the Western historical experience, in which disenfranchised groups had to wage a protracted struggle for the rights to suffrage. The struggle for women to get the vote is well known, as is the continuing difficulty that African Americans and other minorities face in order to exercise their voting "rights." In most of the debates about the extension of suffrage, literacy was not the primary reason for denying these groups the right to vote. Thus, there was almost no historical precedent when the Indian state decided after Independence to conduct the experiment of universal suffrage in a country where literacy rates hovered around 30 percent.[14] Given that India's population constituted one-third that of the non-Western world, the decision to grant universal suffrage to the entire adult population dramatically increased the proportion of the world's population living in a democracy. To appreciate how radical a decision universal suffrage constituted in India shortly after Independence in 1947, we need to remember that universal suffrage obtained in Great Britain only in 1928, with the granting of voting rights to women after a lengthy struggle.

Less than two decades separated full voting rights for all citizens in a long established democracy and in the first of the new nation-states from which the yoke of colonial rule had just been lifted. In this context, we have to think about the exact relationship between literacy and democracy. What does one mean by "democracy"? Much of the discussion about whether illiterate people can be "responsible" citizens centers on the *procedures* for voting. Literacy is taken as the necessary condition of democratic politics because it is assumed that illiterate citizens would find it hard to be "informed" voters. Even something like reading the names on a ballot becomes a challenge not only for the voter but also for election officials, who have to design the ballot to accommodate voters who are illiterate.

The Indian experience demonstrates that the procedures of democracy do not require literacy and that a vigorous democracy can flourish in the absence of formal literacy. What is far more essential is political literacy, and my point here is that political literacy does not depend on formal literacy as a precondition. A fully or largely literate population is neither necessary nor sufficient for political literacy. If it were necessary, then flourishing democracies like India could not exist. If it were sufficient, then we would find functioning democracies everywhere that literate populations are to be found, and we know from the histories of dictatorships that this is often not the case.[15]

My point is that arguments positing literacy as a requirement for democracy operate with a notion of democracy that is largely formal instead of substantive.[16] The excitement in scholarly, as well as political, circles over the rapid expansion of democracy in the wake of the Cold War is largely limited to the institution of formal democracy. This includes, most importantly, the conduct of "free and fair" elections. But it also emphasizes universal suffrage for all adults, including ethnic, linguistic, and religious minorities, and the commitment to a competitive electoral system of government with at least two parties. The emphasis here is on procedural fairness and "transparency."

When we begin to ask about the connection between literacy and substantive democracy as political and economic empowerment, the questions raised become even more acute. By "substantive" democracy, I mean what

Kaviraj describes as "an alternative, Tocquevillian reading of democracy's success—which is not just a continuation of a system of [elected] government, but the capacity of this government to produce long-term egalitarian effects" (Kaviraj 2003:146). Is it possible to think about upward mobility of the most disenfranchised segments of a nation-state's population without the benefit of literacy? How, exactly, can empowerment and enfranchisement occur among groups that are illiterate or on the margins of functional literacy? Also, is it not ironic that multilateral institutions, acting on the behest of powerful nation-states in the global North, are urging Third World governments to cut expenditures on elementary schooling in the name of "fiscal discipline" while heavily promoting formal democracy and "voter education" in those very countries? The appearance of democracy seems to be increasing in symbolic significance at the same time that the "conditionalities" imposed by multilateral institutions and foreign aid undermine governments' ability to determine their own economic and financial future.

But we should be careful not to dismiss formal democracy. Ideally, the "rule of law" and the creation of a space for public discussion and debate enable citizens to live without the fear of arbitrary state violence. Stripped of its utopian possibilities, such a space of public debate emerges with its dual properties of publicness and stratification. Language hierarchies, for instance, may make debates among elites in fora like newspapers and television simultaneously public and yet inaccessible to the majority of the population. In this regard, it behooves us to pay attention to the terms in which "democracy" is understood and negotiated in different languages: what are the words and concepts *through* which people participate in "democracy" (Nugent, chapter 2; Schaffer 2000; West, chapter 4)? The importance of deepening democracy was one chief reason the leadership of the postcolonial Indian state reorganized regional states along linguistic lines. Kaviraj comments sardonically that "Nehru agreed to linguistic reorganization because of the undeniable force of the argument of democracy that use of the vernacular in administration would bring government closer to the people, because that was the language they were illiterate in" (Kaviraj 1992:56–57).

What we find in the Indian case is that, unlike Western nation-states, which have witnessed a rolling back of substantive democracy over the past few decades under neoliberal regimes, formal democracy over the past fifty years has metamorphosed into an expansive, state-led project that is ideologically committed to equality. Kaviraj (2003:159) argues that such an egalitarian commitment has not taken the form of equalizing incomes, but of "a real redistribution of dignity." By this, he is referring to a fundamental shift in formal politics in which lower-caste parties have successfully pressed for recognition and representation. One of the chief forms in which such demands for dignity are pursued is in the sphere of employment.[17] Although the Indian Constitution does not allow private firms to be forced to hire a certain percentage of lower-caste workers, this is not the case with government agencies and the entire publicly funded higher education system. Quotas arouse some of the same ire among upper classes and conservatives in India as in the United States, but quotas are an important, and enduring, feature of government policy.

What makes the Indian case unique is that no major political party—not even the right wing, conservative, Hindu nationalists who have become dominant on the national political scene—has publicly opposed the system of quotas. For any major party to come out openly against these would be political suicide; it would have to face potentially massive retaliation at the ballot box. Instead, the strategy has been to pursue a neoliberal agenda in which cutting the size of government and making government jobs less attractive compared with the private sector makes the quantity and quality of these positions less important. Similarly, by allowing private higher educational institutions to exist, the significance of a reserved quota of seats for admission into government colleges declines. These processes are slow, however: setting up a high-quality, prestigious new college or slashing the number of government employees is difficult. So, for the medium run, quotas will continue to play an important economic and political role.

In the public sphere, there is little contestation of quotas, but, in everyday conversation, quotas for lower castes become the object of the articulation of acute class and caste antagonisms. Every government job has specified minimum educational qualifications and maximum-age requirements. If a job is reserved for a lower-caste person, then the minimum educational requirements are usually lower and the maximum age usually higher than for a "general" position, that is, one for which eligibility is not restricted to lower-caste candidates. This system of quotas, which has been put into place to remedy extensive, deep-seated, and continuing discrimination against lower-caste people, runs up squarely against exam-centric conceptions of meritocracy. So much are the two sets of prejudices conjoined that when (upper-caste) officials see evidence of "incompetence," they automatically assume that the (incompetent) person must be lower caste and must have obtained his position (illegitimately) by meeting lowered standards of competence.

Historically, it is unclear whether the ubiquity of meritocratic discourse among upper-caste bureaucrats has arisen with the system of quotas for lower-caste groups; however, it has certainly intensified since there have been enough lower-caste people whose educational qualifications enable them to meet the quotas left unfilled for many years. In my experience, even lower-caste people rarely contested the idea that selection for state jobs should be meritocratic. Very few people argued that a commitment to the principles of justice, or of equality, required one to support the granting of positions to less qualified members of oppressed groups in society.[18] Oddly enough, neither did the debate hinge on how merit was to be ascertained: almost everyone agreed that grades and educational qualifications were appropriate guides to merit. The sole difference lay in whether one argued that it was appropriate to lower the educational qualifications necessary to obtain jobs in the reserved quota. Of course, such an argument did bring questions of justice and equality to the table, but in a limited framework.

If we were to translate the views of bureaucrats in order to situate them in the history of academic theorizing on the bureaucracy, there would appear to be widespread consensus in India that a bureaucracy *ought* to be Weberian: recruitment ought to be done on the basis of "specialized examinations or tests of expertise" that are "increasingly indispensable for modern bureaucracies" (Weber 1968:999). Against Weber's background assumption—that bureaucratic selection is meritocratic if it accords with the results of exams and respects educational qualifications—is the view that educational achievement effectively reproduces class hierarchies rather than reflects fairly the distribution of talent and ability. "Success" in competitive exams depends not only on access to schooling but also, and more important, on the quality of schooling, both of which are heavily dependent on class and on social and geographic location. Then there is the "invisible curriculum" shaped by teachers and also by the cultural capital of the family to which the child belongs (Bourdieu 1996). Finally, there is the ability of translating capital in money form (to pay bribes, for example) into educational capital (a diploma obtained by cheating) and social capital (a job in the police force) (Bourdieu 1986). Far from being "meritocratic," Bourdieu argues, educational achievement largely reproduces existing social hierarchies of different forms of capital, allowing for some upward mobility but mainly reflecting conversions from one type of capital to another. A system that thus depends on success in educational achievement militates against the democratic aspirations of subaltern and lower-caste people. The emphasis on written documents in bureaucratic procedure helps prevent the sweeping changes brought about by democratic processes from radically altering the relations of inequality reproduced by the actions of bureaucratic offices, including caste and class relations within the bureaucracy itself.

In sum, two large social processes are moving in opposite directions, and conflict is inevitable. On the one side is a renewal of democratic politics enabled by the charismatic qualities of the spectacle and oral performance. Television, audio- and videocassettes, and "cable" television enable the reproduction of the spectacle, which does not rely as much on the mediation of written language. At the same time, political "events" are now increasingly produced with an eye toward their televisual transmission.[19] The technologies enabling a second epoch of orality in the West have a very different role to play in a social setting in which literacy was never widespread. No longer restricted by the audience that can be reached by written language, a vigorous popular democracy is unleashed in a public sphere marked by competitive politics. Although there is much to celebrate in such a situation, we must be wary of its vulnerability to demagoguery, to co-optation by a "passive revolution," or to the real dangers posed by a consolidation of ownership as domestic and global monopoly capitalists eye an increasingly lucrative "market."

On the other side stands the fetish of educational qualifications and degrees, which has received a fresh impetus from India's emergence as a world power in coding and back-office work. The lure of degrees and documents has never been stronger; all that stands in the way of access to global consumer goods is an education that has market value with the corporations, both Indian and multinational, involved in that economy. For those people whose aspiration is that their children participate in this new global economy, writing and literacy are more important than ever before. The lure of degrees, documents, and the written word therefore shows no signs of abating.

However, the value of degrees and documents is ultimately guaranteed by the state (Bourdieu 1996:376). Even when institutions such as private universities and schools issue certificates of educational achievement, the state ultimately ensures their authenticity. Private institutions may mimic the state in using elaborate seals, watermarks, and signatures to mark degrees, official transcripts, and other records of educational achievement, but the state's ability to prosecute and incarcerate people who use forged documents underlines private institutions' dependence on it as the guarantor of symbolic credit. Unlike the theft of personal property, in which the criminal's gain is someone else's loss, producing a fake degree is not a zero-sum game. The person who gains a fake certificate does not thereby take away the certificate of someone else; the action becomes a crime entirely because of its potential impact in devaluing certification as symbolic property.

Counterfeit Writing

Processes of writing that mimic and copy official writing in another register therefore become most important. This is the register of the fake, the forged, and the counterfeit. The chief argument I develop here is that the counterfeit is not to the authentic as the copy is to the original. Not every original work of art or fiction begets a copy. By contrast, every official device that marks a document as authentic begets its shadowy double, the counterfeit. The counterfeit and the authentic are coeval; like Saleem Sinai, the protagonist of *Midnight's Children* (Rushdie 1981), every authentic document brings into the world a shadowy, illegal, and usually subaltern, twin. Forgery, Clanchy (1979:2) reminds us, is probably as old as writing itself.

Forgery is a creative, positive act ("to forge ahead") that challenges the right of the state to authenticate, to adjudicate between the true and the false. Forgery can be a subaltern strategy to undermine the authority of state writing.[20] Perhaps not surprising, its etymology leads back to artisanship, with the same connotations of skill and lower-class location (Radnóti 1999:6). Bourdieu (1996:376) reminds us that the certification or validation of educational degrees is one of the ways in which the state acts as "the central bank of symbolic credit." Whether in the form of currency notes, diplomas, or driver's licenses, the counterfeit challenges this symbolic credit.[21] There is no "originality" in currency notes, which, after all, gain their "currency" by being *exactly* like other notes (with identical watermarks, seals, inserted metal, and signatures) except for their serial number. Mwangi (n.d.:116) points out that fake money differs from real currency in that it is an exact duplicate, with an identical serial number. What makes the copy fake is who authorizes its production, rather than any intrinsic property it might possess. Radnóti (1999:14) observes that "forgery is the democratic satire and parody of the aristocracy of art"; not until the Renaissance was forgery seen to be a moral sin. Even so, forgers have been largely seen as rogues, rascals, and imposters rather than as criminals, and stories about forgers correspondingly stress the picaresque rather than the illegal.[22]

In the case of the programs I studied, it was the "illegibility" of village society in the eyes of state officials that created the conditions for the success of the "duplicate" document (Scott 1998). In the monthly meeting of

Anganwadi Workers at the main office in Mandi, several women talked about *going* to their centers. This suggested that, contrary to official policy, some of them were commuting to their centers and did not actually live in the villages where they worked. The head of the ICDS office was telling me about the difficulties she encountered in determining the residency status of prospective Anganwadi Workers. Proof of residence consisted of getting a "certificate" from the headman testifying to that fact. The result of this policy was that many women managed to obtain certificates for villages where a position of Anganwadi Worker had opened up but where they did not, in fact, live. Headmen would provide such certificates of residence in exchange for cash or as a favor to a relative. Recognizing this problem, a new Government Order had made such certificates of residence harder to obtain. According to the new policy, not only did the headman have to certify that a woman was resident in a village, but so did another, higher official (the *tehsildar*). All that this did, from the standpoint of potential job applicants, was require them to make many additional trips to the tehsildar's office and bribe two officials instead of just one. I found it incomprehensible why the solution to a problem caused by a lack of information about the details of village life (did an applicant actually live in the village that she claimed to be from?) was thought to be resolved best by involving an official *further* removed, institutionally and geographically, from the village.

Thus existed a vigorous trade in the production of "true" documents that was critically mediated by money. The ability to create "authentic" certificates, whether of residence, educational achievement, or physical fitness (for military service), depended on access to money. But money was not enough; one often needed personal connections to get the attention of the relevant official who would agree to produce a fake document at short notice. In this way, symbolic capital (in the form of money) and social capital (in the form of connections and kinship) were tightly linked together.

The counterfeit document flourished in that space of indeterminacy created by the illegibility of rural society in official circles. Even when such information was officially collected, it was not always retrievable, nor could it always be trusted. For example, to figure out whether claims to residency were authentic, it might have been possible to use census data or the information collected to ensure the accuracy of electoral rolls. But such data was not easily available to officials such as the CDPO, and even if it was, that it would have been of much use, given the unreliability of the collection techniques, was unclear. Women and children were especially scarce in the official record, a situation that the ICDS program was quickly changing.

However, this absence of women and children from the official record furnished the background for "duplicate" certification to flourish.

Asha Agrawal was telling me how she checked whether the school certificates that potential job applicants brought to her were genuine. The educational requirements to become an Anganwadi Worker had been recently raised, and even Dalit women now needed at least a junior high school certificate. The problem, according to Asha, was that almost anyone could get a forged certificate from a junior high school and that determining its authenticity was impossible. She was concerned about this. Can a woman with a counterfeit degree shoulder her responsibilities as an Anganwadi Worker? "For if a person is not educated," Asha said, "how is she going to teach others? And how will she understand what she is told?"

As a result, Asha asked all prospective applicants to write out sentences on a sheet of paper and to perform basic arithmetical tasks. She took out a sheet of paper from her purse and showed me the writing samples of eight candidates who had applied in response to a recent advertisement. She was sympathetic to women who complained of being out of practice; despite clear differences in their abilities, she felt that all the candidates met the basic requirements for the job. Of course, this informal test that Asha administered had no official standing, and candidates who would have otherwise passed such a test still had to attach a copy of their junior high school certificates to the application. The fear of forgery, therefore, created its own parallel economy of unofficial procedures employed by officials.

Even if the job applicants whom Asha was screening had completed junior high school as required, it was highly unlikely that they were given a certificate of completion or had managed to preserve it and carry it with them to the village where they moved after marriage.[23] Because such certification was necessary to get the job of Anganwadi Worker, they were likely to obtain a counterfeit document that could be submitted with their application.[24] Thus, the "fake" document attested to an achievement (finishing junior high) that was very likely to be true: what was being forged here was not the underlying property—ability or merit—but the documentary evidence attesting to that ability. Mwangi (n.d.:115) makes an acute observation in this regard when she says, "Forgeries, confusingly, are real until they are not." In other words, only at the moment of unmasking, of the revelation of falsity, does it become a forgery; until then, it functions like the real. In this case, the forgery attested to an ability that was real, so there was no fear that a lack of ability would be "unmasked."

It is often assumed that the counterfeit functions to undermine the legitimacy of state writing. But Das proposes a radically different way to think about forgery. She argues that forgery and mimicry should not be seen as enfeebling the state; rather, they are necessary to the state's legitimacy. Iterability "becomes not a sign of vulnerability but a mode of circulation through which power is produced" (Das 2004:245). She offers examples of community groups and NGOs producing and employing documents that mimic the processes of the Indian state, ironically, often to commute, mitigate, or reverse the ill effects produced by that very state, such as police participation in riots against minorities. Similarly, Tarlo demonstrates how the mimicry of official writing operates in a field where the lines between the unofficial and the official become blurred. Tarlo (2003:74) shows that the Slum Department officially recognized people as "unauthorized occupants," which gave them certain rights belied by the category. In order to be so recognized, the supplicant had to produce papers drafted by an attorney that offered official proof that they had paid for an illegal purchase of the plot in question.

The counterfeit thus shadows the authenticating procedures of the state. While doing fieldwork, I found that the fear of the counterfeit profoundly influenced the mode in which bureaucracies operated. Mr. Malik, the BDO, signed documents with a looping flourish that was more art than signature. He was pleased that it was extremely difficult to copy. He told me very proudly that he had a "special" signature for drawing money from the treasury, which could be executed only by holding a fountain pen at a particular angle and was even more artistic than his normal signature. "This special signature," he boasted, "makes it almost impossible for people to copy [it]."

To the extent that stamp papers, degrees from certified educational institutions, signatures of notaries, government seals, and watermarks authenticate, they create a parallel economy of the inauthentic: the forged and the counterfeit, which constantly threaten, simultaneously, to undermine the authoritativeness of state writing and to multiply its effects and effectiveness. From their vantage point, officials were habituated to see this parallel, and often subaltern, economy as a threat to the value of official writing. Therefore, the search for ever-more elaborate strategies of authentication, whether these took the form of informal (and, strictly speaking, illegal) tests or consciously elaborated signatures (which functioned in the same manner as the elaborately carved calligraphic seals described by Messick [1993:241–246]). Such strategies of inscription acknowledged the ambivalent authority of state writing. From the perspective of subaltern peoples, "duplicate" certificates were merely ways to circumvent the arbitrariness of state procedures. Counterfeiting was one more device in a series of measures that enabled subaltern resistance to bureaucratic domination. Educating children and participating in the political system to influence people and programs were other strategies effectively employed at the same time.

CONCLUSION

This chapter complicates a straightforward narrative of literate bureaucrats dominating a hapless and illiterate peasantry. It is true that the Indian bureaucracy places an inordinate emphasis on the written word. In the context of widespread rural illiteracy, such an emphasis appears excessive and can only reinforce the suspicion that it is in place *because* it enables bureaucrats to control their rural subjects and clients more easily. However, it is useful to reconsider carefully the role of literacy in domination in the Indian context.

I have argued that this narrative of "literacy as domination" presumes the inherent superiority of written modes of communication over oral ones. In such a view, written procedure is essential to institutions such as bureaucracies because written documents better preserve and record events and actions, transmit meanings in a more stable and reliable manner across time and space, are less liable to corruption and contradiction, and, in general, are less prone to interpretive error and play. But to what extent are these purported "properties" of the written defensible? Are such evaluations of the superiority of the written word not the outcome of a teleological view of history, in which societies gradually move from illiteracy to full literacy, from barbarism to civilization, from primitive to modern? Taking the example of societies in which restricted literacy has always been the norm, can we reconsider the relationship between the oral and the written such that the first is not merely an inferior version of the second?

Villagers, in fact, contested the power of literate bureaucrats in a number of ways that were not mutually exclusive. First, almost all poor villagers were extremely keen that their children learn to read and write so that they would be better able to negotiate the world of bureaucratic institutions and perhaps even obtain a government job. Second, participation in the political sphere, facilitated by the new possibilities unleashed by televisual and telecommunication technologies, enabled subaltern rural peoples to put pressure on recalcitrant bureaucracies to act in their favor. Finally, when all else failed, there was always the recourse to mimic state writing by producing counterfeit certificates and affidavits in order to receive benefits and services. The emphasis on writing by bureaucracies was combated by mimicry, subversion, and counterdomination through the political process.

Notes

1. Notable exceptions are Goody 1968, 1986, and Messick 1993.

2. Tarlo (2003:77–79) reports, for instance, that the illiterate and semiliterate people who filed petitions with the Slum Department did so in an archaic English, with the mediation of professional letter writers.

3. Tarlo (2003:75) goes on to say: "For 'paper truths,' despite their flimsiness and elasticity, despite their potential to be forged or destroyed, none the less have authority, belonging as they do to the world of the modern state where the written word reigns supreme."

4. I am not suggesting that such a process will result in greater access or justice, but it places the onus of responsibility onto officials. Das has convincingly demonstrated that when state officials are complicit in perpetrating violence on citizens or exploiting clients, such a process hides as much as it reveals. For instance, riot victims who came to report crimes against them were forced to include a formulaic paragraph framing their complaint in a way that mitigated the act of violence (Das 2004:227–229).

5. This practice does not differ much from that of the Islamic courts in Yemen described by Messick (1993:209), where oral testimony lay at the center of court processes, which otherwise relied heavily on the written word.

6. As we shall see, the charge of "logocentrism" or "phonocentrism" makes more than a little sense here. The motif of presence, the metaphysics of presence, as authorizing the "truth" of oral testimony is central and does, in fact, trace directly to the Greek sources that Derrida critiques in *Of Grammatology* (1976). Speech is seen as offering an unmediated, or less mediated, access to truth.

7. I put these terms in quotes to indicate the difficulty and insufficiency of translating *sharia'* into either of these categories.

8. I am using the term *prejudice* here not in its colloquial sense, but in its literal meaning as "prejudgment."

9. Given that email is written, one would have expected the opposite response, namely, that what may be forgotten or misrepresented in speech can be set down unambiguously in writing. Indeed, sometimes people do take this position, but it is surprising how often the skepticism of writing in this context hinges on the uncertainty of whether the reader's interpretation will follow the writer's intent.

10. For example, speech is broken down into five stages, of which the first three are "internal" to the speaker and have no shape in the form of words or sentences.

11. I am grateful to Raka Ray for bringing this point to my attention.

12. Other justifications of fiction's pedagogic functions include the following: it allows one to travel to other places without leaving home; it allows empathy for people

whose life situations one might not otherwise share; in the case of historical novels, it allows one to experience history "from the inside" in all its immediacy; and, finally, it allows one to think about and resolve moral dilemmas in one's own life through vicarious participation in someone else's life.

13. Kaviraj (2003:157) claims that "the electorate at the last election under colonial administration was about 14 percent of the adult population."

14. If we were to subtract the urban literate from this number, the rates of literacy would be even lower. The majority of the population lived in the countryside, and in 1950 the overwhelming proportion of this population was illiterate.

15. I am grateful to Saba Mahmood and Anjali Arondekar for suggesting these points to me.

16. Kaviraj (2003) calls it a "minimal" interpretation of democracy and contrasts it to an "expansive" interpretation.

17. It might appear paradoxical to state that dignity is pursued through the quest for government jobs, which are about redressing income inequality as much as anything else. However, at least at lower levels in the hierarchy, government jobs carry a special, high status that jobs in private corporations do not.

18. In this context, we should not forget that the state is the largest employer in the formal sector. Therefore, a state position did not just mean the chance for a secure, (relatively) prestigious career: it often represented the only avenue for a decent job. Alternative sources of employment in the formal, organized sector of the economy (private corporations) were small, and self-employment or a job in the informal sector gave much smaller monetary rewards and correspondingly higher risks.

19. I am thinking, for example, of the "Rath Yatra" led by the leader of the BJP, L. K. Advani. The spectacle of riding in a replica of a chariot (*rath*) to Ayodhya was made for television and resulted in the incendiary events that led to the destruction of the Babri Masjid in 1992.

20. It can also be a strategy used by an underground parallel government such as a resistance movement, an independence movement, or the Mafia.

21. See the wonderful discussion of counterfeit money in the context of colonial Africa in Mwangi n.d.

22. For a fuller discussion, see Radnóti 1999:9–12.

23. Because all marriages in this area were exogamous, women's homes after marriage were always in a different place from where they grew up and went to junior high school.

24. In this case, one might ask why they did not just get a certificate from their junior high school. The difficulties of such a task cannot be underestimated: the place could have been far away from their new homes, and the journey hard to make at

short notice (women could not travel alone); the junior high school was unlikely to have preserved older records; even if such records existed, officials in the junior high school were unlikely to take the trouble to dig them up and, in any case, would have been happy to produce a certificate in exchange for money. It was therefore simpler, cheaper, and more efficient to have such a document produced locally.

8

Fractured Discourse

Rethinking the Discursivity of States

Carol J. Greenhouse

This chapter is about discursive manipulation in the Bush administration's political buildup to war. Its source material is drawn entirely from public documents. Viewed from the United States, the normalization of the war on terror poses steep challenges for an anthropology of democracy. Some are ethnographic: within the federal government, the sustained state of emergency after the attacks of September 11, 2001, was a fast-moving front, realigning and restructuring political institutions, indeed, political space itself. In the aftermath of September 2001, executive orders and congressional action in deference to the White House yielded significant retrenchments on the rights of the subjects of searches, detainees and the criminally accused, civil and criminal rules of evidence and procedure, immigration rules and border controls, separation of powers among the branches of federal government, and the relationship of the United States to transnational legal institutions such as the United Nations and the International Criminal Court, among other developments.[1] In the first year after the attacks, key legal landmarks—the Military Order of November 13, 2001, the USA PATRIOT Act (October 26, 2001), the National Security Strategy (September 20, 2002), and the White House's campaign for advance authorization by Congress for presidential use of force in Iraq (culminating in congressional passage on October 11, 2002)—were responses to the new state of affairs, elaborate assertions of presidential control over a wide range of federal powers. Yet at the same time, they were constitutive of it, stagings for a serial trade-off between security and civil liberty, widely proclaimed as necessary in a milieu now described axiomatically as new.

Some of the post-9/11 legal and administrative reforms were novel (for example, the creation of the Department of Homeland Security and new lines of communication between the FBI and the CIA), but others (including the ones just mentioned) were not. Beneath the obvious currency of developments were long-standing conservative commitments to expanded presidential power, as well as specific types of law reform (promoting deregulation, privatization, curtailment of federal unions, wider investigatory and prosecutorial powers in law enforcement, and loosening rules of evidence in criminal trials, among other issues). These were revivals of old partisan debates that, for the most part, liberals had won a generation before—gains now, to some extent, trumped in the name of security.

Meanwhile, throughout that uneasy era simultaneously strange and familiar, united and partisan, the case for war in Iraq was both a driver and an outcome. The most vivid example (discussed below) was the president's request for advance authorization for use of military force in Iraq in fall 2002 (just before the midterm elections), supported by some advocates as a diplomatic tool against war and by others as a prologue to war itself. In this and other respects, an adequate narrative of the eighteen months between the attacks in the United States in 2001 and the beginning of the war in Iraq in 2003 would defy any conventional notion of historical chronology or political process. Many of the key developments were both cause and effect, absorbing (if not wholly dissolving) partisan antagonism.[2] Detemporalization (the suspension of chronological processing) and depoliticization (the implosion of political debate) are just some of the ethnographic challenges of those events, even leaving aside logistical questions such as confidentiality, secrecy, and access.

For anthropological students of democracy who were—are—engaged by these developments, the challenges are also ethical. The prevailing rhetoric of *response*, as well as the official nostalgia for *before*, politicized memory and rescripted hope as endorsement. In relation to the purposes of this volume, the glare of events (recalled even now, in 2007) made—makes (tenses become political acts)—plainly visible the difficulty of cleaving simultaneously to one's hopes for democracy as a political check on this president's immediate power claims and one's hopes for an *anthropology* of democracy in more general terms yet without relativizing or universalizing democracy's form, content, or functional value. From this stand-point, it is not an option to resolve these contradictory commitments by a double standard, proclaiming ourselves citizens at home and scientists abroad. The relevance of states and national borders to an anthropology of democracy, let alone the personal sense of belonging, is by no means a pri-ori clear (not to speak of the fact that many anthropologists work "at home"). On the one hand, if there is no theoretical relevance to the war on terror for anthropologists concerned with democracy, then this would mean that it was normal, within the ambit of what we already knew and understood. On the other hand, if it exceeded the normal and there is no room to register the shock in theoretical terms, then theorizing would be consigned to indifference. "A choice among ultimate commitments cannot be made with the tools of science" (Weber 1978:1381). Still, for those who would not willingly let go of either sort of hope, there is no choice but to embrace the difficulty, that is, to act on both forms of hope at once. There might be many such responses in that spirit. One is to acknowledge the shock of events as legitimate knowledge, that is, as a prompt for theoretical and critical inquiry (Greenhouse 2002). Such a response neither escapes nor trivializes (as one skeptical reviewer put it) the scale and grave stakes of circumstances but defends the mutual productivity of both forms of engagement even in times of crisis.[3]

In what follows, I focus especially on the buildup to the war in Iraq dur-ing the long winter of 2002–2003. As an anthropologist primarily interested in the cultural and political dimensions of federal power in the United States, I choose this interval because it was a sustained period of maximum tension over presidential powers and one in which dissent, though in-tensely expressed in many private quarters, barely registered in the public square. To blame the media for missing or misrepresenting that part of the story is, I believe, simplistic.[4] Rather, the situation invites the question of why the discourse of war occupied the field so totally, without any evident sense of necessity to defend itself against its most vigorous opponents.

My thesis is that the administration's success was due, in part, to adroit handling in that the question of war never, technically, arose. The issue came to the US public (and the world community) in the form of questions overtly having to do with shaping a diplomatic strategy for the conduct of weapons inspections for nuclear and other weapons of mass destruction (WMD) in Iraq by the United Nations and the coordination of US policy in relation to that diplomatic effort. This situation points to a theoretical question—arising from the war but, having arisen, not limited to those circumstances—about how discourse works between states and citizens.

To conceptualize *discourse* as if it involves a dialogic exchange between states and citizens is misleading, as I argue below. The widespread lament that "the White House isn't listening" reflects classical state theory, which posits state and society as two sides of a conversation. Such a construction of the political process tended to suppress dissent in the buildup to war, or so it seemed anecdotally. Be that as it may, imagining political agency as a conversation with the state as interlocutor can only be a fantasy. Rather, the political agency of conversation lies in the self-expression of actual communities (face-to-face or virtual), sustaining their claims to discourse as their own. In what follows, I refer to *discursive fracture* as a name for the way powerful actors control the significance of opposition through their active management of discourse by means of selective appropriation and recomposition. But the oppositional force of such claims is never guaranteed; it is contingent on the nature and circumstances of response. Conversation can be an antidote to such hegemonic reworkings. Later, I explain these terms more fully but for now (in the spirit of this prologue) flag the extent to which an understanding of discursive fracture in theory supports a pragmatic challenge to the administration's master narrative of popular consensus for war. The broadest connection to each of the other chapters in this collection is in our respective emphasis on localized forms of sociability and self-expression as the ethnographic ground for an anthropology of democracy.

DISCURSIVE FRACTURE AND THE CASE FOR WAR

In the United States, the Bush administration's case for war in Iraq threaded through a series of rhetorical maneuvers, most obviously for public consumption but also for audiences within the administration itself. As we shall see, through successive redefinitions of what was most compelling in the brief for war, the White House was able to co-opt, interrupt, and redirect opposition, permitting the president and his circle to profit politically from antagonisms even when these could not be reconciled. The Bush administration has been particularly and consistently adept at appropriating moral discourse from communities whose collective self-identity is outside the US state—notably, at this time, fundamentalist Christians, but also dissident Iraqis—in the interests of justifying the creation of a privileged zone of executive legality within the government.

Making opposition moot (but not mute) was crucial to the appearance of a consensus for war. Paradoxically, perhaps, *unity* as such is a potential encumbrance to the extent that it makes external claims on legitimacy that may prove difficult to control; an actor committed to maximum prerogative has more room for maneuvering in a context in which opposition can be fragmented and then selectively neutralized. Still, the *appearance of unity* is obviously a political asset to a chief executive. We find the makings of discursive fracture in such scenarios, that is, where the political value of apparent consensus exceeds the expediency of consensus in fact. The conditions for discursive fracture are ripe wherever conflict, secrecy, or other technologies of communicative control—including access to the media, official protocol, and restrictions on access—make it possible to control the representation and significance of opposition.

The scaffolding of events leading up to war in 2002–2003 involved four main elements, in the form of major political tests involving, respectively, the United Nations, the US Congress, the US midterm elections, and the mobilization of an international coalition in support of the war. These elements lapped one another in a braided chronology of events.

From early September 2002, the administration pressed the Security Council to resolve on a military option in the face of Saddam Hussein's response to the weapons inspection program. The president addressed the General Assembly on September 12, 2002. On September 19, the administration sent a bill to Congress requesting advance authorization to the president for use of military force in Iraq. On September 20, the White House issued the National Security Strategy, outlining the rationale for preemptive war in response to terrorism. The advance authorization bill passed on October 11, 2002. The elections returned a Republican majority to the Congress on November 8, 2002. After the elections, the main public theater shifted to the United Nations, where France led the opposition to the US initiative. After a series of final ultimatums to Saddam Hussein, the coalition went to war on March 19, 2003.

The inconsistency of the administration's case for war was critical to preempting opposition from those who were unconvinced by any single rationale. The end result was that the week before the war began, a *New York Times*/CBS poll found that more Americans supported the war than endorsed any one of the principal rationales. For example, 55 percent supported the war, and 58 percent believed that the United Nations "was doing a poor job." Yet a majority preferred continuation of the weapons inspection program. Most believed that the desire for regime change motivated the president (Nagourney and Elder 2003).[5] It should be noted, too, that the public case for war succeeded in mobilizing those who would have opposed the war on any single ground, leaving those who opposed the war on *any* grounds essentially without recognition in the field of political discourse. To compromise on *that* ground was to lose out altogether, because any middle ground could be swept up and incorporated into the administration's position.

In fall 2002, public debate over the war—as made accessible through the media—was taking place mainly in Congress, the Security Council, and outside the United States. Public anti-war protests came to the US national news initially in the context of reporting a worldwide day of protest on February 15, 2003. Marches, vigils, and other protest action continued through the start of the war (for example, see *New York Times* coverage on February 16 and March 21, 2003). One indication of the displacement of protest is that the protests in New York at the start of the war were covered in a news story under the rubric "Foreign News" (Tagliabue 2003). But protest quickly became a metropolitan story. More than ninety city councils across the country adopted anti-war resolutions (Olson 2003; Whitaker 2003). At the national level, there were no resignations from the president's cabinet. Three ministers resigned from the Blair cabinet during the weeks immediately preceding the war, and, notwithstanding strong opposition from Labor, Blair survived two parliamentary votes on the war, with the majority of his own party intact (Cowell 2003b; Hoge 2003).

Within the Bush administration, the buildup to war involved a series of overlapping moves and counter-moves in which divisions internal to the "group of principals" (that is, cabinet-level officials) appear to have sought to engage or preempt one another, playing for time with leaks to the press, diplomatic bargains, and serial attempts at persuasion. In this sort of economy of political energy, the multiplication of opposition is a more expedient tactic of control than persuasion or compromise. Within the administration, fundamental debate over objectives and strategy appears to have taken place only indirectly, as discussion about the public's likely tolerance for war (Woodward 2004). The policy-making core—that is, the conversational core—of the administration appears to have been strikingly small and, at that, meeting only rarely as a group for sustained discussion on any single issue. Under these circumstances, sequencing of meetings and selective access to the president became forms of co-optation and silencing.

In the long period of buildup, there was never any one discourse of war, but rather a highly fractured process during which elemental rationales—about WMD, terrorism, and tyranny—moved on and off the table as gambits or responses aimed at different sectors of domestic and international communities. During the fall and winter of 2002–2003, war proponents pressed the case in terms of three main claims: (1) Saddam Hussein had (or intended to create) a program for the development of WMD; (2)

he had ties to Al Qaeda cells, perhaps even the ones that carried out the attacks of September 11, 2001; and (3) he was a murderous oppressor of the Kurds and the Iraqi people.

These rationales moved in and out of top billing, and, with them, the spotlight on key arenas. For example, President Bush led with the WMD claims in his speech before the UN General Assembly on September 12, 2002, seeking a Security Council resolution against Iraq (Sanger and Bumiller 2002). In a televised address to the nation on October 7, 2002, he led with terrorism in publicizing his request to Congress for advance authorization to use military force if it proved "necessary, to enforce UN Security Council demands." Explaining the advance authorization bill then before Congress, he emphasized regime change:

> Approving this resolution does not mean that military action is imminent or unavoidable. The resolution will tell the United Nations and all nations that America speaks with one voice and is determined to make the demands of the civilized world mean something. Congress will also be sending a message to the dictator in Iraq that his only chance—his only choice—is full compliance. And the time remaining for that choice is limited. [The White House 2002b]

The moral argument for war, cast as the liberation of Iraqis from oppression, harmonized with prime minister Tony Blair's principal argument to Parliament and the British public. "Ridding the world of Saddam would be an act of humanity," Blair said, "It is leaving him there that is in truth inhumane" (Cowell 2003a). The moral argument for regime change appears to have been crucial to marshalling the support of US constituencies unconvinced (or unmoved) by the arguments based on WMD and terrorism (Nagourney and Elder 2003). The moral argument also contributed to an image of President Bush as convinced beyond compromise or reassessment, an image reinforced by his own comments regarding his prayerful resolve and personal sense of leadership (Sanger and Barringer 2003). The image of the president as morally resolute was inseparable from his political role in the pre-war context yet simultaneously—key to the discursive fracture of the moment—cast as the opposite of politics. Asked by a reporter for a response to massive anti-war demonstrations around the world in mid-February, President Bush responded: "Size of protest—it's like deciding, well, I'm going to decide policy based upon a focus group.... The role of a leader is to decide policy based upon the security, in this case, the security of the people" (Stevenson 2003). Earlier, he seemed to take a similar stance, casting opposition at the United Nations as a technical impediment rather than a substantive challenge in the context of pressing the Security Council to a vote so as to force the issue (in the president's phrase) "to come to a head" (Sanger and Barringer 2003:A1; see also Nagourney and Elder 2003).

While making the case variously but unambiguously, the language of the administration's claims respected the technicalities of uncertainty. For example, in President Bush's address to the General Assembly, he made the case in terms of anti-terrorism without linking Saddam Hussein directly to Al Qaeda:

> The entire world has witnessed Iraq's 11-year history of defiance, deception and bad faith. We must also never forget the most vivid events of recent history. On Sept. 11, 2001, America felt its vulnerability even to threats that gather on the other side of the earth. We resolved then and we are resolved today to confront every threat from any source that could bring sudden terror and suffering to America. [The White House 2002a]

Even so, language occasionally became the focus of sustained interpretive disputes as speakers wrestled the precision of their words away from rereading by the press or critics inclined to find ordinary meanings in terms that had acquired special cachet. For example, the idiom of "gathering threat" (in wide use by White House staff in 2002–2003) and President Bush's 2003 State of the Union reference to what turned out to be erroneous British intelligence data yielded extensive debates and competition over implications and allowable inferences of particular words. Such forced lapses in ordinary language via assertions of control over meaning are integral to the process of discursive fracture.

The administration was highly successful in achieving a political and diplomatic process that guaranteed the eventuality of war. As noted above, the administration's doctrine of preemptive war won the support of Congress on October 11, 2002.[6] The United Nations' weapons inspection process and related Security Council resolutions enabled the administration to talk openly, while maintaining a public commitment to diplomacy, about the prospect of imminent war on the international stage (for example, Vice President Cheney in his negotiations with the Turkish administration beginning in September 2002 [Washington Institute 2004]). Indeed, the administration was adept at detemporalizing war, bracketing it outside the scope of both international law and domestic law processes. All the threats were hypothetical, cast as future possibilities. All the contingencies that might deflect war were assigned to Saddam Hussein. The relevance of time was always negative; it was always either running out or gone. The detemporalization of war was integral to its depoliticization. The administration focused debate on presidential *powers* rather than on specific *policies*, making the war, in effect, a technical legal question instead of a matter of overt political debate. The congressional debate over the president's request for advance authorization to use military force in Iraq reflected this effect. Indeed, the most fundamental case for advance authorization was the president's claim that "if you want to keep the peace, you've got to have the authorization to use force" (Purdum and Bumiller 2002). Debate in Congress and in the Security Council rested on hypotheticals (Saddam Hussein's intentions) and unknowns, undermining the possibility of a debate on factual grounds. For example, Senator John Kerry (D-Massachusetts) rejected regime change as an end in itself but justified his support for the resolution in the interest of debilitating Hussein's alleged weapons program (*New York Times* 2002).

The multistrandedness and flexibility of the rationales for military intervention constitute part of the long history of the Iraq campaign— effectively combining advocates for war and, at the same time, dividing the war's opponents by presenting them with rationales that crosscut conventional partisan divisions (security, economic liberalization, and democratization of the Middle East). President Bush's consistently moralizing rhetoric (for example, his references to "evil ones" and "the axis of evil") trumped these discursive distinctions by containing them under one broad rhetorical umbrella.[7] In the end, the official logo for the war was "Operation Iraqi Freedom." It is important to remember, however, that as a matter of public relations the moral argument was initially secondary to other rationales aimed at other audiences. The line of argument concerning WMD was aimed at neutralizing UN opposition to war, repeatedly asserting claims that the weapons inspections process led by Hans Blix had not proved the absence of WMD. The argument concerning Hussein's links to terrorism was especially potent in mobilizing the US public behind the war policy. The argument for regime change echoed precisely the language of the influential neoconservative group Project for a New American Century (discussed below). The president's moral language, constituted as a language above politics, rendered each of these planks subordinate to the larger agenda and the performance of discursive unity it entailed.

The multiplication and strategic control of rationales, arenas, and their associated time frames did not preclude opposition or dissent but sustained a scenario in which opposition on any single issue could be contained or set aside without losing forward momentum along other lines. In the buildup to war in 2002 and 2003, discursive fracture became both a tactic and an effect of the administration's energetic quest for maximum presidential prerogative. The development of war as policy did not emerge from a coherent *discourse* in favor of war, but rather from the war proponents' agility in fracturing the discourse of their opposition inside and outside the government—within the administration, within its closest circles in the private sector, between the United States and countries in Europe and the Middle East, and among key non-state constituencies (including the Iraqi opposition, notably Ahmed Chalabi's Iraqi National Congress).

MISSING CONVERSATIONS, CONTROLLING CONTINGENCIES

Notwithstanding the force these arguments might have had among the public, there is no evidence that they circulated within the White House as rationales for war. Subsequent published accounts and interviews with administration officials suggest that the administration's internal conversations were about strategies and plans on military, diplomatic, and political fronts (Clarke 2004; Suskind 2004; Woodward 2004). Within the White House, according to journalist Bob Woodward's account, in 2001 the president requested plans of operations for an Iraq invasion, long before the case for war became an issue for public address by the White House. Such contingency planning and updating of battle plans are routine; even the principals who produce such plans do not necessarily know whether these are hypothetical or actual. Richard Clarke's (2004) book details the history of such contingency planning with respect to Al Qaeda as he knew it from his years of service in the National Security Adviser's office in the White House, especially during the Clinton and George W. Bush years. With respect to Iraq, Clarke's account parallels that of former treasury secretary Paul H. O'Neill, who reports that, from the very earliest days of the Bush administration, regime change in Iraq was understood to be an objective yet there was "no real questioning of why Mr. Hussein had to go or why it had to be done then" (Stevenson 2004). Such circumstances are reminders that no automatic equation exists between personal participation "on the inside" and individual political agency.

Whatever the chronology of decision making, it is clear that by fall 2002 the public case for war was a redirection of an internal administration debate that was already moot. The *object* of the public debate was the war policy, but its *functions* were political in the conventional sense of partisan electoral competition. The rationales for war (as we have seen) were keyed hermeneutically (that is, iconically) to the main constituencies within the United States (fundamentalists, neoconservatives, and neoliberals, among others), as well as outside (Tony Blair and other potential coalition partners).

The buildup to war spanned the midterm elections (November 8, 2002). As the elections approached, the president increasingly adopted the language of moral conviction, conspicuously distancing himself from the force of public debate. This did not obviate his active participation in the interpretation of that debate; he sought to anchor its key terms in his own administration's position. In the fall, he pressed for advance authorization to use military force on the grounds that doing so would give essential support to the international diplomatic effort. Later, however, in his address to the nation on March 7, 2003, President Bush reinterpreted that vote, post facto designating the election as a referendum on the war itself: "What we're inviting people to do is come to the conclusions that they voted for on the 8th of November" (Sanger and Barringer 2003). Democrats were more divided over the war than were Republicans, and open dissent itself became a sign of partisanship—and a partisan political issue (Firestone 2003; Nagourney 2003). This is but one example of a larger point about how discursive fracture works. The means and ends of discursive fracture flourish in democratic institutions as strategic actors invite debate on controversial questions and subsequently appropriate and recombine discursive elements to counter their oppositional force.

Although the administration's case for war emphasized the war against terrorism, the policy decisions committing the United States to contributing military aid to the Iraqi opposition had already been made during the Clinton administration by Congress and the president. The earliest public proponents of the current US campaign in Iraq were a neoconservative group formed in 1997, self-designated as the Project for the New American Century (PNAC).[8] On January 26, 1998, PNAC representatives wrote a public letter to President Clinton, urging him to commit the United States to regime change in Iraq. Their argument focused on Saddam Hussein's capacity to produce and—sometime in the unspecified future—deliver weapons of mass destruction. The letter concluded: "In the long term, it means removing Saddam Hussein and his regime from power. That now needs to become the aim of American foreign policy" (PNAC 1998a).[9] A few months later, the same group wrote to House speaker Newt Gingrich (R-Georgia) and Senate majority leader Trent Lott (R-Mississippi) in similar terms, but this time emphasizing a latent democracy movement in Iraq awaiting American agency for its full realization: "Only the US can lead the way in demonstrating that his rule is not legitimate and that time is not on the side of his regime" (PNAC 1998b).[10]

Subsequently, Congress passed three laws important in the cause of regime change in Iraq: on May 1, 1998, $5 million were dedicated to the Iraqi opposition (Public Law 105-174); on August 14, 1998, Saddam Hussein was declared in material breach of UN resolutions regarding weapons inspection (Public Law 105-235); and on October 31, 1998, the Iraq Liberation Act (Public Law 105-338) authorized $97 million to support the transfer of military equipment to Iraqi opposition groups. Congress passed this legislation with bipartisan support, and President Clinton—impeachment looming—signed the bills into law.[11] In the text of the Iraq Liberation Act, the sense of the Congress is phrased in terms precisely parallel to the PNAC letter: "It should be the policy of the United States to support efforts to remove the regime headed by Saddam Hussein from power in Iraq and to promote the emergence of a democratic government to replace that regime" (Congress 1998).[12] President Clinton signed the bill into law, but he did not spend the money. That did not happen until December 2002, when President Bush authorized a drawdown of $92 million on behalf of six Iraqi opposition groups (The White House 2002c).

Within the Bush administration, vice president Dick Cheney and assistant secretary of defense Paul Wolfowitz—charter members of PNAC—became the leading advocates for war (for example, see Woodward 2004:21, 175). The spate of books on the Bush administration in 2004 presents diverse assessments of where and when the war became policy, as opposed to a tactical threat aimed at securing Saddam Hussein's cooperation with weapons inspectors or galvanizing Iraqi dissidents. Bob Woodward (2004:1) begins his account on November 21, 2001, but Richard Clarke puts the date earlier, recalling Secretary of Defense Rumsfeld and Wolfowitz linking Al Qaeda to Saddam Hussein in the hours immediately following the attacks of September 11, 2001 (Woodward 2004:30–31).

The PNAC documents are evidence that at least some key officials *entered* the administration already convinced that the war was necessary, even if the US role was initially envisioned as a commitment of funds and matériel, not troops on the ground. Direct US military involvement was quickly added to the PNAC agenda after the attacks of September 11, 2001. Just a few days later, on September 20, 2001, PNAC renewed its campaign, writing to President Bush:

> Even if evidence does not link Iraq directly to the attack, any
> strategy aiming at the eradication of terrorism and its sponsors

must include a determined effort to remove Saddam Hussein from power in Iraq. Failure to undertake such an effort will constitute an early and perhaps decisive surrender in the war on international terrorism. The United States must therefore provide full military and financial support to the Iraqi opposition. American military force should be used to provide a "safe zone" in Iraq from which the opposition can operate. And American forces must be prepared to back up our commitment to the Iraqi opposition by all necessary means. [PNAC 2001]

By September 2001, then, Iraq had already been the target of massive investment (literally and figuratively) from multiple locations inside and outside the administration, during the Clinton interregnum and after the George W. Bush administration came to power in 2001. In this sense, the war in Iraq was arguably a project of the private sector—Cheney and Wolfowitz *as private citizens* mobilized PNAC. A private public relations firm under contract to the CIA, the Rendon Group, meanwhile advised and funded Ahmed Chalabi and his dissident group (Foer 2002; Hersh 2002; Mayer 2004). The war shifted into the public sector with the transfer of key personnel from the private sector into the Bush administration in early 2001.

Even this thin history of the buildup to war underscores the vulnerability of public discourse (that is, in public arenas) to fracture, displacement, and recomposition, as well as the contingencies of social hierarchy that make participation in the production of discourse a specialized index of power and privileged social access.[13]

RETHINKING DISCOURSE

In the United States, as well as on the home fronts of the main coalition countries, the war on terror has involved a massive depoliticization of national government—literally, a withdrawal of issues from the political process—revealing the imbrication of the national executives not only with one another's political objectives and institutions but also with powerful elements of the transnational private sector relatively sheltered from the risks of scandal. In this sense, the war on terror has intensified and streamlined the conditions of "democracy deficit" already prevalent within the administrative state (see Aman 2004). In this sense, too, the war on terror is both anomalous and normal, the very possibility suggesting the limitations of remembered assumptions (from "before") about the social character of states.

The social character of the state is classically a question directed at the civil service, especially the question of whose interests it serves. The question Marx and Weber urge upon us asks what the people who work in the state's name actually do, in real time.[14] But the very question points to a vein of irrationality within the state, *irrationality* in the Weberian sense of multiple regimes of authority (for example, personal and bureaucratic) and value (for example, legal and moral) operating simultaneously. For Marx (1975[1843]), governmental bureaucracy sustains a fantasy association of the state with the people, allowing special interests to rule through the state in their name. For Weber, it is the bureaucrat's personal, even erotic, identification with power that compromises his (masculine, for Weber) ability to act "sine ira et studio, without hate and without love... [and] as closely as possible in accordance with the rational regulations of the modern power system" (Weber 1978:600).

These lines of analysis put state bureaucrats on different sides of the question of whom the state serves. This difference (and the stakes in it) is sharpened by the modern retheorizings of bureaucracy in the aftermath of the Holocaust. The two leading theorists of that turn, Hannah Arendt and Zygmunt Bauman, ask the classic question in the negative: how is it that a state bureaucracy can work against the very lives of citizens, authorizing and administering a program of mass violence? Both make this into a question of personal agency within state bureaucracies. For Arendt, personal agency is a question of moral philosophy. For Bauman, it is a question of organizational sociology and modern bureaucratic rationality.

"The present-day significance of the Holocaust" (Bauman 1989:207) is in the ongoing relevance of a critique of that aspect of a hierarchical "bureaucratic culture" that suppresses the "moral significance" of violence. It does so by separating acts from their consequences in the course of the routine division of labor, that is, by attenuating moral debate in the social distances inherent in bureaucratic organization (Bauman 1989:18, 25). For Hannah Arendt, individuals, no matter what they are systematically asked to do or cannot refuse to do, remain ultimately and personally responsible for their actions. The "dehumanization" of the bureaucratic actor—"the essence of bureaucracy and its inevitable tendency to make functionaries of men, mere cogs in the administrative machinery" (Arendt 2003:58)—should not be seen as the cause of the wholesale evasion of personal moral responsibility that normalizes the unthinkable as daily administrative routine. Rather, she argues, it is the failure to think. For Arendt (2003:98ff), thinking is a function of an inner narrative that situates the individual amidst others, in a social nexus at once imaginative, ethical, and political.

These lines of argument point to a horizon where collective well-being is contingent on particular qualities of discourse within state agencies— qualities of discourse specifically linked to conversation. It is *conversation* that yields the form and content of inner narrative; in conversation, that discourse yields occasions for ethical choice and individual action (through debate, consent, refusal); in conversation, civil servants retain or renounce their attitudes and identifications, contributing or withholding, obeying or refusing, expressing or reserving doubts. In short, conversation makes individuals "morally accessible" (Cavell 1976:23) in their capacity as agents of the state.[15]

Pursuing the connections between conversation and thinking means asking how these forms of social exchange circulate through the state. *Governmentality* would seem to be one response to this question. Foucault offers this term to emphasize the contiguity of "juridical state power" and "disciplinary power," that is, the power effects of knowledge construction (Santos 1995:3–4, 405), primarily through a mutual (if asymmetrical) process of reception (see Foucault 1978, 1980: chs. 5, 10). Viewed from one side, within Foucault's concept of governmentality looms a limitless field for state power through discourse, given the infinite recombinant quality of discourse after it is unhooked from accountability to the moral or political community of which it is the sign. Viewed from the other side, knowledge relations—and the power of conversation—are constrained and constraining, if only because they are held accountable to organic social relations by social conventions of authority, form, and content. Conversation is inherently subject to external checks, in other words, in a way that discourse is not. To be sure, conversation is not immune to manipulation; however, even under such circumstances, the other party remains relevant, even necessary. This is not the case in the tactical situations I refer to as discursive fracture, because once the key terms are in circulation, the other party becomes, at best, redundant. In this sense, discourse and conversation involve substantially different accounts of power.

Foucault (1980:97) stipulates that state power is not a question of the sovereign's intentions, but of how intentions come to be "invested in...real and effective practices."[16] He looks for the sovereign's effects in the constitution of subjects through their bodies, as objects of punishment, discipline, gaze, diagnosis, treatment, and myriad forms of control. Accordingly, Foucault envisions the "ascent" (his metaphor) of power as arising from the "infinitesimal mechanisms" of the body in a social field:

> Between every point of a social body, between a man and a
> woman, between the members of a family, between a master and

> his pupil, between every one who knows and every one who does not, there exist relations of power which are not purely and simply a projection of the sovereign's great power over the individual; they are rather the concrete, changing soil in which the sovereign's power is grounded, the conditions which make it possible to function. [Foucault 1980:187]

But indifference is also a relation, marking the locations where the sovereign is exempt from the obligation to converse and therefore from the constraints of substantive social exchange. From this perspective, the state is perhaps not the external visage of power, but a Dali-esque carapace protecting a hidden mouth and a sensitive inner ear. *Discursive fracture* helps clarify the protean specificity of states in relation to the ways state agencies and processes are discursively bound to "the people," as well as the critical difference (and distance) between "the people" in that sense and the milieus in which actual people join in common purpose.

To say that state power is *discursive* is not to suggest that it is only symbolic or superficially textual. One implication of the discussion in this section is that the consolidation of executive power is for its own sake, not subject to social motivations in the conventional sense. Another implication is that social domination (for example, comprehensive registration requirements for visitors, immigrants, and students)[17] may not be the motivated objective of executive power. Rather, it may be a form of indifference, an artifact of the process of discursive fracture within the registers of bureaucratic communication that vests social control with political value, independent of its functional value in other terms.[18]

DISCURSIVE STATES

The appeal to *conversation* supplements the critical specificity of recent cultural theories of state discursivity. From the mid-1980s through the 1990s, Foucauldian concepts of discourse and governmentality, in a sense, came to replace the state as a theoretical object for cultural theorists concerned with politics (Abrams 1988; Mitchell 1991; Schmitt 1996:19; Weber 1978). A new canon emerged around the interplay of imagination and identity as elements of "stateness."[19] As more recent critical syntheses emphasize, the relevance of the state to social theory, in effect, shifted to its salience as "a" discourse, that is, the *idea* of the state (Alonso 1994; Axel 2002; Hansen and Stepputat 2001; Steinmetz 1999). A theory of discourse helped account for how states are rendered social through language and the interplay of subjective experience among ordinary people in their everyday lives, as well as how states figure in history through collective identities created in these very processes. As formulated by Corrigan and Sayer (1985:180), "the enormous power of 'the State' is not only external and objective; it is in equal part internal and subjective, it works through us.... State formation is cultural revolution."

Corrigan and Sayer's analysis has been influential primarily for what follows the semicolon in the passage just quoted. In retrospect, what comes before is equally important and, even more so for our purposes, the connection between them. Read together, they point to a specific historical window framed by identity politics, on the one hand (especially in terms of race and class), and a rising ideological response antagonistic to the claims of identitarian movements, on the other. By the late 1980s, at least in the United States, the increasingly conservative climate militated against continued state investment in response to the demands of new social movements, for example, in the areas of rights, remedies, welfare, and urban renewal. Instead, the increasingly neoliberal climate retained the strong federal state of the civil rights period, but primarily to assert and extend an anti-rights, anti-regulatory program of reform on the grounds that the national interest compelled a level of agility that only an open market could provide. Jumping to the present, although political rhetoric and public celebrations (such as those associated with electoral politics) might retain strong symbolic links with cultural "communities," the federal government increasingly consigns the management of those connections to specialists in public relations and business brokerage, for example, the Rendon Group and other consultants (Foer 2002; Mayer 2004).

In short, *discourse* and *governmentality* displaced the state as a theoretical object for cultural theorists at the precise historical juncture at which liberalism reached its maximum point of tension within the emergent neoliberal state in the United States (and, in different terms, in the United Kingdom). The ideological commitment to bringing an end to "big government" and state regulation under Reagan and Thatcher made privatization the cornerstone not just of the new economic order but also of a new political and social order in which identity was to be specifically devalued as a basis for collective action and claims making. Although the "state idea" may be inseparable from contemporary practices of collective self-identity, the state does not reciprocate this gesture, that is, when it is available at all as an addressee (for example, see Gregory 1998). Modern circumstances suggest that the state is not reducible to a discourse—and specifically not to a discourse of identity condensed as representations and representational practices. That association was key to liberalism's legislative phase, which, in the United States, ended in the 1980s.[20]

The idea that the state had become an abstraction, internalized as social effects or merged with political identity, can perhaps be accounted for (in retrospect) in the novelty of privatization and the intense competition for markets of cultural expression in the 1980s. In its generality, discourse theory preserved the form of an organic connection between state and society past its actuality, tending to conceal the withdrawal of the state from the contingencies of everyday social security. The theoretical preoccupation with the internalization of state power by individuals and non-state institutions—as discourse, hegemony, subalterity, identity, or consciousness—may also be understood as a theoretical response to the political situations of the time: the end of the Cold War, the collapse of the Soviet Union, the end of apartheid in South Africa, the rise of the new conservative right in the United States and the United Kingdom, the emergence of globalization. States did not disappear. Their powers remained highly concrete, as we see in the new security context. Discourse and the "mythification" of the state may be central to states' "legitimation work" (Corrigan and Sayer 1985:185), but such performances for external consumption are not states' primary function, even if they are (for now) still politically necessary.

In retrospect, those studies, dating from the early years of the Reagan-Thatcher era, were prescient formulations of the means by which neoliberal states could, in effect, rule without governing by promoting (literally and figuratively) the equation of privatization and democratization.[21] But today the evolution of neoliberal reform brings out a different element. Today, the combination of militarized and marketized elements of the Bush administration's war on terror at home and abroad underscores an ongoing state of affairs in which the state has neither "withered away" (per Marx) nor yielded ground to forms of authority outside the state (as early privatization advocates predicted it would).

In the United States, we find a strong state *and* a strong private sector, working together and borrowing each other's forms of power. Indeed, in many respects, the executive branch resembles a multinational corporation nestled within the institutions of the federal government, with corresponding demands for autonomy, secrecy, and exemption from external regulation. This transformation of the executive branch should make a difference to how we theorize democracy, for our canons were developed in an earlier period when the representative branch was most prominent and the judiciary was in activist mode.

As "neoliberal governmentalities" take hold, the hybrid zone where the government operates through the private sector (for example, Vice President Cheney's Energy Task Force), or vice versa (for example, PNAC), is especially prone to the expedient of secrecy or concealment by other means (Ferguson and Gupta 2002).[22] Important sectors of the state function in uncharted interstices between established political communities. The hegemonic potency of discursive fracture is particularly strong in these zones because it is a tactic for realigning dissent and reworking its key terms as consent in the absence of an actual forum for participation. Accordingly, these are also important sites for political and material investment that obfuscate the extent to which the public and private sectors are nowadays fused. Specifically, the rhetoric of hybrid public-private arrangements tends to construct "society" as the state's "other," but this is seriously misleading as to the location and substance of political agency in both the public and private sectors, as well as its potentially ad hoc nature.

Read in new light, then, it would seem that Corrigan and Sayer's insight for our own times is not the discursivity of states in identitarian terms, but instead the constant availability of *identity discourse*—constant because it is democratically produced in conversation—for autonomous reworking by state agents. That external play on self-knowledge is what makes states at once real and chimerical, mirror and myth. In this context, it is tempting to consider, with Agamben (2005:3), that "the immediately biopolitical significance of the state of exception [reveals] the original structure in which law encompasses living beings by means of its own suspension." But the search for an original structure is a diversion from the more fundamental, critical implication of Agamben's formulation. The significance of the state of exception is what it reveals about the expediency of rendering actual people redundant as their self-knowledge is reworked to confirm their *having been already taken into account* by the security state. The unauthorized double is among the preconditions of the death that is not a sacrifice—Agamben's (1998) formulation of human dispensability under the law.

In theory and practice, *discourse*—conceived as a generalized exchange encompassing state actors and citizens—continually opens new ground for juridical power. State power escapes political checks through processes of discursive fracture, a political asset to whoever can mine its "repetition value" (see Deleuze 1988:10–11). But the tactic of discursive fracture meets its check in conversation, which, by its inherent nature, regulates and sustains the coherence of meaningful exchange, preserving discourse from unilateral appropriation and recomposition. Ethnography, epistemologically grounded in conversation even when it is in the archive, is also a means of specifying discursive associations and making visible (or audible) their connections to particular communities of interest, solidarities, and antagonisms.

Discursive fracture creates situations in which the difference between speech and silence is irresolvably, even if momentarily, ambiguous. This means that, in political and interpretive terms, the "agency of response" (Spivak 2004:81) is not automatic. Indeed, precisely to avoid prejudgments of this kind, discursive fracture is relevant to expanding the repertoire of interpretive practices ethnographers bring to politics. Discursive fracture is not limited to the high levels of government or, indeed, to government. It might be anyone's tactic, but it is not a tactic that an individual can manage alone, given the necessary intricacy of its workings through the authorizing institutions of democratic government, as well as the immense expense of providing large constituencies with a convincing media image of themselves.

Discursive fracture is neither inherently negative nor inherently affirmative. Its primary relevance is as a reminder that states produce and circulate discourse but do not speak. *Society* is not the state's other; the state has no other. Thus, the metaphor of conversation for *democracy* is potentially *anti*-democratic in drawing political communities ever closer to a zone of erasure where their words are drained of oppositional value. Under such conditions, state power has no *theoretical* limits, but it is subject to *practical* limits. Even if the representative branch and some sectors of the public square are merely *locations* for discourse, stagings for discursive *display*, one can take assurance from the fact that even the high institutions of a democratic state offer no automatic check on power as strong as that which individuals, communities, and social movements present when speaking to one another in their own names. Theorizing democracy entails ethnographic acknowledgment of discursive fracture, lest discourse in theory misplace political agency and obviate attention to the potential for pragmatic checks on state power.

CODA: TALKING OUTSIDE

The play of discursive fracture across actual and mythical social fields—people and "the people"—points to locations where states come into their social existence through signs that are already legible and in wide circulation as the discursive practices "on the ground." For this reason, as noted above, an ethnography of the state necessitates an interpretation of its hermeneutics, if only to decode those associations, retemporalizing discourse as political contestation and rekeying lines of discursive fracture to their reference points in the politics of everyday life.

It is in those realms, too, rather than in state recognition, that political agency is clearest. Perhaps the most available means of political agency is the interpretive and dramatic work of rendering state action discursive through conversation, that is, reformulating its broken elements as coherent narrative, if only to establish the grounds for accountability through syntax and conversational exchange. At a minimum, this would mount a broad-based challenge to the political monopoly and exclusiveness of political communication that appear to have shaped the developments discussed in this chapter.

An unaccustomed resource for pursuing such prospects is the work of feminist scholars, for whom political agency is at once a conversational gambit, a theoretical object, a confrontation with legality, and a subjective (even comedic) gamble. Recent scholarship amply demonstrates the complexities of gender not only in mapping the impact of new social institutions and practices but also, more fundamentally, in articulating political and cultural transition itself, for example, in Eastern Europe (Gal and Kligman 2000), South Africa (Comaroff and Comaroff 1997), China (Anagnost 1997), Latin America (Lazarus-Black 2001; Paley 2001; Warren 1998), and the United States (Coutin 2000; Ginsburg 1989; Merry 2000). In each of these contexts (among others), ethnographers detail the locations and social processes whereby state and civil society are constituted in terms that resignify gender in fundamental ways. The ambiguous qualification of women as icons of both *modernity* (in the public sphere) and *tradition* (in the private sphere) genders any formulation of state and society that rests on a binary opposition between those two terms.

An association between state legality and a sexual binary is the critical core of Luce Irigaray's challenge to Freud and Lacan. Irigaray argues that women are discursively sublimated within the terms of male sexuality; therefore, the category *woman* can be no more than the Other to a male self. Contesting that arrangement means overturning the binary, not just inverting it or equalizing its terms: "It is not a matter of toppling that order so as to replace it—that amounts to the same thing in the end—but of disrupting and modifying it, starting from an 'outside' that is exempt, in part, from phallocratic law" (Irigaray 1985:68). Irigaray's various lines of argument converge on the psychoanalytic construction of male/female difference as inherent in the very ideas of complementarity and equivalence. She rejects the neat binary of self/Other, asserting the nonequivalence of men and women's pleasures:

> So there is, *for* women, no possible law for their pleasure. No more than there is any possible discourse. Cause, effect,

> goal...law and discourse form a single system. And if women—
> according to [Lacan]—can say nothing, can know nothing, of
> their own pleasure, it is because they cannot in any way order
> themselves within and through a language that would be on
> some basis their own. Or...his? [Irigaray 1985:95, original
> ellipses]

Irigaray's gambit toward a new conversation from outside the male/female binary extends beyond the scope of this chapter. Still, it is no mere analogy to the questions at its core. The history of social science, no less than the public discourse of the current Bush administration, positions the theoretical significance of law at the precise juncture where heterosexual partnership would symbolize an idealized, but never reciprocal, fusion of state and society. The state *engenders* citizens from the feminine side of this binary, by the very nature of its claims (when it tenders them) to cover its citizens, borrowing their liberty in return for security, speaking for them, and making moral cause of their pleasures. Thus, states are potentially deeply invested in the meanings of male and female because those meanings sustain the fundamental partability of identity discourse.

Ethnography has tended to take the state as a mythical aggrandizement of the terms *within* such partnerships, a total social fact that can be explored from anywhere. But the buildup to war shows that states are relatively restricted as social facts—although, to be sure, this does not mean that they lack consequence. Indeed, events press us to reconsider the assumptions about political power and popular sovereignty that underwrite anthropology's long-standing practices of substituting state discourse for state action as its ethnographic object. State actors' deployments of discourse such as we have been reviewing here also constitute state action, even if not the totality of whatever the phrase "state action" might mean. The state is not an empty sign, in other words, but rather (to paraphrase Irigaray) this state which is not one.

Such a claim does not make states disappear (any more than Irigaray's critique of discourse makes men and women disappear; see Grosz 1994: especially ch. 8). The implication of Irigaray's analysis of gender discourses underscores the creative potential for an ethnography of the state that relinquishes the state/society binary implicit in a notion of state discursivity conceived as a generality or whole. As abundant new scholarship confirms, there are endless fresh questions to be asked in relation to stateness, personhood, security, and discourse, among other things, as local specifications of what I have elsewhere called "empirical citizenship"

(Greenhouse 2003). In that context, *discourse* is not the mechanism of stateness, but a register of contestation—both methodological and political—that underscores the social embeddedness and unevenness of the stakes when it comes to anyone's changing the subject.

Acknowledgments

It is a pleasure to acknowledge the contributions of participants in the SAR seminar through their engagements with an earlier version of this chapter in Santa Fe—and especially Julia Paley, for her collegial readings then and since. The kernel of the original paper was a short commentary prepared for the Fellowship of Woodrow Wilson Scholars at Princeton in fall 2001; this chapter subsequently emerged from the continuation of that project in relation to the events of winter and spring 2002–2003. I have presented it in various forms to the Law and Public Affairs Program at Princeton, the Seminar on Social Medicine at Harvard, the Anthropology Colloquium at the University of Pennsylvania, the Law & Society Workshop at Indiana University, and the American Anthropological Association—on each occasion reaping the benefit of critical perspectives from hosts and colleagues, for which I am very grateful. Any errors of fact and interpretation are my own.

Notes

1. I have written elsewhere on other aspects of the war on terror: the partisanship and the hegemonic restructuring of political space in relation to the Military Order of November 13, 2001 (Greenhouse 2005a), the transnational entanglements of executive power among coalition partners (Greenhouse 2005b), the National Security Strategy and the Bush administration's use of the preemptive war doctrine (Greenhouse 2006a), the expansion of presidential power (Greenhouse n.d.), and the methodological implications of the war on terror for sociolegal research (Greenhouse 2006b).

2. I omit here other crucial developments that were secret at the time: for example, the treatment of detainees at Guantánamo, the abuse of prisoners at Abu Ghraib and other detention centers in the war zone, CIA renditions of prisoners for detention and interrogation in secret prisons, and domestic surveillance in the form of wiretaps and sweeps (for which the White House subsequently claimed legal justification).

3. Our SAR seminar was convened in March 2005, and the original version of this chapter was written over the course of the long fall and winter of 2004–2005, when George W. Bush won election to a second presidential term and the Republicans swept the Congress. The 2004 elections were evidence of a new discursivity of state power—

that is, a rhetorical mandate for institutional reform and realignment—in which security appears to have figured most prominently in determining the outcome (Menand 2004). Public opposition to the policy governing the war registered in the midterm elections of 2006, gradually consolidating bipartisan congressional opposition to the war itself in 2007, as I write this.

4. The "mediatization" of the war on terror poses overlapping but complex issues; see Morris 2002.

5. For discussion of security as an influence on the outcome of the 2004 presidential election, see Menand 2004.

6. The Joint Resolution to Authorize the Use of United States Armed Forces Against Iraq was passed by the Congress on October 11, 2002, by a vote of 77–23 in the Senate and 296–133 in the House (Mitchell and Hulse 2002:1).

7. The administration's moral discourse articulates an instrumentalist and depoliticized vision of "society" as the product of administrative technique. Bauman writes: "The bureaucratic culture...prompts us to view society as an object of administration, as a collection of so many 'problems' to be solved, as 'nature' to be 'controlled', 'mastered' and 'improved' or 'remade', as a legitimate target for 'social engineering', and in general a garden to be designed and kept in the planned shape by force" (Bauman 1989:18). See also p. 208 above.

8. See PNAC's "letters and statements" section on its website (PNAC n.d.).

9. The letter, dated January 26, 1998, was signed by Elliott Abrams, Richard L. Armitage, William J. Bennett, Francis Fukuyama, Zalmay Khalilzad, William Kristol, Richard Perle, Donald Rumsfeld, Paul Wolfowitz, R. James Woolsey, and Robert B. Zoellick, among others.

10. This letter, dated May 29, 1998, was signed by Dick Cheney, Francis Fukuyama, Zalmay Khalilzad, I. Lewis Libby, Norman Podhoretz, Dan Quayle, Donald Rumsfeld, and Paul Wolfowitz, among others.

11. The Iraq Liberation Act was decried by the Pentagon but welcomed as a "policy reversal" by Ahmed Chalabi, head of the Iraqi National Congress and lobbyist for the legislation (Risen and Crossette 1998).

12. Previous legislation had authorized $5 million in aid to opposition groups (PL105-174, May 1, 1998). See Shenon 1998. On December 16, President Clinton launched a massive air strike against Iraq, incurring bitter division in Congress, where an impeachment vote was imminent. See Schmitt 1998.

13. Moreover, the obligation to render discourse coherent (and even more so, the obligation to realize coherent discourse in action) becomes a crucial mark of political subordination; aspirations to virtuoso control of meanings in public may be anyone's, but the means for doing so are not.

14. In this sense, war making also challenges conventions of sociological and historical explanation, as Durkheim makes clear in *Who Wanted War?* (Durkheim and Denis 1915). The book chronicles the buildup to war over the summer of 1914, detailing Kaiser Wilhelm's "diplomacy of omission" (Durkheim and Denis 1915:59). The book opens with an observation on the entanglements of explanation and agency:

> Like all historical events, the present war depends in part on deep and distant causes....But, whatever the importance of these impersonal causes, they are not effective in themselves. In order for them to yield effects, human will must set them in motion. When war erupts, it is because a State has willed it....If, then, this time, catastrophe was the result, it is because these wills, or certain among them, made it happen. And so a question arises: Which is the people that wanted war instead of peace, and for what reason? [Durkheim and Denis 1915:3–4]

15. Cavell (1976:31) excludes official orders from moral discourse: "Commands, pure imperatives, are not paradigms of moral utterance, but represent an alternative to such utterance."

16. "Therefore we should not ask: 'What is power and where does it come from?' but 'How is it practised?'" (Deleuze 1988:71).

17. My thanks to Peg Sutton for these examples in this context.

18. On the limits of individualist explanations in relation to the executive branch's conduct of the war on terror, see Hooks and Mosher 2005:1628.

19. See Abrams 1988; Corrigan and Sayer 1985; Mitchell 1991; for comprehensive reviews, see Alonso 1994; Hansen and Stepputat 2001; Steinmetz 1999. In the context of globalization and the collapse of the Iron Curtain, transnational capitalism also provided a context for the new studies of states, identity, and hegemony: see B. Anderson 1991; Appadurai 1996; Corrigan and Sayer 1985; Laclau and Mouffe 2000[1985].

20. Observers of the mid- to late 1980s might well have imagined that the future of the state lay in the private orderings of community, market, media, and so-called popular culture, making the newly opened public spheres appear to be a new and volatile locus of the public sector, that is, outside the state (see Corrigan and Sayer 1985: ch. 6).

21. Ethnographers and sociolegal scholars' concerns with identity, representation, agency, and discourse in the terrains of everyday legal and political practice at this time may be read as specialized articulations of these same social currents, in effect, tracking the escape of neoliberal legality into the categories of everyday life. This trend was most vivid in the domains of politics and law, in which "identity" and "discourse" began to feature prominently as themes for research in the late 1980s and early 1990s (see Mertz 1994; Riles 1998, 2004; see also Greenhouse 2003). Pierre

Clastres (1989:19) referred critically to "the gradual dissolution of the political" in the anthropological literature on power. But, in fact, the opposite was the case: the very notion of identity was becoming a political necessity as counterweight to the increasingly global sweep of neoliberalism's claims with respect to markets and civil society (Comaroff and Comaroff 1999, 2006; Cowan, Dembour, and Wilson 2001).

22. For a synthetic discussion of neoliberalism, see Pieterse 2004.

9

Habits of Mind, Deliberative Democracy, and Peace

Conversatorios *among Military Officers, Civil Society, and Ex-guerrilleros in Colombia*

Jennifer Schirmer

I have been carefully listening to everyone these past two days in this Conversatorio, and I find I have a question to ask ourselves here at the table. If the government wants peace, if the armed forces want peace, if the guerrillas want peace, if the international community wants us to want peace, then where lies the problem?

—Military participant in a Conversatorio

Democracy rests in large measure on rather surprisingly simple social foundations. "Small questions that countless citizens confront concerning whom they associate with, listen to, and engage in conversation with, carry —in the aggregate—large consequences for democracy's public quality" (Fishman 2004:171).[1] Conversations that join socially dissimilar persons whose perspectives and discourse grow and create boundary-crossing ties are not insignificant. Studies show that the ties that most influence public life are those in which the participants listen to one another (Fishman 2004:173).

This suggests that, rather than focus on the health of public institutions to judge the quality of democracy in Colombia, we should approach democracy more as part of the "republican" tradition of democratic theory: the creation of conditions favoring a genuine and lively exchange of perspectives and ideas in the public sphere and, in this particular case, as part and parcel of a peace-building effort.[2] This tradition views democracy as a *process of deliberation,* an avenue for providing access to other opinions and a space for welcoming differences of opinion, thereby creating a political literacy, a habit of mind and an enthusiasm to learn about various political analyses and political visions. Such democratic deliberation, in turn, depends on the capacity to cross social and political boundaries. So, too, does the peaceful resolution of conflicts.

If the political essence of democracy includes establishing linkages for deliberation by way of discussion, conversation, argument, and, potentially, persuasion rather than bargaining for the advantage of established interests or ideological positions, then political actors must be able to formulate their agendas in ways that transcend the narrow defense of self-interest. Jon Elster (1998) writes about "deliberative democracy" in terms of the translocal and globalizing discourses among broadly dispersed publics across the globe, but cross-boundary connections and deliberation can also be built *within* a country that has been fragmented by conflict and bounded by social exclusion. This chapter focuses on an understanding of the potential for expanding "discursive horizons" (Fishman 2004:28) in the shaping of democratic peace building.

COLOMBIA

Colombia today is witness to a fundamental irony. On the one hand, it is a country with a rich electoral and institutional culture and vibrant democratic discourse in the form of an essentially free media and vigorous public debates. On the other hand, it is a country with an enduring history of political exclusion and marginality for a significant part of the population; profound social and economic inequality; and assassinations, forced disappearances, and other forms of repressive practices against public intellectuals, university professors, trade unionists, politicians, journalists, and many other sector representatives.[3]

As such, Colombia is a precarious democracy and faces a myriad of contradictions. For one, although there is vigorous political discourse within socially similar sectors of society, there has been little or no political engagement—no cross-boundary ties—*between* sectors of society. It has strong and vibrant *intra*sectoral debate, yet *inter*sectoral silence. For another, even as Colombia provides evidence of a democratic culture, it is also a society with the longest, internal, armed conflict in the hemisphere. It might even be said that Colombia is a country with stable democratic institutions that is at war with itself.

Fraught with irony and contradiction, Colombia faces an uncertain future unless it can find ways to create a basis for ending its internal strife, addressing its profound inequalities, and building a democratic culture that includes all of its various sectors in lively dialogue and debate. Yet this entails the final irony of all: how can the basis for peace be created through democratic dialogue when democratic dialogue demands that there first be peace? Within any society, opportunities for forming social ties with someone from a different class, race, or subculture are limited.[4] This is all the more true when conflict slices the social map and creates boundaries that are crossed only occasionally and at great risk.

[handwritten margin note: the classroom + can, diversity]

Divisions, after forty years of war, exist at all levels of the Colombian social order: between civil society and the military, rebels and the government, left and right, and rich and poor. At best, this makes Colombian democracy fragile. What is more critical is that only certain sectors embrace a deliberative vision of democratic debate and openness in the public sphere. Others have a more exclusionary vision of what the "appropriate" political space and its discourse should be, and they have gone to great lengths to maintain the privilege of defining "the appropriate space" for the majority. The mindset of these Colombians, both military and civilian, is guided by a vision in which they serve as the "permanent guardians of internal and external peace" against the "multiple enemies of the citizenry and of the State" (Cruz and León 2005:16–17): leftists, subversives, common delinquents, and "extremists" in social and labor protests. This one-sided vision is particularly apropos for the military, a critical component of any effort to build a more durable peace based on a truly deliberative democracy in Colombia.

For the military, not only ideological but also social reasons account for its reluctance to cross boundaries. Military and police officers and their families live apart, in military ghettos.[5] They are locked into a significant, hermetically sealed, collective endeavor of war that breeds its own form of exclusion and "outsiderness." For Colombian military officers to form social ties with academics, intellectuals, and analysts from other than the conservative and right-wing persuasion is extremely unlikely.

Therefore, officers are part of the citizenry of a democracy in only an abstract sense; they are not part of its "public sphere," despite the fact that the armed forces and police are referred to in Colombia as the "Public Force" (la Fuerza Pública). Although they learn of the various ideological options present in Colombia, these habits of mind are most often understood as operational threats to stability, not differences of opinion to be debated. As a consequence, the "public sphere," filled with politicians, ideologies, and everyday debates, may be viewed from the officers' mental universe as a threatening, "conflictive" social and political arena rather than as an opportune space for deliberating informed political choice, as well as for deliberating on political resolution of conflict.

Similarly, most progressive intellectuals and academics in Colombia have their own form of social isolation, keeping to their own, similar, social worlds, with little access to the armed forces, partly from disdain or lack of interest. Many admit to not pursuing the proper "forum" generative of political debate, analysis, and reflection with officers. For example, one academic argued that the officers' presentations at the one conference he had attended with military officers were "mere rhetoric." And he said, "[As a result] I very quickly lost interest in conversing with them."

An exception to this is a critical mass of former *guerrilleros* from the handful of revolutionary groups in Colombia who, during the multiple peace negotiations in the 1990s, chose to accept a peace agreement, demobilize, and "reinsert" themselves back into civil society after electing to work outside civil society. Thus, they made their own "deliberations" to "cross" a number of social boundaries—of class, of ideology, sometimes of culture and the nuclear family. Although still isolated in certain ways, these ex-guerrilleros are sometimes adept at crossing intersectoral boundaries in conversations.

How does one bring the republican tradition of *processes* of deliberative democracy, political literacy, and habits of mind to bear on the issue of negotiations and peace processes within such a conflictive society? How does one transform anti-democratic habits of mind of key armed actors in the conflict, such as the military, whose vision of politics has historically been cynical? At best, for them, all politics and politicians on the left or in the center are driven either by ideology or by self-interest and are therefore not to be trusted. At worst, the left political opposition and the guerrilla movements amount to one and the same and must be controlled by violent means. And how does one change habits of mind of the political left, which assumes that officers of the Public Force are not worth talking to? How does one cross such boundaries of separation to begin a conversation to reshape the potential for the makings of an inclusive, democratic peace?

ARMED ACTORS AND PEACE

During negotiations for a potential peace process, can armed actors give up isolating habits of mind that are so much a part of their ghettoized subculture without some form of preparation in crossing boundaries?[6] How does one draw armed actors who are effectively outside the "public sphere" and those civilians and government officials who define that sphere into the process of debate and engage them in democratic dialogue long before a peace is negotiated? What might a third party do to make the armed actors comfortable with speaking and listening to civilians and ex-guerrilleros (and, possibly, eventually, to guerrillas), and vice versa, in order to move the discussions toward peace?

Along with lessons learned from other peace processes that have failed to include the armed actors early on in preparatory discussions,[7] a project under my direction, titled "Skilling the Armed Actors for Peace in Colombia" and funded by the Norwegian Foreign Ministry, has worked with the armed actors in Colombia for the past eight years establishing such a dialogue, in what is called the "Conversatorio project."

To set the Conversatorio project in motion, extensive interviews and conversations were undertaken with members of the officer core in the field, in the academies, and in the defense ministry and also with representatives of government and civil society and politicians from the left and the right. Instead of focusing solely on civil society sectors, as is the wont of much of the international community, I brought armed actors of the state together with civilians in "conversations" in the midst of the conflict, in preparation for peace. Without a doubt, this task is fraught with difficulties. Career military officers, trained for decades in national security doctrine and threat mentality, do not easily forfeit their demonized image of the guerrilla as enemy (and, in the twenty-first century, as "terrorist") to live magically side by side peacefully. Taking this into consideration, the project maintains a long-term view of engagement—building trust among parties takes time—and locates the dialogue in a low-profile, more academic setting. This allows a generative process of reflection upon the role of the armed forces in resolving the conflict peacefully in conjunction with civil society and the international community.

What follows is a brief discussion of the following aspects of the "conversation" project: (1) the context of the project and how it has progressed and (2) the basis for the approach and why and how it has developed.

PROJECT

The distinct possibility exists that militaries perceive themselves as outside both the peace process and the democratic public sphere of their country. They may feel that they lack the skills to listen to differing opinions, to participate in dialogue, and eventually to negotiate. They may become anxious and resentful about such a process, making them potential spoilers to a negotiated settlement and easy prey for the anti-democratic narratives of right-wing elites.

In the beginning, I looked to the models of human rights training for military officers and found that these are used to good effect in changing military rhetoric but apparently to little effect in changing military mentalities. One argument is that the same military educational instruments and personnel—referred to as Mil-to-Mil (a model used by the US military)—of both active and retired officers is the best approach. This approach, however, begs the question of whether a conceptual paradigm shift occurs or humanitarian principles are merely placed atop military ones instead. Can peace building be taught by addressing the technicalities of war alone? It may be possible, but does this not forfeit the opportunity to move officers out of their mental universe and be comfortable with dialoguing in a democratic manner with civil society, thereby creating respect for democratic pluralism? As a result of these questions, I began to shift my thinking to develop new ways of approaching the military.

Based on my initial conversations, it became clear that the Colombian officers were potentially open to new ways of interacting. With this in mind, I began to establish, together with a two-member Colombian team, informal, neutral, and off-the-record Conversatorios, in which the primary rule is to respect and listen to one another's opinions. Conversatorios work anthropologically by framing the dialogue in terms of the multiple mindsets present in the room. Military officers and other participants are encouraged to articulate their beliefs about the issues at hand and express what they see as the issues emanating from their experiences in the field and their frames of reference.

CONVERSATORIOS

Genuine conversation entails listening, as well as talking. Between 2000 and 2005, I organized fifteen Conversatorios, which covered themes generative of political debate, analysis, and reflection, with more than 175 officers participating. The fifteen Conversatorios included themes of humanitarian accord with the guerrilla, paramilitarism, forced displacement, land reform, the economic costs of war, policies of new progressive mayors and governors regarding trade unionism, and rehabilitation and work programs for ex-paramilitary youths. (This project is ongoing today and is dealing with similar issues.)

To create a group dynamic, an event typical of all those held to this day begins with a late afternoon gathering at the airport, with the officers out of military uniform and the civilians in casual dress. This is only the tip of the ice-breaking process. It is difficult to get both groups to sit together on the airplane and later on the bus: both parties display shyness and awkwardness. Everyone checks in at the hotel, selected for its quiet, retreat-like setting away from cell phones and the Internet. After check-in, there is a welcoming reception and toast and, over dinner, the participants are reminded that the event is entirely off the record, with no attribution permitted.[8] (Most officers later admit that they very much appreciate this opportunity to speak their minds—an indication of how seldom they have the opportunity to do so in their seminars.) I always emphasize in my opening remarks that I am not the "owner" of the dialogue and that its success will be due entirely to their own initiatives in speaking with and listening to one another: "This is *your* Conversatorio, your opportunity to speak with people on an informal level about how, together, we can begin to resolve this conflict in Colombia." During dinner, conversation between officers and civilians remains cordial and informal. Most officers later admit that they had expected to be "hammered" by "leftist NGO types" and are pleasantly surprised that this did not occur.

The next morning begins with breakfasting together. Again, most officers and civilians eat at separate tables (it is the continual task of our team to distribute ourselves at different tables). As talk moves increasingly into political discussions that emerged from the morning Conversatorio, separation softens at lunch, and even more so at dinner.

The Conversatorio takes place for the next two days in a room set up to be as tranquil as possible—no outside noise, no microphone, no PowerPoint, no slide projectors. The table equally distributes twenty-five people, mixed by rank, branch, gender, and (civilian and military) status and located by name cards displaying first names only, with no titles or ranks. Rules of the table are that each civilian facilitator gives a presentation on the topic (previously negotiated with the director of the military school, along with his liaison officers) for a maximum of twenty-five minutes. Then, the discussion opens to everyone equally, with respectful questions and comments. Often (but not always), a higher-ranking officer speaks first, to "balance" any perspective that is too progressive for his liking, especially one given by an ex-guerrilla. This "shoring up" by higher-ranking officers usually does not have the effect of dampening the discussion, with some officers of the Navy and Air Force, for example, disagreeing with their esteemed colleagues of the Army or, to their own surprise, agreeing with the civilian facilitator. In one instance, an officer frowned and stated that he was "exceedingly worried" because he found himself in agreement with a statement by one of the ex-guerrillas at the table. There was a collective drawing in of breath, and then everyone laughed. By late morning, most officers and civilians readily participate, saying how much they appreciate the openness and "equal making" of the methodology.

It is important to emphasize that one of the primary rules of the

Conversatorio is that respect does not necessarily mean agreement. Nor does it mean that we simply take in the view of the other side. Rather, dialogue here tries to step aside from this vision of ideological politics to a much more continual stream of conversation, allowing us to see that, no matter how different our experiences and perspectives, we can arrive at areas of agreement and formulate new analyses of the conflict.

Removing the conversation from the polemical world, to a large extent, and placing it within a world of open discussion of ideas in a neutral space in which all ideologies are treated in a leveling way results in some interesting concurrences of thinking and transformations of attitude. For example, when ex-guerrillas have talked about their view of political and economic inequalities and the need for social justice, military officers have talked about their resentment of the upper class. From this dialogue, at times, they have come to a realization that they have similar ideas about social justice but different vocabularies with which to describe their understandings, because of different experiences, histories, and narrative traditions.

As the Conversatorios on peace building proceed, we can begin to see a slow disintegration of the military's resistance to the perceptions and predispositions of those they originally believed to be intrinsically antagonistic to their institutional and individual interests. For example, military "alumni" of past Conversatorios are relaxed and fluent in conversing with "the other side" whenever they are invited to another Conversatorio, readily serving as "mediators" between new officers and their civilian counterparts during the first evening. On the other side, many an ex-guerrilla, leftist politician, and human rights lawyer has admitted to me that his own prejudgments of the military were erroneous. These dialogues, then, are an ethnographic education for all parties—officers, academics, parliamentarians, human rights lawyers, businessmen, international organization representatives (the United Nations, the European Union), and ex-guerrillas. They have been able to overcome their initial predispositions and begin to see the other as a legitimate and ultimately helpful participant in dialogue about the future of peace in Colombia.

Meeting the "enemy" face to face, officers learn that the ex-guerrilleros hold views with which some of the officers can agree and others cannot. Also, officers learn that the ex-guerrilleros, too, disagree among themselves, critically transforming the way officers see the guerrilleros, and vice versa. The meetings also enable officers to familiarize themselves with the history of peace negotiations in Colombia and to reflect positively on the concerns of peace making, in general, through the optic of an ex-combatant. In particular, the ex-guerrilleros' experiences with previous peace processes in Colombia and elsewhere, and the lessons learned from these, are an education for officers.

From my experiences during these past five years (and continuing into the present), it is clear that the more the participants engage in these Conversatorios, the more curious they become about the "other." They learn to listen without adopting the identity or perspective of the "other" and without having to agree with it. They come to see the advantages of having the option to become literate in political choice.

DELIBERATION

I would hazard to say that the Conversatorios achieve two objectives. The project engages officers in a structure that is dialogic and democratic to the core, encouraging a frank and respectful exchange of ideas unprecedented in their world. It also introduces officers to ideas and progressive intellectuals who challenge their habits of mind, making them comfortable with differences of opinion.

(1)

A

(2)

A Conversatorio is not a one-sided exchange in which the civilians talk *at* the military: it is decidedly a dialogue. It allows the officers to raise issues about operations that civilians never confront, and it challenges the civilians' preconceptions of the military's mindset. The central premise is that participants learn about one another rather than impose their own viewpoint. It is a long-term process of engagement and co-ownership, not a one-off lecture. What is encouraged in these discussions is an anthropological frame of mind that seeks to understand the experience of others. This → How? approach allows the military to speak from its prejudices, ideas, and frames of mind rather than passively attend a lecture or be subject to hectoring, as is so often the case in seminars on human rights. Gradually, this approach generates dialogue with left-wing parliamentarians—many of whom are ex-guerrilleros—whose consistently progressive vision and analysis of the roots of the conflict, as well as the political solution to it, are very much at odds with the national security logic in which the officers are trained. Moreover, the discussion with human rights lawyers, local civilian authorities, and university academics provides another layer of analysis to all parties about how, together, they might resolve the conflict. Equally as critical, representatives from civil society learn that the officers do not think as one but have different, individual experiences and viewpoints and that differences exist especially across forces. The goal is not consensus, but a plural democratic discourse in which, more often than not, people disagree but come away appreciating the richness of democratic dialogue and feeling at ease with people who are critical of them in a situation that is not entirely structured or controlled.

One Air Force general commented:

> These Conversatorios have been a learning experience because
> they represent unique neutral spaces where one can discuss
> themes with people with whom one is normally on an antagonistic
> footing. Where else can a general sit down with an ex-guerrillero
> and leftist parliamentarian and calmly discuss the conflict? Every-
> thing is off the record, and this creates trust and friendship for
> the necessary long-term dialogue towards peace.

[handwritten margin note: Civil society: classroom]

[handwritten arrow pointing to "the necessary long-term dialogue towards peace"]

But, as with all processes, there are questions and dilemmas. There are
questions about the implications of these Conversatorios for the peace
process. Will participants use the Conversatorio to confirm their own vision
of the world or to explore what they see as serving the state's best interests?
More crucially, will participants learn how to utilize the vocabulary of
human rights and peace and the imagery of rule of law to create what I
refer to as justificatory narratives (Schirmer 1996, 1998)?

Notwithstanding these important questions, the inclusion of armed
actors in such a dialogue is predicated on the belief that the act of dialogue
with one's "enemy" is transformative. It humanizes and legitimizes the
other party and its ideas by virtue of a democratic, participatory mode and,
in doing so, prioritizes dialogue over the operational logic of violence.
Even though concerns about the wisdom of engaging armed actors in the
process of peace building are certainly legitimate, we must ask ourselves,
Would it not be better to *engage* the armed actors, in an effort to influence
how they think about peace? Would not access to and dialogue with non-
state guerrillas and state security forces provide a significant advantage in
building toward a peace? And might not this process lead to the discovery
that the armed actors are indeed willing to participate in meaningful dialogue about peace building and conflict resolution?

CONCLUSION

A durable democracy in the midst of conflict demands dialogue, most
particularly with the armed actors. Ironically, these powerful actors are the
most likely to be excluded or marginalized from pluralistic dialogue during peace processes, leaving in serious question the sustainability of such a
democracy.

The work undertaken in Colombia rests on two key premises: (1) dialogue
is a necessary precursor to building both a durable peace and an effective
democracy, and (2) conversation, or the habit of examining together whatever
comes to pass, as Hannah Arendt (1971) averred, can be transformative.

What the project has set out to build is a dialogue among previously separate, indeed segregated, social groups to establish the basis for peace and a more effective and pluralist discourse. More critically, this work has centered on a social group conventionally ignored in efforts to build peace and a democratic culture: the military and other armed actors. Without the active participation of these groups in dialogue with civil society, sustaining peace and creating a democratic culture are problematic at best. Unsurprisingly, in attempting to promote such a dialogue in Colombia, we have encountered resistance not only among the military but also among members of civil society. Mutual dialogue has needed to revolve less around abstract issues of human rights, peace building, and democracy than around the building of a process that fosters dialogical debate and deliberations about substantive issues that have significant consequences for all the various groups in Colombian society. The goal is not to build consensus or to develop a singular viewpoint about how to solve the challenges raised in the Conversatorios. Rather, *through the very process of inter-action* defined by the Conversatorios, groups are brought together that have been previously set apart, to create the basis for informal deliberation and provide a model for democratic interaction leading toward a peaceful resolution of the conflict. Therefore, it is not so much what is said in the conversation, but that groups previously not on speaking terms are now in deep conversation, creating a space and a model for deliberation about overcoming political differences and economic exclusion, elements necessary for resolving Colombia's internal conflict.

Notes

1. Robert Fishman's *Democracy's Voices: Social Ties and the Quality of Public Life in Spain* (2004) was of inestimable help in formulating the issues on democratic deliberation.

2. This is in contrast to the more traditional focus on how well public institutions are functioning, to calibrate the "health" of a democracy (see Putnam, Leonardi, and Nanetti 1994, among others).

3. For example, see the report that Colombia has the highest rate of assassinations of trade unionists in the world (Perillo 2006). Another report details the use of the paramilitaries by the National Intelligence Office (DAS) between 2004 and 2005 to target "trade unionists and leaders of the left," especially those working with the new left party, El Polo Democrático Alternativo (*El Tiempo* 2006).

4. Culture here is used as "a repertoire of meanings and values"; a subculture

could be seen as one in which there is a set of understandings, expectations, and ideologies that you see as setting you apart from others.

5. This ghettoization even exists *between* the police and the army, with only a handful of "cross-force" couples intermarrying.

6. Herb Kelman's workshops, which I attended while teaching at Harvard, and his general work on transforming the relationship between enemies in the Israeli-Palestinian conflict have been of inestimable help to me in addressing this issue and in formulating my methodology (Kelman 1999, 2005a, 2005b).

7. For example, in the Oslo years, during the Israeli-Palestinian negotiations, Hamas remained outside the Palestinian Authority, opposing the peace process. In 2005 the Palestinian president believed that "[if Hamas is going to remain in opposition,] it will be better to bring it inside Palestinian institutions to persuade them to relinquish violence and integrate its armed wing into the authority's security services. To those who criticize Abu Mazen's approach, his response is to ask for a credible alternative" (Agha and Malley 2005). Hamas's electoral victory in 2006 illustrates even further the need to include the participation of armed actors early on in the peace process.

8. This rule has not been breached in all the years of the Conversatorios.

References

Abrams, Philip

1988   Notes on the Difficulty of Studying the State. Journal of Historical Sociology 1(1):58–69.

Africa Watch

1992   Conspicuous Destruction: War, Famine, and the Reform Process in Mozambique. New York: Human Rights Watch.

African American Institute

1997   Relatório sobre Círculos de Trabalho e Discussão. Maputo: African American Institute.

Agamben, Giorgio

1998   Homo Sacer: Sovereign Power and Bare Life. Daniel Heller-Roazen, trans. Palo Alto, CA: Stanford University Press.

2005   State of Exception. Kevin Attell, trans. Chicago: University of Chicago Press.

Agha, Hussein, and Robert Malley

2005   Now Hamas Must Be Put to the Test. The Guardian, May 18: 26.

Albó, Xavier

2002   Bolivia: From Indian and Campesino Leaders to Counsillors and Parliamentary Deputies. *In* Multiculturalism in Latin America: Indigenous Rights, Diversity, and Democracy. Rachel Sieder, ed. Pp. 74–102. New York: Palgrave Macmillan.

Alden, Chris

1995   The UN and the Resolution of Conflict in Mozambique. The Journal of Modern African Studies 33(1):103–128.

2001   Mozambique and the Construction of the New African State: From Negotiations to Nation Building. New York: Palgrave.

Alden, Chris, and Mark Simpson

1993   Mozambique: A Delicate Peace. The Journal of Modern African Studies 31(1):109–130.

Alexander, Jocelyn

1997   The Local State in Post-war Mozambique: Political Practice and Ideas about Authority. Africa 76(1):1–26.

Alonso, Anna-Maria

1994   The Politics of Space, Time, and Substance: State Formation, Nationalism, and Ethnicity. Annual Review of Anthropology 23:379–405.

Alves, Armando Teixeira, and Benedito Ruben Cossa

1997   Guião das Autarquias Locais. Maputo: Ministério da Administração Estatal.

Aman, Alfred C., Jr.

2004   The Democracy Deficit: Taming Globalization with Law Reform. New York: New York University Press.

Anagnost, Ann

1997   National Past-times: Narrative, Representation, and Power in Modern China. Durham, NC: Duke University Press.

Anderson, Benedict

1991   Imagined Communities: Reflections on the Origin and Spread of Nationalism. 2nd edition. London: Verso.

Anderson, Perry

1974   Lineages of the Absolutist State. London: New Left Books.

Appadurai, Arjun

1996   Modernity at Large: Cultural Dimensions of Globalization. Minneapolis: University of Minnesota Press.

Ardant, Gabriel

1975   Financial Policy and Economic Infrastructure of Modern States and Nations. In The Formation of National States in Western Europe. Charles Tilly, ed. Pp. 164–242. Princeton, NJ: Princeton University Press.

Arendt, Hannah

1971   The Life of the Mind. New York: Harcourt.

2003   Some Questions of Moral Philosophy. In Responsibility and Judgment. Jerome Kohn, ed. Pp. 49–146. New York: Schocken.

Axel, Brian, ed.

2002   From the Margins: Historical Anthropology and Its Futures. Durham, NC: Duke University Press.

Baez, Sara, Mary García, Fernando Guerrero, and Ana María Larrea

1999   Cotacachi: Capitales comunitarios y propuestas de desarollo local. Quito: Abya Yala.

Banerjee, Mukulika

N.d.   Leadership and Political Work. *In* Leaders in South Asia. Pamela Price and
         Arild Ruud, eds. New Delhi: Routledge.

Basadre, Jorge

1980   Elecciones y centralismo en el Perú. Lima: Centro de Investigación de la
         Universidad del Pacífico.

Bauman, Zygmunt

1989   Modernity and the Holocaust. Ithaca, NY: Cornell University Press.

Berry, Sara

2002   Debating the Land Question in Africa. Comparative Studies in Society and
         History 44(4):638–668.

Beteille, Andre

1987   On Individualism and Equality. Current Anthropology 28(5):669–677.

Biolsi, Thomas

2005   Imagined Geographies: Sovereignty, Indigenous Space, and American Indian
         Struggle. American Ethnologist 32(2):239–259.

Bledsoe, Caroline

1980   Women and Marriage in Kpelle Society. Palo Alto, CA: Stanford University
         Press.

Bourdieu, Pierre

1986   The Forms of Capital. *In* Handbook of Theory and Research for the Sociology
         of Education. John G. Richardson, ed. Pp. 241–258. New York: Greenwood
         Press.

1996   The State Nobility: Elite Schools in the Field of Power. Loretta C. Clough,
         trans. Cambridge: Polity Press.

1999   Rethinking the State: Genesis and Structure of the Bureaucratic Field. *In*
         State/Culture: State Formation after the Cultural Turn. George Steinmetz, ed.
         Pp. 53–75. Ithaca, NY: Cornell University Press.

Boyd, William, and Edmund J. King

1995   The History of Western Education. 12th edition. Lanham, MD: Barnes and
         Noble Books.

Brenner, Neil

1997   Global, Fragmented, Hierarchical: Henri Lefebre's Geographies of
         Globalization. Public Culture 10(1):135–167.

Brysk, Alison

2000   From Tribal Village to Global Village: Indian Rights and International Relations
         in Latin America. Palo Alto, CA: Stanford University Press.

Burawoy, Michael, and Katherine Verdery

1999   Uncertain Transition: Ethnographies of Change in the Postsocialist World.
         Lanham, MD: Rowman & Littlefield.

Buur, Lars, and Helene Maria Kyed

2003   Implementation of Decree 15/2000 in Mozambique: The Consequences of State Recognition of Traditional Authority in Sussundenga. Copenhagen: Centre for Development Research.

Cameron, John D.

2003   Municipal Democratization and Rural Development in Highland Ecuador. *In* Rural Progress, Rural Decay: Neoliberal Adjustment Policies and Local Initiatives. Lisa North and John D. Cameron, eds. Pp. 164–186. Bloomfield, CT: Kumarian Press.

Cárdenas, Víctor, Laureano Carnero Checa, Hector Cordero Guevara, and Orestes Romero Toledo

1952   El APRA y la revolución: Tesis para un replanteamiento revolucionario. Buenos Aires: II Congreso Postal de Desterrados.

Carothers, Thomas

1997   The Observers Observed. Journal of Democracy 8(3):17–31.

The Carter Center

2005   Postelection Statement on Mozambique Elections. http://www.cartercenter. org/news/documents/doc1999.html, accessed January 2008.

Cavell, Stanley

1976   Must We Mean What We Say? *In* Must We Mean What We Say? A Book of Essays. Stanley Cavell, ed. Pp. 1–43. Cambridge: Cambridge University Press.

Centeno, Miguel

1997   Blood and Debt: War and Taxation in Nineteenth-Century Latin America. American Journal of Sociology 102(6):1565–1605.

2001   Blood and Debt: War and the Nation-State in Latin America. College Park: Pennsylvania State University Press.

Chakrabarty, Dipesh

2000   Provincializing Europe: Postcolonial Thought and Historical Difference. Princeton, NJ: Princeton University Press.

Chan, Stephen, and Moisés Venâncio

1998   War and Peace in Mozambique. Houndsmills, UK: MacMillan Press Ltd.

Chandra, Kanchan

2004   Why Ethnic Parties Succeed. Cambridge: Cambridge University Press.

Clanchy, M. T.

1979   From Memory to Written Record: England, 1066–1307. London: Edward Arnold.

Clark, A. Kim, and Marc Becker, eds.

2007   Highland Indians and the State in Modern Ecuador. Pittsburgh: University of Pittsburgh Press.

Clarke, Richard A.

2004   Against All Enemies: Inside America's War on Terror. New York: Free Press.

Clastres, Pierre

1989   Society against the State. Robert Hurley and Abe Stein, trans. New York: Zone Books.

Clemens, Dave

2002   Requiem for a Dream of Mozambique? Mozambican Journalist Carlos Cardoso's Suspected Killers on Trial. December 16. http://www.worldpress.org/Africa/864.cfm, accessed January 2008.

Clinton, William Jefferson

1998   Remarks to the People of Accra in Ghana. March 23. http://findarticles.com/p/articles/mi_m2889/is_n13_v34/ai_20969083, accessed January 2008.

Coles, Kimberley

2004   Election Day: The Construction of Democracy through Technique. Cultural Anthropology 19(4):551–580.

2007   Democratic Designs: International Intervention and Electoral Practices in Postwar Bosnia-Herzegovina. Ann Arbor: University of Michigan Press.

Collins, James, and Richard K. Blot

2003   Literacy and Literacies: Texts, Power, and Identity. New York: Cambridge University Press.

Comaroff, John L., and Jean Comaroff

1997   Of Revelation and Revolution: The Dialectics of Modernity on a South African Frontier. Vol. 2. Chicago: University of Chicago Press.

1999   Introduction. In Civil Society and the Political Imagination in Africa. J. L. Comaroff and J. Comaroff, eds. Pp. 1–43. Chicago: University of Chicago Press.

Comaroff, John L., and Jean Comaroff, eds.

2006   Law and Disorder in the Postcolony. Chicago: University of Chicago Press.

Commission of the European Communities

2000   Communication from the Commission on EU Election Assistance and Observation. Brussels: Commission of the European Communities.

Congress of the United States of America

1998   Public Law 105-338: Iraq Liberation Act of 1998. http://news.findlaw.com/hdocs/docs/iraq/libact103198.pdf, accessed April 2005.

Cooper, Frederick

1979   The Problem of Slavery in African Societies. Journal of African History 20(1):103–125.

Corrigan, Philip, and Derek Sayer

1985   The Great Arch: English State Formation as Cultural Revolution. Oxford: Basil Blackwell.

Coutin, Susan Bibler

2000   Legalizing Moves: Salvadoran Immigrants' Struggle for US Residency. Ann Arbor: University of Michigan Press.

Cowan, Jane K., Marie-Bénédicte Dembour, and Richard A. Wilson

2001   Culture and Rights: Anthropological Perspectives. Cambridge: Cambridge University Press.

Cowell, Alan

2003a   Threats and Responses: Britain; Blair, Increasingly Alone, Clings to Stance. New York Times, February 17.

2003b   Threats and Responses: London; British Dissent over an Iraq War Imperils Blair's Political Future. New York Times, March 12.

Creed, Gerald W.

2006   The Seductions of Community: Emancipations, Oppressions, Quandaries. School of American Research. Santa Fe, NM: SAR Press.

Cruz, Atehortua, and Adolfo León

2005   Militares: Otra visión, otros estudios. Bogota: Universidad Pedagógica Nacional.

Das, Veena

2004   The Signature of the State: The Paradox of Illegibility. *In* Anthropology in the Margins of the State. Veena Das and Deborah Poole, eds. Pp. 225–252. School of American Research. Santa Fe, NM: SAR Press.

Deleuze, Gilles, ed.

1988   Foucault. Minneapolis: University of Minnesota Press.

Democratization Policy Institute

2001   Focus on Africa. Vol. 2005. Unpublished paper, Washington DC. http://www.anonime.com/dpinstitute/africa/index.htm, accessed January 2008.

Derrida, Jacques

1976   Of Grammatology. Gayatri Chakravorty Spivak, trans. Baltimore, MD: Johns Hopkins University Press.

Dias, António Jorge, and Margot Schmidt Dias

1970   Os Macondes de Moçambique, vol. III: Vida Social e Ritual. Lisboa: Centro de Estudos de Antropologia Cultural, Junta de Investigações do Ultramar.

Dubner, Stephen, and Steven Levitt

2005   Freakonomics: Why Vote? New York Times Magazine, November 6. http://freakonomics.blogs.nytimes.com/2005/11/06/freakonomics-in-the-times-magazine-why-vote/, accessed February 2008.

Dunn, John

1980   The History of Political Theory and Other Essays. Cambridge: Cambridge University Press.

Durkheim, Emile

1898 [1969] Individualism and Intellectuals. S. Lukes and J. Lukes, trans. Political Studies 17(1):19–30.

1904   Professional Ethics and Civic Morals. New York: Routledge & Kegan Paul.

Durkheim, Emile, and Ernst Denis
1915   Qui a voulu la guerre? Les origines de la guerre d'après les documents diplomatiques. Paris: Armand Colin.

Egerö, Bertil
1987   Mozambique: A Dream Undone: The Political Economy of Democracy, 1975–84. Uppsala: Scandinavian Institute of African Studies.

Elster, Jon, ed.
1998   Deliberative Democracy. Cambridge: Cambridge University Press.

El Tiempo
2006   En nueva declaración, ex-director de informática del DAS revela detalles de listas negras. El Tiempo, May 26.

Englund, Harri
2002   From War to Peace on the Mozambique–Malawi Borderland. Edinburgh: Edinburgh University Press.

Fauvet, Paul
2000   Mozambique: Growth with Poverty: A Difficult Transition from Prolonged War to Peace and Development. Africa Recovery 14(3):12–19.

Ferguson, James
1994   The Anti-politics Machine: "Development," Depoliticization, and Bureaucratic Power in Lesotho. Minneapolis: University of Minnesota Press.
1999   Expectations of Modernity: Myths and Meanings of Urban Life on the Zambian Copperbelt. Berkeley: University of California Press.

Ferguson, James, and Akhil Gupta
2002   Spatializing States: Toward an Ethnography of Neoliberal Governmentality. American Ethnologist 29(4):981–2001.

Finer, Samuel E.
1975   State and Nation Building in Europe: The Role of the Military. *In* The Formation of National States in Western Europe. Charles Tilly, ed. Pp. 84–163. Princeton, NJ: Princeton University Press.

Finnegan, William
1992   A Complicated War: The Harrowing of Mozambique. Berkeley: University of California Press.

Firestone, David
2003   Threats and Responses: The Politics; House Republican Leader Faults Democrats Who Oppose Iraq War. New York Times, February 26.

Fishman, Robert
2004   Democracy's Voices: Social Ties and the Quality of Public Life in Spain. Ithaca, NY: Cornell University Press.

REFERENCES

Foer, Franklin
2002   John Rendon's Shallow PR War on Terrorism. The New Republic, May 20. http://www.prfirms.org/resources/news/redon051402.asp. Full text available at http://web.ebscohost.com/ehost/detail?vid=3&hid=1098&sid=a35bcf3-424b-47b9-9543-ec62658cc4c6%40sessionmanager104, accessed March 2008.

Foucault, Michel
1978   The History of Sexuality, vol. 1: An Introduction. Robert Hurley, trans. New York: Pantheon.

1980   Power/Knowledge: Selected Interviews and Other Writings, 1972–1977. Colin Gordon, trans. and ed. New York: Pantheon.

1991   Governmentality. In The Foucault Effect: Studies in Governmentality. Graham Burchell, Colin Gordon, and Peter Miller, eds. Pp. 87–104. Chicago: University of Chicago Press.

Freire, Paulo
1968   Pedagogy of the Oppressed. Myra Bergman Ramos, trans. New York: Seabury Press.

Fry, Peter
1997   Final Evaluation of the Decentralization/Traditional Authority Component of the African American Institute's Project "Democratic Development in Mozambique" (Cooperative Agreement #656-A-00-4029-00). Maputo: USAID.

Funk, Patricia
2005   Theory and Evidence on the Role of Social Norms in Voting. http://graphics8.nytimes.com/images/blogs/freakonomics/pdf/FunkVoting.pdf, accessed February 2008.

Gal, Susan, and Gail Kligman
2000   The Politics of Gender after Socialism: A Comparative-Historical Essay. Princeton, NJ: Princeton University Press.

García Bravo, Mary
2002   Proceso organizativo y gestión en la Unión de Organizaciones Campesinas de Cotacachi (UNORCAC). In Construyendo capacidades colectivas: Fortalecimiento organizativo de las federaciones campesinas–indígenas en la sierra ecuatoriana. Thomas Carroll, ed. Pp. 283–350. Quito: Soka University of America, The World Bank Group, PRODEPINE, OXFAM, and Heifer International.

Geffray, Christian
1990   La Cause des Armes au Mozambique: Anthropologie d'une Guerre Civile. Paris: Karthala.

Gerlach, Allen
1973   Civil–Military Relations in Peru, 1914–1945. Ph.D. dissertation, University of New Mexico.

Geschiere, Peter
1997   The Modernity of Witchcraft: Politics and the Occult in Postcolonial Africa. Charlottesville: University Press of Virginia.

Gilbert, Andrew

2005 Humanitarianization and Politika in the Refugee Return Process in Bosnia-Herzegovina. Paper presented at the conference "Politics and Society Ten Years After Dayton," Sarajevo, November 10–13.

2006 The Past in Parenthesis: (Non)Post-socialism in Post-war Bosnia-Herzegovina. Anthropology Today 22(4):14–18.

Gilmartin, David

2007 Election Law and the "People" in Colonial and Postcolonial India. *In* From the Colonial to the Postcolonial: India and Pakistan in Transition. Dipesh Chakrabarty, Rochona Majumdar, and Andrew Sartori, eds. Pp. 55–82. New Delhi: Oxford University Press.

Ginsburg, Faye D.

1989 Contested Lives: The Abortion Debate in an American Community. Berkeley: University of California Press.

Goody, Jack

1968 Introduction. *In* Literacy in Traditional Societies. Jack Goody, ed. Pp. 1–26. Cambridge: Cambridge University Press.

1986 The Logic of Writing and the Organization of Society. Cambridge: Cambridge University Press.

Gowa, Joanne S.

1999 Ballots and Bullets: The Elusive Democratic Peace. Princeton, NJ: Princeton University Press.

Greenhouse, Carol J.

2002 Altered States, Altered Lives. Introduction. *In* Ethnography in Unstable Places: Everyday Life in Contexts of Dramatic Political Change. Carol Greenhouse, Elizabeth Mertz, and Kay Warren, eds. Pp. 1–34. Durham, NC: Duke University Press.

2003 Identity, Law, and the Dream of Time. *In* Looking Back at Law's Century. Austin Sarat, Bryant Garth, and Robert Kagan, eds. Pp. 184–209. Ithaca, NY: Cornell University Press.

2005a Hegemony and Hidden Transcripts. American Anthropologist 107(3):356–368.

2005b Nationalizing the Local: Comparative Notes on the Recent Restructuring of Political Space. *In* Human Rights in an Age of Terror. Richard Wilson, ed. Pp. 184–208. Cambridge: Cambridge University Press.

2006a Lear and Law's Doubles: Identity and Meaning in a Time of Crisis. Law, Culture, and Humanities 2(2):239–258.

2006b Fieldwork of Law. *In* Annual Review of Law and Social Science, vol. 2. Pp. 187–210.

N.d. Discourse and Democracy: New Challenges to the Ethnography of Law. *In* Law, Culture, and Power. Anne Griffiths, Keebet von Benda-Beckmann, and Franz von Benda-Beckmann, eds. Oxford: Berghahn.

References

Gregory, Steven
1998   Black Corona: Race and the Politics of Place in an Urban Community. Princeton, NJ: Princeton University Press.

Grosz, Elizabeth
1994   Volatile Bodies: Toward a Corporeal Feminism. Bloomington: Indiana University Press.

Grupo Democracia y Desarrollo Local
1999   Ciudadanías emergentes: Experiencias democráticas de desarrollo local. Quito, Ecuador: Ediciones Abya Yala.

Guerrero, Fernando, and Pablo Ospina
2004   El poder de la comunidad: Movimiento indígena y ajuste estructural en los Andes ecuatorianos. Buenos Aires: CLACSO, IEE.

Guizot, Francois
1977[1822]   History of Civilization in Europe. William Hazlitt, trans. New York: Penguin Books.

Gupta, Akhil
1995   Blurred Boundaries: The Discourse of Corruption, the Culture of Politics, and the Imagined State. American Ethnologist 22(2):375–402.

Gustafson, Bret
2002   The Paradoxes of Liberal Indigenism: Indigenous Movements, State Processes, and Intercultural Reform in Bolivia. In The Politics of Ethnicity: Indigenous Peoples in Latin American States. David Maybury-Lewis, ed. Pp. 267–306. Cambridge, MA: Harvard University Press.

Gusterson, Hugh
1997   Studying Up Revisited. Political and Legal Anthropology Review 20(1):114–119.

Guyer, Jane
1995   Wealth in People as Wealth in Knowledge: Accumulation and Composition in Equatorial Africa. Journal of African History 36(1):91–120.

Habermas, Jurgen
1989   Structural Transformation of the Public Sphere. Cambridge, MA: MIT Press.

Hall, Margaret
1990   The Mozambican National Resistance Movement (RENAMO): A Study in the Destruction of an African Country. Africa 60(1):39–68.

Hanlon, Joseph
1990   Mozambique: The Revolution under Fire. London: Zed Books.
1991   Mozambique: Who Calls the Shots? London: James Currey.
1994   Report of AWEPA's Observation of the Mozambique Electoral Process, 1992–1994. Amsterdam: African-European Institute.
2000   New Decree Recognises "Traditional Chiefs." AWEPA Mozambique Peace Process Bulletin (August):4–5.

2004   How Northern Donors Promote Corruption: Tales from Mozambique. Oldham, UK: The Corner House.

Hansen, Thomas

2005   On Legality and Authority in India. *In* Sovereign Bodies: Citizens, Migrants, and States in the Postcolonial World. Thomas Hansen and Finn Sepputat, eds. Pp. 169–191. Princeton, NJ, and Oxford: Princeton University Press.

Hansen, Thomas Blom, and Finn Stepputat

2001   States of Imagination: Ethnographic Exploration of the Post-colonial State. Durham, NC: Duke University Press.

Harrison, Graham

1999   Corruption as "Boundary Politics": The State, Democratisation, and Mozambique's Unstable Liberalisation. Third World Quarterly 20(3):537–550.

Harriss, John

2006   Middle Class Activism and the Politics of the Informal Working Class: A Perspective on Class Relations and Civil Society in Indian Cities. Critical Asian Studies 38(4):445–465.

Haya de la Torre, Víctor Raúl

1927   Por la emancipación de América Latina: Artículos, mensajes, discursos, 1923–1927. Buenos Aires: Gleizer.

Helms, Elissa

2003a   The "Nation-ing" of Gender? Donor Policies, Islam, and Women's NGOs in Post-war Bosnia-Herzegovina. Anthropology of East Europe Review 21(2):85–93.

2003b   Women as Agents of Ethnic Reconciliation? Women's NGOs and International Intervention in Post-war Bosnia-Herzegovina. Women's Studies International Forum 26(1):15–33.

Henriksen, Thomas H.

1983   Revolution and Counter-revolution: Mozambique's War of Independence, 1964–1974. Westport, CT: Greenwood Press.

Hersh, Seymour

2002   Annals of National Security: The Debate Within. The New Yorker, March 4. http://www.newyorker.com/printable/?fact/020311fa_fact. Full text available at http://proquest.umi.com/pqdlink?did=110242079&sid=2&Fmt=2&clientId=172108RQT=309&VName=PQD, accessed March 2007.

Herzfeld, Michael

1993   The Social Production of Indifference: Exploring the Symbolic Roots of Western Bureaucracy. Chicago: University of Chicago Press.

Hintze, Otto

1975   Military Organization and the Organization of the State. *In* The Historical Essays of Otto Hintze. F. Gilbert, ed. Pp. 178–215. New York: Oxford University Press.

REFERENCES

Hoge, Warren

2003   Threats and Responses: London; Blair Survives a Mutiny over Joining US in
        War. New York Times, March 19.

Hooks, Gregory, and Clayton Mosher

2005   Outrages against Personal Dignity: Rationalizing Abuse and Torture in the War
        on Terror. Social Forces 83(4):1627–1646.

Hume, Cameron

1994   Ending Mozambique's War. Washington DC: United States Institute of Peace.

Institutions for Natural Resource Management

N.d.   Implementing CBNRM in M'punga. http://www.geog.sussex.ac.uk/research/
        development/marena/pdf/mozambique/Moz09.pdf, accessed January 2008.

Irigaray, Luce

1985   This Sex Which Is Not One. Catherine Porter and Carolyn Burke, trans.
        Ithaca, NY: Cornell University Press.

Israel, Paolo

N.d.   The "War of the Lions": Lion-Killings and Witch Hunts in Muidumbe
        (Mozambique), 2002–2003. Unpublished ms.

Jaffrelot, Christophe

2007   Voting in India: Electoral Symbols, the Party System, and the Non-individual
        Vote. *In* The Hidden History of the Secret Ballot: Cultures of Voting. Peter
        Pels, Romain Bertrand, and Jean-Louis Briquet, eds. Pp. 78–99. London: Hurst
        and Co.

James, Wendy

2003   The Ceremonial Animal. Oxford: Clarendon Press.

Joseph, Miranda

2002   Against the Romance of Community. Minneapolis: University of Minnesota
        Press.

Kaviraj, Sudipta

1992   Writing, Speaking, Being: Language and the Historical Formation of Identities
        in India. *In* Nationalstaat und Sprachkonflikte in Süd—Und Südostasien.
        Dagmar Hellmann-Rajanayagam and Dietmar Rothermund, eds. Pp. 25–68.
        Stuttgart: Franz Steiner Verlag.

2003   A State of Contradictions: The Post-colonial State in India. *In* States and
        Citizens: History, Theory, Prospects. Quentin Skinner and Bo Strath, eds. Pp.
        145–163. New York: Cambridge University Press.

Keane, John

1998   Civil Society: Old Images, New Visions. Palo Alto, CA: Stanford University Press.

Kelman, Herbert

1999   Transforming the Relationship between Former Enemies: A Social-
        Psychological Analysis. *In* After the Peace: Resistance and Reconciliation.
        R. L. Rothstein, ed. Pp. 193–205. Boulder, CO: Lynne Rienner.

2005a   Interactive Problem Solving in the Israeli-Palestinian Case: Past Contributions and Present Challenges. *In* Paving the Way: Contributions of Interactive Conflict Resolution to Peacemaking. R. Fisher, ed. Pp. 41–63. Lanham, MD: Lexington Books.

2005b   Building Trust among Enemies: The Central Challenge for International Conflict Resolution. International Journal of Intercultural Relations 29(6):639–650.

Kittler, Friedrich A.

1999   Gramophone, Film, Typewriter. Geoffrey Winthrop-Young and Michael Wutz, trans. Palo Alto, CA: Stanford University Press.

Korovkin, Tanya

2001   Reinventing the Communal Tradition: Indigenous Peoples, Civil Society, and Democratization in Andean Ecuador. Latin American Research Review 36(3):37–67.

Laclau, Ernesto, and Chantal Mouffe

2000[1985]   Hegemony and Socialist Strategy: Toward a Radical Democratic Politics. 2nd edition. Winston Moore and Paul Cammack, trans. London: Verso.

Larson, Brooke

1988   Colonialism and Agrarian Transformation in Bolivia: Cochabamba, 1550–1900. Princeton, NJ: Princeton University Press.

Lazarus-Black, Mindie

2001   Law and the Pragmatics of Inclusion: Governing Domestic Violence in Trinidad and Tobago. American Ethnologist 28(2):388–416.

Lean, Sharon

2004   The Transnational Politics of Democracy Promotion: Election Monitoring in Latin America. Ph.D. dissertation, University of California, Irvine.

Limbombo, Oscar

2003   Leões de Muidumbe. "Questão de Fundo" radio show. Pemba: Radio Moçambique, radio broadcast (date unknown).

Linz, Juan, Alfred Stepan, and Yogendra Yadav

2007   "Nation State" or "State Nation"? India in Comparative Perspective. *In* Democracy and Diversity: India and the American Experience. K. Shankar Bajpai, ed. Pp. 50–106. New Delhi: Oxford University Press.

Lipset, Seymour Martin

1981   Political Man: The Social Bases of Politics. Baltimore, MD: Johns Hopkins University Press.

Lokniti

1999   National Election Studies. New Delhi: Centre for the Study of Developing Societies.

Lopez-Alves, Fernando

2000   State Formation and Democracy in Latin America, 1810–1900. Durham, NC: Duke University Press.

Lubkemann, Stephen

2001   Rebuilding Local Capacities in Mozambique: The National Health System and Civil Society. *In* Patronage or Partnership: Local Capacity Building in Humanitarian Crises. Ian Smillie, ed. Pp. 77–106. Bloomfield, CT: Kumarian Press.

Lukes, Steven

1975   Political Ritual and Social Integration. Sociology 9(2):289–308.

Lundin, Iraê Baptista

1995   A Pesquisa Piloto Sobre a Autoridade/Poder Tradicional em Moçambique— Um Somatório Comentado e Analisado. *In* Autoridade e Poder Tradicional, vol. I. Iraê Baptista Lundin and Francisco Jamisse Machava, eds. Pp. 7–32. Maputo: Ministério da Administração Estatal/ Núcleo de Desenvolvimento Administrativo.

Lutz, Catherine

2004   Militarization. *In* A Companion to the Anthropology of Politics. David Nugent and Joan Vincent, eds. Pp. 318–331. Malden, MA: Blackwell.

Machel, Samora

1978   Produzir é Aprender: Aprender para Produzir e Lutar Melhor. Maputo: FRELIMO.

Mallon, Florencia

1983   The Defense of Community in Peru's Central Highlands. Princeton, NJ: Princeton University Press.

1995   Peasant and Nation. Berkeley: University of California Press.

Mann, Michael

1986   The Sources of Social Power. Vol. 1. Cambridge: Cambridge University Press.

1988   States, War and Capitalism. Oxford: Basil Blackwell.

1993   The Sources of Social Power. Vol. 2. Cambridge: Cambridge University Press.

Manning, Carrie

2001   Competition and Accommodation in Post-conflict Democracy: The Case of Mozambique. Democratization 8(2):140–168.

2002   The Politics of Peace in Mozambique: Post-conflict Democratization, 1992–2000. Westport, CT: Praeger Publishers.

Marx, Karl

1975[1843] Critique of Hegel's Doctrine of the State. *In* Early Writings by Karl Marx. Rodney Livingstone and Gregor Benton, trans. Pp. 57–188. New York: Vintage.

Masterson, Matthew

1976   The Peruvian Armed Forces in Transition, 1939–1963: The Impact of National Politics and Changing Professional Perspectives. Ph.D. dissertation, Michigan State University.

Mattingly, Garrett

1988[1955] Renaissance Diplomacy. New York: Dover.

Mayer, Jane
2004 Reporter at Large: The Manipulator. The New Yorker, June 7. http://www. newyorker.com/archive/2004/06/07/040607fa_fact1, accessed March 2008.

Mazula, Brazão
1995 Moçambique: Eleições, Democracia e Desenvolvimento. Maputo: Embassy of Holland.

Menand, Louis
2004 Postcard from Stanford: Permanent Fatal Errors. The New Yorker, December 6: 54–60.

Meneses, Maria Paula, Joaquim Fumo, Guilherme Mbilana, and Conceição Gomes
2003 As Autoridades Tradicionais no Contexto do Pluralismo Jurídico. *In* Conflito e Transformação Social: Uma Paisagem das Justiças em Moçambique, vol. II. Boaventura de Sousa Santos and João Carlos Trindade, eds. Pp. 341–420. Porto: Edições Afrontamento.

Merry, Sally Engle
2000 Colonizing Hawaii: The Cultural Power of Law. Princeton, NJ: Princeton University Press.

Mertz, Elizabeth
1994 Legal Language: Pragmatics, Poetics, and Social Power. Annual Review of Anthropology 23:435–455.

Messick, Brinkley
1993 The Calligraphic State: Textual Domination and History in a Muslim Society. Berkeley: University of California Press.

Miers, Suzanne, and Igor Kopytoff
1977 Slavery in Africa: Historical and Anthropological Perspectives. Madison: University of Wisconsin Press.

Miller, J.
1988 Way of Death: Merchant Capitalism and the Angolan Slave Trade, 1730–1830. Madison: University of Wisconsin Press.

Mines, Mattison
1994 Public Face, Private Vices: Community and Individuality in South India. Berkeley: University of California Press.

Minter, William
1994 Apartheid's Contras. London: Zed Books.

Mitchell, Alison, and Carl Hulse
2002 Threats and Responses: The Vote; Congress Authorizes Bush to Use Force against Iraq, Creating a Broad Mandate. New York Times, October 11.

Mitchell, Timothy
1991 The Limits of the State: Beyond Statist Approaches and Their Critics. American Political Science Review 85(1):77–96.

REFERENCES

Monteiro, José Oscar
1989   Power and Democracy. Maputo: People's Assembly.

Moore, Barrington, Jr.
1966   Social Origins of Dictatorship and Democracy. Boston: Beacon Press.

Morris, Rosalind C.
2002   Theses on the Questions of War: History, Media, Terror. Social Text 20(372):149–175.

Municipalidad de Cotacachi
1997   Plan de Desarrollo del Cantón Cotacachi. Cotacachi, Ecuador.
N.d.a   Remuneraciones Unificadas de Funcionarios y Empleados del Municipio de Cotacachi. http://www.cotacachi.gov.ec/htms/esp/Municipio/sueldos.htm, accessed March 2008.
N.d.b   Asemblea de Unidad Cantonal. http://www.cotacachi.gov.ec/htms/esp/asamblea/Asamblea.htm, accessed March 2008.

Munslow, Barry
1983   Mozambique: The Revolution and Its Origins. London: Longman.

Mwangi, Wambui
N.d.   The Stutter of the Real: Counterfeit Currency and Colonialism in East Africa. Unpublished paper.

Myers, Gregory
1994   Competitive Rights, Competitive Claims: Land Access in Post-war Mozambique. Journal of Southern African Studies 20(4):603–632.

Nader, Laura
1972   Up the Anthropologist—Perspectives Gained from Studying Up. *In* Reinventing Anthropology. Dell H. Hymes, ed. Pp. 248–311. New York: Pantheon Books.

Nagourney, Adam
2003   Threats and Responses: Democrats; Divided Democrats Concerned about 2004. New York Times, March 29.

Nagourney, Adam, and Janet Elder
2003   Threats and Responses: The Poll; More Americans Now Faulting UN on Iraq, Poll Finds. New York Times, March 11.

Negrão, José Guilherme
1984   A Produção e o Comércio nas Antigas Zonas Libertadas. Maputo: Arquivo Histórico de Moçambique.

New York Times
2002   Excerpts from Senate Debate on Iraq Policy. New York Times, October 10.

Nugent, David
1997   Modernity at the Edge of Empire: State, Individual and Nation in the Northern Peruvian Andes, 1885–1935. Palo Alto, CA: Stanford University Press.

1999a   Democracy, Modernity and the Public Sphere: Latin American Perspectives on North American Models. Paper presented at the 1999 international conference "Visions and Voices, Manchester, England," Manchester, October.

1999b   State and Shadow State in Turn-of-the-Century Peru: Illegal Political Networks and the Problem of State Boundaries. *In* States and Illegal Practices. Josiah Heyman, ed. Pp. 63–98. London: Berg.

2002   Erasing Race to Make the Nation: The Rise of "the People" in the Northern Peruvian Andes. *In* Locating Capitalism in Time and Space: Global Restructurings, Politics, and Identity. David Nugent, ed. Pp. 137–174. Palo Alto, CA: Stanford University Press.

2004   Disordered and Altered States: A View from the Peruvian Margins. Paper presented at the Annual Meeting of the Latin American Studies Association, Las Vegas, Nevada.

2006   Victor Raúl Haya de la Torre and APRA. *In* Heroes and Hero Cults in Latin America. Samuel Brunk and Benjamin Fallaw, eds. Pp. 202–228. Austin: University of Texas Press.

2007   Dark Fantasies of State: Notes from the Peruvian Underground. Paper presented at the Annual Discussion Group on the State Conference, Lancaster University, England, April.

2008   Alternative Democracies: Discipline, Democracy and State Formation in the Northern Peruvian Andes. Unpublished manuscript.

Office of the High Representative (OHR)

2000   Office of the High Representative Information. http://www.ohr.int/info/info.htm, accessed April 2003.

Olson, Elizabeth

2003   Threats and Responses: Dissent; City Leaders Carry Message against War to President. New York Times, February 14.

Organization for Security and Co-operation in Europe (OSCE)

2001   Survey of OSCE Long-term Missions and Other OSCE Field Activities. http://www.osce.org/publications/survey/survey.pdf, accessed April 2003.

Ortiz, Santiago

2004   Cotacachi: Una apuesta por la democracia participativa. Quito: FLACSO-Sede Academica de Ecuador.

Ortner, Sherry B.

1984   Theory in Anthropology since the Sixties. Comparative Studies in Society and History 26(1):126–166.

Orvis, Stephen

2001   Civil Society in Africa or African Civil Society? *In* A Decade of Democracy in Africa. S. N. Ndegwa, ed. Pp. 17–38. Leiden: Brill.

Osborne, Thomas

1994   Bureaucracy as a Vocation: Governmentality and Administration in Nineteenth-Century Britain. Journal of Historical Sociology 7(3):289–313.

Paley, Julia

2001   Marketing Democracy: Power and Social Movements in Post-dictatorship Chile. Berkeley: University of California Press.

2002   Toward an Anthropology of Democracy. Annual Review of Anthropology 31:469–496.

2004   Accountable Democracy: Citizens' Impact on Public Decision Making in Postdictatorship Chile. American Ethnologist 31(4):497–513.

Pallares, Amalia

2002   From Peasant Struggles to Indian Resistance: The Ecuadorian Andes in the Late Twentieth Century. Norman: University of Oklahoma Press.

Papić, Zoran, ed.

2001   International Support Policies to SEE Countries—Lessons (Not) Learned in Bosnia-Herzegovina. Sarajevo: Open Society Fund Bosnia-Herzegovina.

Parker, Geoffrey

1976   The "Military Revolution," 1550–1660—A Myth? Journal of Modern History 46(2):195–214.

Perillo, Bob

2006   The Struggle for Workers' Rights in Colombia. AFL-CIO Solidarity Center Report. http://www.solidaritycenter.org/files/ColombiaFinal.pdf, accessed December 2006.

Pieterse, Jan Nederveen

2004   Globalization or Empire? New York: Routledge.

Pitcher, M. Anne

2002   Transforming Mozambique: The Politics of Privatization, 1975–2000. Cambridge: Cambridge University Press.

Plato

1995   Phaedrus. Alexander Nehamas and Paul Woodruff, trans. Indianapolis, IN: Hackett Publishing Company.

Polanyi, Karl

1944   The Great Transformation: The Political and Economic Origins of Our Time. Boston: Beacon.

1957   The Economy as Instituted Process. In Trade and Market in the Early Empires. Karl Polanyi, Ben Pearson, and Conrad Arensberg, eds. Pp. 243–270. Glencoe, IL: Free Press.

Postero, Nancy

2004   Articulations and Fragmentations: Indigenous Politics in Bolivia. In The Struggle for Indigenous Rights in Latin America. Nancy Grey Postero and Leon Zamosc, eds. Pp. 189–216. Portland, OR: Sussex Academic Press.

Project for the New American Century (PNAC)

1998a   Letter to President Clinton on Iraq. http://www.newamericancentury.org/iraqclintonletter.htm, accessed April 2005.

1998b   Letter to Newt Gingrich and Trent Lott on Iraq. http://www.newamericancen
         tury.org/iraqletter1998.htm, accessed April 2005.

2001   Letter to President Bush on the War on Terrorism. http://www.newamerican
         century.org/Bushletter.htm, accessed April 2005.

N.d.   Letters and Statements. http://www.newamericancentury.org/lettersstate
         ments.htm, accessed April 2005.

Purdum, Todd S., and Elizabeth Bumiller

2002   Bush Seeks Power to Use "All Means" to Oust Hussein. New York Times,
         September 20.

Putnam, Robert, Robert Leonardi, and Raffaella Nanetti

1994   Making Democracy Work: Civic Traditions in Modern Italy. Princeton, NJ:
         Princeton University Press.

Radcliffe, Sarah A.

2001   Development, the State, and Transnational Political Connections: State and
         Subject Formations in Latin America. Global Networks 1(1):19–36.

Radcliffe, Sarah, Robert Andolina, and Nina Laurie

2002   Re-territorialised Space and Ethnic Political Participation: Indigenous
         Municipalities in Ecuador. Space and Polity 6(3):289–305.

Radnóti, Sándor

1999   The Fake: Forgery and Its Place in Art. New York: Rowman & Littlefield.

Ramón, Galo, and Víctor Hugo Torres Dávila

2004   El desarrollo local en el Ecuador: Historia, actores y métodos. Quito: Ediciones
         Abya Yala.

Rao, Ritu

2004   A Positive Verdict. Economic and Political Weekly (December 18):5437–5440.

Ray, James L.

1997   The Democratic Path to Peace. Journal of Democracy 8(2):49–64.

Red Interamericana Agricultura y Democracia

1998   Organizaciones campesinas e indígenas y poderes locales: Propuestas para la
         gestión participativa del desarrollo local. Quito: Ediciones Abya Yala.

Rhoades, Robert E., ed.

2006   Development with Identity: Community, Culture and Sustainability in the
         Andes. Cambridge, MA: CABI Publishing.

Riles, Annelise

1998   Infinity within the Brackets. American Ethnologist 25(3):378–398.

2004   Real Time: Unwinding Technocratic and Anthropological Knowledge.
         American Ethnologist 31(3):392–405.

Risen, James, and Barbara Crossette

1998   Even US Sees Iraq Opposition as Faint Hope. New York Times, November 19.

Roberts, Michael
1967   The Military Revolution. *In* Essays in Swedish History, by Michael Roberts. Pp. 195–225. Minneapolis: University of Minnesota Press.

Rose, Nikolas
1996   Governing "Advanced" Liberal Democracies. *In* Foucault and Political Reason: Liberalism, Neo-Liberalism, and Rationalities of Government. Andrew Barry, Thomas Osborne, and Nikolas Rose, eds. Pp. 37–64. Chicago: University of Chicago Press.

Rose, Nikolas, and Peter Miller
1992   Political Power beyond the State: Problematics of Government. British Journal of Sociology 13(2):173–205.

Roseberry, William
1994   Hegemony and the Language of Contention. *In* Everyday Forms of State Formation: Revolution and the Negotiation of Rule in Modern Mexico. Gilbert M. Joseph and Daniel Nugent, eds. Pp. 355–366. Durham, NC: Duke University Press.

Ruggie, John Gerard
1998   Constructing the World Policy: Essays on International Institutionalization. New York: Routledge.

Rushdie, Salman
1981   Midnight's Children. New York: Knopf.

Russett, Bruce
1993   Grasping the Democratic Peace: Principles for a Post–Cold War World. Princeton, NJ: Princeton University Press.

Salzman, Todd A.
1998   Rape Camps as a Means of Ethnic Cleansing: Religious, Cultural, and Ethical Responses to Rape Victims in the Former Yugoslavia. Human Rights Quarterly 20(2):348–378.

Sanger, David E., and Felicity Barringer
2003   Threats and Responses: The President; President Readies US for Prospect of Imminent War. New York Times, March 7.

Sanger, David E., and Elisabeth Bumiller
2002   Threats and Responses: The President; Bush Presses UN to Act Quickly on Disarming Iraq. New York Times, September 13.

Santos, Boaventura de Sousa
1995   Toward a New Common Sense: Law, Science, and Politics in the Paradigmatic Transition. New York: Routledge.
2003   O Estado Hetrogénio e o Pluralismo Jurídico. *In* Conflito e Transformação Social: Uma Paisagem das Justiças em Moçambique, vol. I. Boaventura de Sousa Santos and João Carlos Trindade, eds. Pp. 47–95. Porto: Edições Afrontamento.

Sassen, Saskia

1996   Losing Control? Sovereignty in an Age of Globalization. New York: Columbia University Press.

Schaffer, Frederic C.

2000   Democracy in Translation: Understanding Politics in an Unfamiliar Culture. Ithaca, NY: Cornell University Press.

Schirmer, Jennifer

1996   The Looting of Democratic Discourse by the Guatemalan Military: Implications for Human Rights. *In* Constructing Democracy: Human Rights, Citizenship and Society in Latin America. Elisabeth Jelin and Eric Hershberg, eds. Pp. 84–96. Boulder, CO: Westview Press.

1998   The Guatemalan Military Project: A Violence Called Democracy. Pennsylvania Studies in Human Rights Series. Philadelphia: University of Pennsylvania Press.

Schmitt, Carl

1996   The Concept of the Political. George Schwab, trans. Chicago: University of Chicago Press.

Schmitt, Eric

1998   Attack on Iraq: Capitol Hill: GOP Splits Bitterly over Timing of Assault. New York Times, December 17.

Schneider, Jane C., and Peter T. Schneider

2003   Reversible Destiny: Mafia, Antimafia, and the Struggle for Palermo. Berkeley: University of California Press.

Scott, James C.

1998   Seeing like a State: How Certain Schemes to Improve the Human Condition Have Failed. New Haven, CT: Yale University Press.

Shenon, Philip

1998   House Votes $100 Million to Aid Foes of Baghdad. New York Times, October 6.

South and Meso American Indian Rights Center (SAIIC)

1996   Pachakutik-Nuevo País: Breaking New Ground in Ecuadorian Politics; Interview with Luís Macas. Abya Yala News 10(2). http://saiic.nativeweb.org/ayn/macas.html, accessed March 2008.

Spalding, Karen

1984   Huarochirí: An Andean Society under Spanish Rule. Palo Alto, CA: Stanford University Press.

Spencer, Jonathan

2007   Anthropology, Politics and the State; Democracy and Violence in South Asia. Cambridge: Cambridge University Press.

Spivak, Gayatri Chakravorty

2004   Terror: A Speech after 9-11. Boundary 31(2):81–111.

Stabilization Force (SFOR)

2001   History of the NATO-Led Stabilization Force (SFOR) in Bosnia and
        Herzegovina. http://www.nato.int/sfor/docu/d981116a.htm, accessed April
        2003.

Steinmetz, George

1999   State/Culture: State Formation after the Cultural Turn. Ithaca, NY: Cornell
        University Press.

Stern, Steve, ed.

1998   Shining and Other Paths: War and Society in Peru, 1980–1995. Durham, NC:
        Duke University Press.

Stevenson, Richard W.

2003   Threats and Responses: The White House; Antiwar Protests Fail to Sway Bush
        on Plans for Iraq. New York Times, February 19.

2004   Bush Sought to Oust Hussein from Start, Ex-official Says: Recounts Discussions
        Months before 9/11. New York Times, January 12.

Stiglmayer, Alexandra, ed.

1994   Mass Rape: The War against Women in Bosnia-Herzegovina. Lincoln:
        University of Nebraska Press.

Suskind, Ron

2004   The Price of Loyalty: George W. Bush, the White House, and the Education of
        Paul O'Neill. New York: Simon and Schuster.

Tagliabue, John

2003   A Nation at War: World Reaction; Wave of Protests, from Europe to New York.
        New York Times, March 21.

Tarlo, Emma

2003   Unsettling Memories: Narratives of the Emergency in Delhi. Berkeley:
        University of California Press.

Taylor, Lewis

1986   Bandits and Politics in Peru: Landlord and Peasant Violence in Hualgayoc,
        1900–1930. Cambridge Latin American Miniatures no. 2. Cambridge:
        Cambridge University.

Thurner, Mark

1997   From Two Nations to One Divided. Durham, NC: Duke University Press.

Tilly, Charles

1975a   Reflections on the History of European State-Making. In The Formation of
        National States in Western Europe. Charles Tilly, ed. Pp. 3–83. Princeton, NJ:
        Princeton University Press.

1985   How War Made States, and Vice Versa. In Bringing the State Back In. Peter
        Evans, Dietrich Rueschemeyer, and Theda Skocpol, eds. Pp. 67–95.
        Cambridge: Cambridge University Press.

1990   Coercion, Capital and European States, AD 990–1990. Oxford: Blackwell.

1993   European Revolutions, 1492–1992. Oxford: Blackwell.

2004   Contention and Democracy in Europe, 1650–2000. New York: Cambridge
          University Press.

Tilly, Charles, ed.

1975b   The Formation of National States in Western Europe. Princeton, NJ: Princeton
          University Press.

United Nations (UN)

2001   United Nations Mission in Bosnia and Herzegovina Mandate.
          http://www.unmibh.org/unmibh/abutus.htm, accessed April 2003.

United Nations Development Program (UNDP)

1998   Human Development Report, Bosnia and Herzegovina 1998. Sarajevo: United
          Nations Development Program.

US Institute of Peace (USIP)

2001   US Online Training Course for OSCE, including REACT. Modeule 2. OSCE
          Mission Structures and Functions. http://react.usip.org/Main.html, accessed
          April 2003.

Van Cott, Donna Lee

2005   From Movements to Parties in Latin America: The Evolution of Ethnic Politics.
          New York: Cambridge University Press.

2006   Radical Democracy in the Andes: Indigenous Parties and the Quality of
          Democracy in Latin America. Working Paper #333. Notre Dame: Kellogg
          Institute for International Studies.

Vansina, Jan

1988   Paths in the Rainforest: Toward a History of Political Tradition in Equatorial
          Africa. Madison: University of Wisconsin Press.

Vega-Centeno B., Imelda

1991   Aprismo popular: Cultura, religión y política. Lima: CISEPA/TAREA.

Verdery, Katherine

1996   What Was Socialism, and What Comes Next? Princeton, NJ: Princeton
          University Press.

2003   The Vanishing Hectare: Property and Value in Postsocialist Transylvania. Ithaca,
          NY: Cornell University Press.

Villanueva Valencia, Víctor

1973   La sublevación aprista del 48: Tragedia de un pueblo y un partido. Lima:
          Editorial Milla Batres.

Vines, Alex

1991   RENAMO: Terrorism in Mozambique. London: James Currey.

Warren, Kay B.

1998   Indigenous Movements and Their Critics: Pan-Maya Activism in Guatemala.
          Princeton, NJ: Princeton University Press.

REFERENCES

Washington Institute

2004   Chronology of US–Turkish Relations: July 2002–January 2004. http://www.was
        hingtoninstitute.org/documents/420a3b30c5e7f.pdf, accessed April 2005.

Weber, Max

1950   General Economic History. Frank H. Knight, trans. Glencoe, IL: Free Press.

1968   Economy and Society: An Outline of Interpretive Sociology. Guenther Roth
        and Claus Witich, eds. Berkeley: University of California Press.

1978   Economy and Society: An Outline of Interpretive Sociology. Guenther Roth
        and Class Wittich, eds. Ephraim Fischoff, Hans Gerth, A. M. Henderson,
        Ferdinand Kolegar, C. Wright Mills, Talcott Parsons, Max Rheinstein,
        Guenther Roth, Edward Shils, and Claus Wittich, trans. Berkeley: University of
        California Press.

Weimer, Bernhard

1996   Challenges for Democratization and Regional Development in Southern
        Africa: Focus on Mozambique. Regional Development Dialogue 17(2):32–59.

Weimer, Bernhard, and Sabine Fandrych

1999   Mozambique: Administrative Reform—A Contribution to Peace and
        Democracy? *In* Local Government Democratisation and Decentralisation: A
        Review of the Southern African Region. Purshottam S. Reddy, ed. Pp. 151–177.
        Kenwyn, South Africa: Juta and Co.

Wengrow, David

2006   The Archaeology of Early Egypt. Cambridge: Cambridge University Press.

West, Harry G.

1997   Creative Destruction and Sorcery of Construction: Power, Hope and Suspicion
        in Post-war Mozambique. Cahiers d'Études Africaines 37(147):675–698.

2003   "Who Rules Us Now?" Identity Tokens, Sorcery, and Other Metaphors in the
        1994 Mozambican Elections. *In* Transparency and Conspiracy: Ethnographies
        of Suspicion in the New World Order. Harry G. West and Todd Sanders, eds.
        Pp. 92–124. Durham, NC: Duke University Press.

2005   Kupilikula: Governance and the Invisible Realm in Mozambique. Chicago: The
        University of Chicago Press.

West, Harry G., and Scott Kloeck-Jenson

1999   Betwixt and Between: "Traditional Authority" and Democratic Decentralization
        in Post-war Mozambique. African Affairs 98(393):455–484.

West, Harry G., and Gregory W. Myers

1996   A Piece of Land in a Land of Peace? State Farm Divestiture in Mozambique.
        Journal of Modern African Studies 34(1):27–51.

Whitaker, Barbara

2003   Threats and Responses: A Vote of "No"; Los Angeles Council Adopts
        Resolution against Iraq War. New York Times, February 22.

The White House

2002a   President's Remarks at the United Nations General Assembly. http://www.white house.gov/news/releases/2002/09/print/20020912-1.html, accessed April 2005.

2002b   Iraq: Denial and Deception; President Bush Outlines Iraqi Threat. Remarks by the President on Iraq. http://www.whitehouse.gov/news/releases/2002/10/print/20021007-8.html, accessed April 2005.

2002c   Presidential Determination on Authorization to Furnish Drawdown Assistance to the Iraqi Opposition under the Iraq Liberation Act of 1998. http://usinfo.state.gov/xarchives/display.html?p=washfile-english&y=2002&m=December&x=20021209184439pkurata@pd.state.gov0.1011 011&t=xarchives/xarchitem.html, accessed April 2005.

Wood, Evelyn Meiksins

1988   Peasant-Citizen and Slave: The Foundations of Athenian Democracy. London; New York: Verso.

1994   Democracy: An Idea of Ambiguous Ancestry. *In* Athenian Political Thought and the Reconstruction of American Democracy. J. Peter Euben, John R. Wallach, and Josiah Ober, eds. Pp. 59–80. Ithaca, NY: Cornell University Press.

Woodward, Bob

2004   Plan of Attack. New York: Simon and Schuster.

Yadav, Yogendra

1999   Electoral Politics in the Time of Change India's Third Electoral System, 1989–1999. Economic and Political Weekly (August 21–28):2393–2399.

Yurchak, A.

2005   Everything Was Forever, Until It Was No More: The Last Soviet Generation. Princeton, NJ: Princeton University Press.

Index

257

School for Advanced Research Advanced Seminar Series

AMERICAN ARRIVALS: ANTHROPOLOGY
ENGAGES THE NEW IMMIGRATION
  Nancy Foner, ed.

VIOLENCE
  Neil L. Whitehead, ed.

LAW & EMPIRE IN THE PACIFIC:
FIJI AND HAWAI'I
  Sally Engle Merry & Donald Brenneis, eds.

ANTHROPOLOGY IN THE MARGINS
OF THE STATE
  Veena Das & Deborah Poole, eds.

THE ARCHAEOLOGY OF COLONIAL
ENCOUNTERS: COMPARATIVE PERSPECTIVES
  Gil J. Stein, ed.

GLOBALIZATION, WATER, & HEALTH:
RESOURCE MANAGEMENT IN TIMES OF
SCARCITY
  Linda Whiteford & Scott Whiteford, eds.

A CATALYST FOR IDEAS: ANTHROPOLOGICAL
ARCHAEOLOGY AND THE LEGACY OF
DOUGLAS W. SCHWARTZ
  Vernon L. Scarborough, ed.

THE ARCHAEOLOGY OF CHACO CANYON: AN
ELEVENTH-CENTURY PUEBLO REGIONAL
CENTER
  Stephen H. Lekson, ed.

THE GENDER OF GLOBALIZATION: WOMEN
NAVIGATING CULTURAL AND ECONOMIC
MARGINALITIES
  Nandini Gunewardena & Ann Kingsolver, eds.

COMMUNITY BUILDING IN THE TWENTY-
FIRST CENTURY
  Stanley E. Hyland, ed.

AFRO-ATLANTIC DIALOGUES:
ANTHROPOLOGY IN THE DIASPORA
  Kevin A. Yelvington, ed.

COPÁN: THE HISTORY OF AN ANCIENT MAYA
KINGDOM
  E. Wyllys Andrews & William L. Fash, eds.

THE SEDUCTIONS OF COMMUNITY:
EMANCIPATIONS, OPPRESSIONS, QUANDARIES
  Gerald W. Creed, ed.

THE EVOLUTION OF HUMAN LIFE HISTORY
  Kristen Hawkes & Richard R. Paine, eds.

IMPERIAL FORMATIONS
  Ann Laura Stoler, Carole McGranahan,
  & Peter C. Perdue, eds.

OPENING ARCHAEOLOGY: REPATRIATION'S
IMPACT ON CONTEMPORARY RESEARCH AND
PRACTICE
  Thomas W. Killion, ed.

NEW LANDSCAPES OF INEQUALITY:
NEOLIBERALISM AND THE EROSION OF
DEMOCRACY IN AMERICA
  Jane L. Collins, Micaela di Leonardo,
  & Brett Williams, eds.

SMALL WORLDS: METHOD, MEANING &
NARRATIVE IN MICROHISTORY
  James F. Brooks, Christopher R. N. DeCorse,
  & John Walton, eds.

MEMORY WORK: ARCHAEOLOGIES OF
MATERIAL PRACTICES
  Barbara J. Mills & William H. Walker, eds.

FIGURING THE FUTURE: GLOBALIZATION
AND THE TEMPORALITIES OF CHILDREN AND
YOUTH
  Jennifer Cole & Deborah Durham, eds.

TIMELY ASSETS: THE POLITICS OF
RESOURCES AND THEIR TEMPORALITIES
  Elizabeth Emma Ferry &
  Mandana E. Limbert, eds.

WRITING CULTURE: THE POETICS
AND POLITICS OF ETHNOGRAPHY
  James Clifford &
  George E. Marcus, eds.

THE COLLAPSE OF ANCIENT STATES AND
CIVILIZATIONS
  Norman Yoffee &
  George L. Cowgill, eds.

Participants in the School for Advanced Research advanced seminar "Toward an Anthropology of Democracy," Santa Fe, New Mexico, March 6–10, 2005. Front row (left to right): David Nugent, Julia Paley, Carol Greenhouse. Back row (left to right): Kay Warren, Mukulika Banerjee, Jennifer Schirmer, and Harry West.